W9-CTL-832

Received On

MAY -- 2018

Magnolia Library

NO LONGER PROPERTY OF
SEATTLE PUBLIC LIBRARY

THE DOHA
EXPERIMENT

THE DOHA EXPERIMENT

ARAB KINGDOM, CATHOLIC COLLEGE, JEWISH TEACHER

GARY WASSERMAN

Foreword by Senator Dick Durbin

Skyhorse Publishing

Copyright © 2017 by Gary Wasserman
Foreword © 2017 by Dick Durbin

All rights reserved. No part of this book may be reproduced in any manner without the express written consent of the publisher, except in the case of brief excerpts in critical reviews or articles. All inquiries should be addressed to Skyhorse Publishing, 307 West 36th Street, 11th Floor, New York, NY 10018.

Skyhorse Publishing books may be purchased in bulk at special discounts for sales promotion, corporate gifts, fund-raising, or educational purposes. Special editions can also be created to specifications. For details, contact the Special Sales Department, Skyhorse Publishing, 307 West 36th Street, 11th Floor, New York, NY 10018or info@ skyhorsepublishing.com.

Skyhorse® and Skyhorse Publishing® are registered trademarks of Skyhorse Publishing, Inc.®, a Delaware corporation.

Visit our website at www.skyhorsepublishing.com.

10 9 8 7 6 5 4 3 2 1

Library of Congress Cataloging-in-Publication Data is available on file.

Cover design by Rain Saukas
Cover photo credit iStock

Print ISBN: 978-1-5107-2172-2
Ebook ISBN: 978-1-5107-2173-9

Printed in the United States of America

To the Wonderful Wasserman Women

Helen, Aunt Ann,

Ann, Eva

Adrienne, Laura

Table of Contents

"Every time you make an experiment you learn more: quite literally, you cannot learn less."

—Buckminister Fuller

Foreword

I have been reading Gary Wasserman's writings for a long, long time.

Gary and I were students and friends at Georgetown University's School of Foreign Service many years ago. (Think Simon and Garfunkel's "Bridge Over Troubled Waters" era). He was the editor of the campus magazine, the *Courier*, and I was a staff writer.

His one feature story I still remember came about when he decided our magazine should lead a campus effort to kill the school mascot, a lovable English bulldog named Jack.

Gary was upset that Jack, who lived in a fenced pen on campus, was being mistreated. When our mutt wasn't being paraded at weekly sports events he was locked in his hot pen with limited attention and occasionally with no water. So Gary ran a cover on our magazine with a blow up photo of Jack's beautiful, sad face and the headline: "Let's Shoot Jack."

The cover story worked. Jack's life improved dramatically.

Reading the account of his years teaching at Georgetown's new campus in Qatar, I was glad to find Gary's sense of humor intact as he introduces his story with "A Jewish Guy Walks into a Catholic School in an Arab Country." But his insights into the formation of the campus, the challenge of teaching, and the lives of his students are thoughtful and timely.

He was clearly learning as much as he taught, witnessing the Muslim tradition in the lives of his students. His stories from the classroom and visits with his students years later show the impact of this transplanted campus on their lives. Though the students never seemed to appreciate his wry American humor, a "liberal education" at Georgetown University in Doha challenged their view of the world.

His overviews of Qatar's history, the intrigues of the royal family, the nation's bountiful economy, and the political perils of the region are timely as this tiny nation of 250,000 natives finds itself in the headlines in 2017. Age-old enmity with Saudi Arabia and edgy relationships with both terrorist groups and the United States government have created new and heated regional rifts.

Gary didn't duck the controversial political issues with his students. Frank dialogue on Israel, the Palestinians, and even the impact of AIPAC, the leading pro-Israel lobby in Washington, revealed the beliefs and prejudices in the next generation of Arab leaders. He finds students who have been taught Al Gore was a Jew and 9/11 an Israeli Mossad venture.

But the most powerful part of the book is the most personal. Gary tells us the struggles his students, particularly the young women, had reconciling their emerging identities with their Muslim faith and their loving but controlling families. A young Muslim woman takes a course on God and decides she is an atheist. Ordinary classroom life is shaken when another young woman switches unexpectedly from the traditional abaya and arrives in class in a blouse and jeans. More than one tells Gary that this Georgetown education is a way to cope with looming family pressures and a life constricted by limited opportunity for women.

He shares aspects of everyday life for the ex-pat: aggressive driving in Doha, socializing with other families, the experience of his LGBT friends, and the plight of migrant workers, an overwhelming part of the local economy.

After eight years Gary retires with a chapter reflecting on the future of our relations in the Middle East and experiments like the

Georgetown campus in Doha. But it's his candid, personal reflection on the "Doha Experiment" that brings an honest, even surprising, conclusion to the work.

Gary quotes an essay written by a student reflecting on the disruption of the Arab Spring. The student writes: "Life is the cruelest teacher because it gives us the test before the lesson." This book despite its many moments of levity offers a serious and important lesson about the possibilities, and limitations, of American education as a bridge between cultures.

—Senator Dick Durbin

INTRODUCTION

A Jewish Guy Walks into a Catholic School in an Arab Country

T his is a true story that sounds like a politically incorrect joke. A Jewish guy walks into a fundamentalist Arab country he has never heard of to teach American politics at a Catholic college. It is a good job offering lots of perks. Assuming survival, of course. The story starts four years after 9/11. The United States was, as it is now, caught in a period of great despair over the Middle East. The Jewish guy's family, only half-smiling, assure him they will recite the Mourners' Kaddish if needed. An elderly aunt quietly and unhelp-fully takes my hand: "Gary, stay away from Arabs."

After eight years, the fears I took with me to the Middle East have subsided. Teaching at Georgetown University's new Foreign Service School in Doha, Qatar, didn't get me killed, kidnapped, or even treated badly. Instead, I became part of a significant, little-known movement of higher education from American institutions into the embattled nations of the Middle East. By accident, I dropped into the front lines of a clash of civilizations—or, more accurately, a confusion of cultures in which liberal universities confront a gaggle of students including fundamentalists, first-rate scholars, gay Muslims, wealthy jet-setters, Arab valley girls, Asian nerds, budding jihadists, and tomorrow's world leaders. The stakes were high, the process often chaotic, the results sur-prisingly positive.

Georgetown University's leaders had the insight and courage to understand that if America wanted to send its best to a difficult region of the world, it should send scholars, not just soldiers. While I can't claim to be one of the best, my vices were my virtues. Not having studied the region before I arrived in Doha gave me some unexpected advantages. For starters, it gave me a certain openness toward what people had to say. I found myself listening, partly because I wasn't committed to many firm ideas of my own, other than my slowly diminishing paranoia.

My ambitions in writing this book, too, are modest. I did not try, while in Doha, to uncover the causes of terrorism, to explain the contradictions of Islam in the modern age, or to explore how Arab regimes have failed to adapt their societies to the challenges of the twenty-first century. Nor will I try to in this book. Others have made that effort, some successfully, some not. My stories are simple, honest, sometimes funny accounts of very different students interacting with one another and their American, Arab, and foreign teachers. The intimacy of the classroom allows candid exchanges. I have tried to capture what I saw: a surprisingly diverse Muslim group of young people struggling to find their way between conflicting worlds.

Not to give away the book's punch line, but this is not a blood-soaked narrative. Georgetown, my alma mater, treated me fairly and provided a scholarly environment that was open and free. The Qataris were generous, if not warm, hosts. The anxiety I brought with me subsided; my fears were not borne out. As a Jew, I never suffered discrimination or harassment from the people of Qatar. If anything, the respect I received as a foreign professor was the respect given to an honored, welcomed guest.

I began my journey both apprehensive and idealistic. I ended it less apprehensive and also less idealistic.

A few things should be said at the outset of this story. The Qataris are a private people. Tribe, religion and, above all, family are the most important loyalties. The nation is important but that, too, in an emirate, is a family matter. "Public affairs" is a mislabeled concept. The local media are cheerleaders for those in power and poster boards for corporate good news. Government means "palace politics" and it happens behind closed doors. Public critiques are not welcomed. My Doha friends will probably be reluctant to embrace a book that they may see as the product of bad manners—of taking the money, running, and then writing.

And yet establishing an American college in Qatar is a bold, interesting, and important experiment. Washington policymakers may view this as an exercise of "soft power," extending an American approach to the world. It makes for an intervention that is embraced in a region that has generally greeted American involvement—including the sending of troops and investments—as, at best, necessary evils. Overseas campuses like Georgetown's do help America's relations with the rest of the world. They give others insight into how we think and what we value. And they establish bonds of trust among friends.

American universities are the world's gold standard in higher education. If a Jesuit-run Catholic university can establish a liberal arts undergraduate school in a conservative Wahhabi Islamic emirate in the Arab Gulf, then some of the early experiences of that project offer lessons that can be applied, or avoided, elsewhere. And Qatar, an increasingly important state, may offer clues to other traditional tribal societies that are rapidly changing how they live, work, and think.

Liberal higher education opens a world of opportunity for the most precious possessions of Arab families: their children. It gives those children new ways to view a host of issues, from women's rights to press freedom. It also establishes networks of foreign professionals who can fill important positions in a globalized world. Products of these American universities can compete with graduates anywhere.

My own experiences may provide insights, if not amusement, to others heading for an overseas posting.

Though Georgetown's experience in Qatar is surely unique, elements of it may encourage similar efforts elsewhere: pairing American universities with sister schools abroad, allowing exchanges of scholars between academic departments, planning interfaith field trips, or delivering online classes from one university to another across the world. I hope this case will excite others to experiment and adapt other educational models to different settings and needs.

A few words on methods. What goes on in a classroom is not quite public, not quite private. It involves trust on both sides of the chasm between teacher and students. I have tried to keep that trust by not identifying my students by their given names. I have further disguised their identities where necessary. They have important things to say, especially to an American audience, and I have tried to convey that while respecting their right to privacy.

In putting together this account, I've done my best to verify facts and check recollections with friends and colleagues from Doha. Since returning to the United States, I've availed myself of some of the books and articles on the region that I studiously avoided in advance of my headlong journey. I've also interviewed dozens of former students, administrators, staff, and colleagues, and I've examined letters and emails. There still may be gaps, mistakes, and misperceptions in my account. If so, I am responsible and regret the unintended errors.

Despite my experience, I sometimes share with my countrymen their exasperation toward the Middle East. The recent crisis over Qatar will pass and, one hopes, without the United States making the conflict worse. I know from my eight years in Doha that the wars, terrorism, and zealotry dominating the headlines miss the full story. They must not compose the organizing narrative that will determine America's future in the region. Georgetown's successful effort to protect and promote a liberal presence in the Middle East should and must be continued.

My own journey was one of insights and confusion, irony and optimism. I recount my experiences knowing that I might reinforce certain unfortunate generalizations made by outsiders to the region. I also hope that I might offer alternatives to these easily grasped myths.

Some years ago, the Palestinian scholar Edward W. Said gave some good advice to those "covering Islam":

Respect for the concrete detail of human experience, under-standing that arises from viewing the Other compassionately, knowledge gained and diffused through moral and intellectual honesty: surely these are better, if not easier, goals at present than confrontation and reductive hostility. And if, in the pro-cess, we can dispose finally of both the residual hatred and the offensive generality of labels like "the Muslim," "the Persian," "the Turk," "the Arab," or "the Westerner," then so much the better.

I have tried to do this in my own journey. Inshallah.

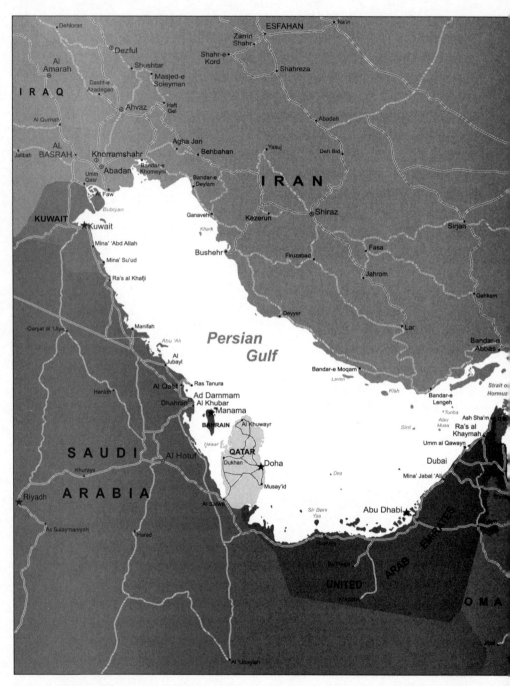

Qatar, with its capital Doha, sticks out into the Arab Gulf surrounded by larger neighbors.

Credit: University of Texas Libraries

CHAPTER 1

Preparing for the Worst: The Early Years

Given the doomsday prophecies I had heard before coming to Doha, I expected the worst. What happened on the first day of teaching the Intro to American Government class was bad enough. And it was all my fault.

Doha, Qatar, Sunday, January 14, 11:05 a.m.: Opening Day

It was Sunday morning, which didn't help my mood. Because the Muslim Sabbath falls on Friday, weekends end on Saturday night. Sunday is the first day of the workweek. I elevated this to a human rights violation, but more to the point, it undermined my ingrained habit of taking Sunday mornings very slowly. My wife, Ann, noted that by working Sundays, my weekly teaching duties—consisting of twice-weekly classes—ended on Tuesday afternoon. Where she came from, this wasn't considered a full-time job—so I wasn't getting much sympathy at home.

My attitude didn't improve much as I watched the last students sluggishly file in. There were only a dozen in the class, which was par for the second year of Georgetown's School of Foreign Service in Qatar, in which only freshman and sophomore classes had been admitted. An additional class would be added each year until the school's full undergraduate complement was in place in the fourth year. That, at least, was the plan.

No one seemed happy that day. First-day classes tend to be fraught with anxiety for students. Add to the mix a new course with a new professor, topped by whatever baggage of expectations the students brought with them.

About one-third of the students were Qataris, about the same ratio as in the school overall. They were easily identified by their dress—the three women were clad in full-length black abayas, their hair covered in equally dark head scarves. Their faces, eyes, and cheeks, framed by their scarves, seemed to have been lavished with feminine attention that morning.

The one Qatari man wore the traditional white thobe, his white head cover or kaffiyeh held down by a black band. A dark, wispy beard hugged his chin. Keeping the head covering on required a straight neck and an erect posture, which added to an appearance of dignity and reserve. I assumed that students dressed in traditional attire were religious. Another rookie mistake.

The rest of the class was evenly divided between men and women, with two of the females covering their hair. Others were outfitted in the uniform of the global teenager: jeans, sneakers, and T-shirts spouting slogans. Most of the class was a shade darker than the teacher.

The class was held in a small, typically bland classroom. It contained a half-dozen unattached, uneven rows of chairs, each armed with its own moveable half desk for taking notes. A frequently glanced-at wall clock monitored the class from over the doorway.

One distinction of the room was its clean floor and sparkling surfaces. A hint of freshly applied ammonia could be detected early in the morning, blending with the ever-present air-conditioning. This tidiness wasn't a surprise given the legions of South Asians—called "blue boys"—scattered around the halls in blue uniforms with black sleeves dusting, sweeping, mopping, and scrubbing, all while trying to stay out of the way of their superiors on appointed educational missions. These slight, brown, inevitably smiling men and women seemed to belong to the building yet to be not quite part of the university.

Appropriately for a sage on the stage, I stood on a slightly raised platform in front of a whiteboard, with a small podium full of never-touched electronics. The dozen students filled about half the available seats. As is customary for the first day of class, the front row was unoccupied, a protective moat of separation. I could delude myself that it reflected a backhanded compliment regarding the feared force of the coming lectures.

I had several goals for the first day. I wanted the students to be excited about the coming semester and to think that the readings, discussions, and issues ahead would be engaging, maybe even fun. Closely related to this, if sometimes in conflict, was the importance of politics in their lives. What we were doing was significant and they should take their studies and assignments seriously.

Halfway through this sermon, I often paused and dramatically pointed to the inevitable migrant workers laboring outside our windows in the midst of their twelve-hour days, constructing yet another of Doha's metastasizing malls or monuments. I reminded them that life's luck separated them from earning a living through the sweat of their brow, having been lifted into this classroom by fortunes unearned—by them. One student later quoted me: "It is the ultimate luxury in the world that we can be here discussing ideas rather than digging ditches."

Perhaps overblown, but I concluded by noting that our privileges must not be wasted. The lesson, while greeted with grim nods, had usually faded by the time the first assignments were due.

One other goal in my first day presentations was for them to think kindly of their professor. I did this by saying something funny, which hardly ever worked, but as well-mannered youth, they politely smiled. I didn't have to be liked but I tried to convey that I was not a monster. At least not yet.

On this particular Sunday, I managed to accomplish none of my objectives.

All because I tried to throw one of the students out of class.

Admittedly, this was not one of my kinder acts as a teacher. But it was designed as a bit of theater to introduce and interest them in politics. After reviewing what we would cover in the semester ahead, I paused for their comments. Then I posed the questions: What is politics? Where does it take place? Most students, in Qatar and America, identified politics with acts of government. I intentionally misled them by voicing sympathy for this view.

But I was trying to get across a different point: that politics is a process of influence involving power and authority in many social settings, including church or mosque, home, even school.

After some prodding by the professor, at least one unsuspecting student responded that, no, politics doesn't go on in this classroom. The teacher, me, feigned anger at this answer and asked the student to leave. The intention was to stop the unhappy student at the door, ask why he or she was obeying, and thus encourage a more energetic discussion of authority and politics in universities, families, etc. That was the idea.

Now, when I carried out this exercise in the United States, there was usually a range of responses. The accomplished students I taught at Georgetown and Columbia reacted with detached bemusement. This display of aberrant behavior was *my* problem, not theirs. Perhaps in their mass-mediated, online-addled minds, they sensed a trap or an angle they had yet to uncover in the plot. Some reacted with smiles; some with smirks; and some quietly calculated whether their schedule would still allow them to transfer out of this wack job's course.

My initial attempt at this form of pedagogy hadn't worked terribly well. Just out of graduate school, I was teaching at Medgar Evers College, a tough inner-city school in Brooklyn. Classes were held in a sort of converted Catholic elementary school in a rundown section of Bushwick. It was bare-bones education. Chalk for the blackboards was scarce. Most of the students were in their twenties, their schooling having been interrupted by babies for the women, jail for many of the men, or poverty for both.

Anyway, I—an allegedly street-smart, recent Columbia University grad—pointed to a slouching student near the front of the room and asked him to leave. He refused to move. "I ain't goin' nowhere," was the gentleman's succinct response.

In full retreat, I quickly explained to the giggling class that this too was an example of politics.

Years later, on that first day of class in Doha, I was again the new guy on the block, a recent arrival. I had picked out a cheerful-looking, chubby Pakistani who frequently leaned over to talk to the guy in the next seat. (Note: I wasn't crazy enough to select anyone wearing traditional Arab dress.) When I asked him to leave, he smiled, disbelievingly. The class halfheartedly grimaced. I insisted: "Will you *pleeeze* leave." He slowly rose and headed for the door. I stopped him and went through my spiel. His relief was sincere; his interest probably faked. He sat down again. But I sensed trouble.

A low murmur of distress had run through the class. I saw looks of pain, discomfort, and even disbelief on the faces staring up at me. Oh boy. I sensed that I had stepped over a line. Ordering a student out of class had violated an unspoken code of public courtesy for me and pride for them. I had used my position to humiliate one of their peers. Perhaps this place did not need lessons on the unpredictable power of the powerful or their ability to shame those beneath them. Curiously, I had stumbled over these students' elevated respect for teachers. Their pain at my display of disapproval was a reminder that I was in another culture with different traditions of education, not to mention authority and politics.

That was one of the few mistakes in teaching I never repeated.

Looking back, I am surprised at my own daring in trying this little stunt so early in my tenure. To use that well-known Semitic tribal phrase, the *chutzpah* I displayed I seldom felt.

Already, some of my more attentive students were Googling my last name to see if they could identify more obviously Jewish people who shared the Wasserman tag. In those early days, I kept my mouth shut on matters of faith. "Don't ask, don't tell" was once good enough for gay GIs; it should be okay for me. To my relief, nobody asked.

Growing Pains

In the months between accepting this teaching position and arriving in Doha, I battled my demons, not all of which I could blame on the Arabs.

Okay, I'll blame the Jews.

Growing up in a Jewish family in the 1950s with parents only one generation away from Eastern Europe's pogroms and fresher received memories of the Holocaust meant breathing in the ghetto's insecurity about the outside world. Although I was born in a working-class garden apartment in southeast Washington, DC, my parents had grown up in New York tenements, the Bronx (Sam) and Brooklyn (Helen). Early on, they discovered that life was not going to be a cushy bed of matzo balls.

Both of Mom's parents died by the time she was twelve, compelling an older brother and sister to raise her with help from the city's welfare system. Dad's father was a tailor, which made Dad the one sitting at the family's Singer sewing machine—this despite a brawny build and huge arms appropriate to the football lineman he had been. My grandparents were never completely comfortable with English; my parents never went to college.

They did get enough education to rise to the middle class, escape New York, and hatch dreams for advancing their two sons. Through night school, Sam could put together sufficient credentials which, added to his considerable native technical skills, had allowed him to pass muster as an engineer, first working for the army and then the navy during and after World War II. It did not go unmentioned at the dinner table that engineering schools in the 1930s and '40s were not admitting Jews. Helen used New York City's public night schools to train as a bookkeeper and work part-time to supplement her career as a mom.

In 1940, with the war looming and the Depression lifting, Dad moved to Washington for a job in the federal government. While it didn't offer much money ($1,500 a year), it did promise enough security that he could marry, rent an apartment in the unfashionable but safe Southeast quadrant of DC, and raise a family. They delayed the birth of their first child—me—almost five years until December 1944, perhaps to make sure the war would be won. Brother Ed followed in 1948.

The initial temptation in looking back is to say that being Jewish was not that important. Sure, both parents were from self-identified Semitic generations—not that anyone spent much time talking about past traumas or ancestors. Ed and I went the expected bar mitzvah route following five years in after-school religious classes. Most of our family's social connections gravitated toward families with shared "Tribe" backgrounds.

Yet we weren't religious and we seldom attended services—except the obligatory once-a-year High Holidays of Rosh Hashanah and Yom Kippur—and ignored kosher dietary restrictions. (I can recall the ever-practical Helen declaring that religion had no business telling a mother what to feed her children.) My brother and I grew up Jewish but what that meant had to be teased out.

One clear meaning was that the family stood for safety while the outside world was uncertain and could be dangerous. Looking back, the connections were reinforcing: the less safe the world, the more important the home. The risks outside reinforced how high the walls of our family fortress had to be.

These life lessons were taught by words and deeds. Mom saying to my brother in getting him to attend some relative's celebration he was resisting: "Your friends will come and go but you'll always have your family." Or to me when I objected to an unwanted religious obligation: "You may not think you're Jewish but the world knows and will treat you that way."

They followed their own advice. Dad switched to the navy from the Army Redstone rocket program when it was moved in 1949 to Huntsville, Alabama. The explanation was that there weren't many Jewish families in Alabama and he wanted his kids raised with "our kind." Which meant, I suppose, forgoing Werner von Braun as a neighbor. ("Once the rockets are up, who cares where they come down? That's not my department," as Tom Lehrer, folksinger of my era, put it about the former Nazi scientist).

I can recall Mom in our changing Southeast neighborhood asking me after the first day of elementary school every year how many other Jewish students were in the new class. And the falling numbers were added to the data bolstering her case for moving to the suburbs. When we left for Silver Spring, it was not just because of the expected influx of blacks, the worsening integrated schools, and the perceived growing danger in the streets. It was also that other Jewish families were moving to places like Montgomery County, Maryland, where we landed in a freshly built, tidy, red-brick, bay window rambler in 1955. My parents paid $18,500, which was a steep enough price to provoke debate between them for years, before and after the purchase.

Of course, my parents' fears weren't unfounded. Southeast Washington soon became unlivable for families like ours with expectations for children's safety and upward mobility. Their "white flight" to the suburbs faintly echoed the upheaval of the previous generation from the shtetls of Ukraine and Poland. The motivations for our minor migration were similar: the push from physical insecurity and the pull of economic opportunity. The memory of historic threats was not clouded because this time the Cossacks were *schvartzes* and generally didn't ride horses.

The neighborhood streets, in both Silver Spring and DC, reinforced parental warnings. There were the usual fights, then considered vaguely acceptable for boys. And any verbal provocations were also deemed normal, including disparagements of race, religion, and size. One I recall involved an eleven-year-old me arriving at our kitchen door with a bleeding nose and a claim to victory over the attackers. The dialogue went like this:

Mom: Why were you fighting?
Me (after some hemming, hawing, and sniffling): He called me a Jew.
Mom: Well, you are a Jew.
Me: Yeah, but he doesn't have to call me that.
Mom: Whaddya gonna do, fight with everyone who calls you a Jew? You should be proud of being Jewish.

Me: Yeah, but that's not what he meant and anyway it's none of his business.

Mom: Sam (who was clearly on my side and just as clearly in the background), talk to your son.

The relevance of all this to my story of travel and work in the Middle East is that despite the intervening years of accomplishments, the advanced degrees, global travel, publications, and semi-important jobs, along with love affairs, marriage, and friendships with people of myriad backgrounds, when push came to shove, well into adulthood I found myself in a defensive crouch. Deep in my own mind, I was facing a bunch of bullies threatening me not for what I had done but for who I was. The years of achievements and layers of defenses fell away and I was again just a skinny kid exploring a strange neighborhood and lost on a darkening corner—alone, vulnerable, and scared.

On the Other Hand

Despite these bleak spasms of memory, I was not without resources in 2006. I had a strong, loving family behind me. My parents had both passed. But besides my wife Ann, there was our son Daniel in medical school and daughter Laura working on becoming a nurse. Brother Ed, who remained close, was then a professor of media ethics at Washington and Lee University in rural Leesburg, Virginia, where he lived with his wife, Eva. There were lots of friends from my varied careers in education, political consulting, journalism, and unemployment. Of course, a good percentage of this support group thought I was out of my mind.

At times when I've told this story, I've described myself as being offered a job teaching American politics in a fundamentalist Arab state I had never heard of. That was true at the beginning of the process when I first learned of Georgetown establishing its School of Foreign Service in Qatar. Ann and I, like most of our countrymen, knew nothing of Doha or Qatar. We looked it up in travel guide *Lonely Planet* only to see it described as "the dullest place on earth." Unhelpfully, the description continued, "There's absolutely no reason to visit Doha." And this is a publication trying to *encourage* foreign tourists.

Drastic shifts in my professional life were nothing new. Since leaving Medgar Evers College, New York City, and full-time teaching, I pursued what after twenty-five years I on occasion called a career. I moved to Washington in 1975 to become the issues coordinator for a presidential campaign. Not so helpful was that it was Fred Harris's spirited, populist, hopeless bid for the Democratic nomination in 1976. (Slogan: "Take the Rich Off Welfare!") After a year of what used to be called a political crusade, it hadn't worked out. Following that, I served a brief stint as a legislative assistant to Congressman Dave Obey, the Democrat from Wisconsin. Then I worked in the US Agency for International Development (USAID) as a special assistant for evaluation, a political appointment. The Reagan Administration put an end to that.

Then there were three years attempting to start a political satire magazine, *Mole*, which left behind good reviews, fond memories, and six-figure debt. I climbed out of that hole by helping my friend Bob Beckel, later a Fox TV commentator, start a political consulting firm. The ten years with Bob and afterward with a well-regarded public communications group (Robinson, Lake, Sawyer Miller) put me in solid financial shape but on less firm ground for the future. I grew to hate clients. And after a while they didn't care for me much either.

I wanted to get back to teaching.

The steps required to go from practicing politics to teaching it were not exactly a hop, skip, and a jump. Sure, I had a PhD from an Ivy League university, Columbia, where I had also taught. I could point to university press publications (an elite English university—Cambridge—had published my thesis) and a popular textbook in American politics that had flowered through a dozen editions. There was teaching as a part-time adjunct at Georgetown University and a year spent in China instructing grad students at the Hopkins-Nanjing Center for Chinese and American Studies. "Yes, that's all fine," said the faceless peers rejecting my application to teach US politics at some dozen American universities, "but where are the strangely neglected scholarly publications? And given your seniority, you'll probably be expensive. And all that time actually practicing politics? Can't have that."

Experience in politics as preparation for university teaching of political science is like trying to get a job in an oncology department by pointing out that you had cancer. Interesting background, but how does it apply? If George McGovern, former Democratic nominee for president, former party chair, senior US senator, and, yes, a PhD in history, could initially be turned down by Columbia's faculty as unqualified to teach a class in presidential politics (he was later hired part-time), then taking a pass on hiring me was not terribly surprising.

Spending the 2004–2005 academic year teaching in China at Johns Hopkins School of Advanced International Studies had opened my eyes to other, not-so-distant opportunities. Much to my surprise, American academics were highly valued overseas. There were jobs for those willing to temporarily give up the unique attractions of America, which at that point in my life—besides family—meant Ben & Jerry's Chocolate Fudge Brownie ice cream and episodes of *Deadwood*. Compensating for these sacrifices, teaching overseas offered income, novel encounters with interesting people, and, in China, exceptional students.

But a year in China was enough. It was a great, engaging place to teach and travel. It was also a year of never seeing stars at night because of air you could hear everyone choking on, not trusting the drinking water because of what floated down the Yangtze river outside our dorm window, and a homesick, environmentalist wife reminding me of the health consequences of all this. The benefits of exporting my teaching skills were, however, not lost.

In contrast to the American teaching posts I wasn't being offered, Doha had a strikingly attractive package of salary ($100,000) and perks (free housing and transportation) rarely seen by a verging-on-retirement, itinerant political scientist. Further, the largesse was coming from Georgetown, where I had done my undergraduate work—a school that had been a roof and refuge throughout my career as well as a source of numerous friends. I am a loyal Hoya.

Going to Doha would not be an act of altruism.

Taking a Look-See

To become a visiting professor, there were still the hiring hoops to jump through. This wasn't my first rodeo. The interviews went okay and my lecture about the writing I was doing on Washington lobbying didn't put the mixed audience of students and teachers to sleep right away. I had friends on the faculty and had taught classes on campus. Washington had taught me the value of maintaining networks. The faculty review committee gave their approval. Helping my chances was a lack of academic competitors interested both in teaching American politics and living in Doha, Qatar.

The next step was the preemployment visit. Georgetown, no fools they, decided that a dose of on-the-ground reality was necessary before they could be assured that approved candidates might actually show up.

So a month later, in April 2006, Ann and I were on a Qatar Airways flight, heading toward three nights at the Four Seasons in Doha, courtesy of my wannabe future employer. Our first impression on landing was the door opening and descending into a late Doha afternoon that resembled stepping into a pizza oven.

But the sales pitch that followed was impressive. The small faculty, less than a dozen, then in their first year of the start-up, were eager cheerleaders, conveying exuberance about how glad they were to see me join them. A year later, I would be sitting beside these smiling colleagues, beaming just as broadly, as we convinced other sadly misinformed skeptics to get their feet wet or at least some sand between their toes.

Even the awkward moments had their positive sides. During one of my interviews, an American dean asked if I was Jewish. After my solemn nod, he noted: "Well, we had to hire some of you guys sooner or later." I took consolation in the fantasy that—should nothing else work out—his very illegal question could be leveraged into explaining to friends and family around the dinner table why I ulti-mately decided not to take the job.

We were shown housing compounds available for faculty. They were walled, sand colored, and built to look like what passed for medieval Arab forts with cable TV. In fact, the residence we picked was called Barzan, which is Arabic for "a palace with watchtowers." It contained fifty-five large town houses, connected on one side to each other with parallel garages and, on the second floor, four bedrooms, each with its own bathroom and bidet. The two concentric, rectan-gular rings of residences surrounded a clubhouse, tennis court, and pool in the center. It was a new structure and the recently trans-planted nonnative palm trees showed an unhealthy droop under the sun of a real Arab spring.

Security was provided by twenty-four-hour-a-day, unarmed, uni-formed, Nepalese men at a gated entrance with retractable truck bar-riers that were raised and lowered out of the ground as traffic stopped at the guard post. Swiveling television monitors topped twelve-foot poles on each corner of the outside walls. We were advised by a secu-rity consultant from Carnegie Mellon who lived in Barzan to follow his example and take a house on the inside ring, a safer bet—from imagined incoming terrorist attacks—than the houses near the outer wall. We decided on a corner house on the inner ring, which was also farther away from one of the neighboring mosques, with a 4:00 a.m. call to prayer loud enough to wake up believers and nonbelievers alike.

Safety was not discussed much. There had been a bombing at the Doha Players' Theater at Doha College in downtown Doha a year ear-lier. *Twelfth Night* was being performed; the American ambassador was supposed to be there but was not. One expat was killed along with the Egyptian national, a Qatar Petroleum employee, who carried out the attack. It was vaguely thought to be a one-off act of a mad-man but not a lot is recalled.

When we asked if we should lock our thick bedroom door at night in addition to our front entrance, we got shrugs. One Georgetown administrator, when asked about security, replied, "It's safe till it's not safe." I am still not sure how reassuring that was supposed to be.

Although the visit could be considered a success, still I hesitated. Partly it was Ann. My wife spent much of the twenty-four-hour return trip sitting next to me sobbing—despite my pointing out all the neat stuff from her first time in business class. She said it was jet lag from our quick turnaround. But I recalled that when she married me twenty years earlier, her move from rural Washington State (on the edge of the North Cascades mountains) to Washington, DC, had covered an emotional distance equivalent to that from Earth to Mars. Doha might yet prove a galaxy farther. A look out the window as we took off hinted why.

Doha was a city that had done the most with what it had. And what it had was money ("Dough-Ahh," one envious colleague in the United States put it). The city skyline filled the jet's window with an array of tall, individually distinctive glass and steel towers. They may reveal more than intended.

Each building seemed to have been flown in from somewhere else, dropped from the sky onto its site as a glowing monument to honor whichever state-run agency paid for the endorsement. Whether they had an actual function was not clear—later we would discover that many were half-empty, some entirely dark for years. Little thought seemed to have gone into how one structure could harmonize with the others or even how they might reach their neighbors with an ordinary sidewalk. They seemed squeezed between a plain brown desert wrapping bordered by a mawkish sea that concealed the natural gas nurturing everything above.

Doha was a global city that might have been located anywhere. Like the supervisors in them, the buildings were imports. At first glance, the thought arose that the people and their buildings might well pack up and leave when their contracts ended. As our flight ascended, there was no way to tell whether these tall, expensive toys in this coastal sandbox would remain very long.

Eventually, I would grow protectively fond of Doha, the way a father cares for his plain teenage daughter who gets all dolled up for her high school prom. You found yourself remarking wistfully to your wife that she has, after all, done the most with what she has been given to work with. And Doha, with her flat, charmless sands bordering a dull, placid sea, would never be labeled a natural beauty. But that could be masked by expensive wrappings, modern technology, and inviting, occasionally exciting, happenings. And Doha, in time, would become almost home.

But it would take time. When I first arrived to teach, Ann wouldn't be with me, delaying her arrival by another couple of months. She explained this as a reasonable way to avoid Doha's heat—we're talking a humid 120°F in August—but I suspected she preferred watching from the slopes of Washington State's Mount Baker to "see how it goes." In other words, she wanted to uncover the on-the-ground truth of our move to the Middle East. Would my indulgent paranoia of "life among the terrorists" play out as nightmare fantasy or prescient insight? I could argue this either way, and I frequently did.

Shrinking the Problem

Still, when we returned from the employment visit, I hesitated.

As a child of the sixties, I was familiar with the acceptable tools for handling conflicting emotions, sleepless nights, and anxiety. Although I had not seen a shrink for several decades, arriving home from our Doha visit I could see this situation called for professional help. Reflecting a culture that responded to threatening challenges by consulting professional experts, I turned to an emotional specialist, a psychiatrist I will call Dr. Irving Strotz.

While I have no idea whether Dr. Strotz was actually Freudian in his psychoanalytical approach, he was certainly of the Vienna school in appearance. A short, trim-bearded gentleman over sixty, he was dressed formally if a little unfashionably in a dark suit, out of place both for the summer heat and for his no-longer-modern glass office in Bethesda, Maryland. He was "old school." When he spoke, which wasn't often, it was in carefully framed sentences, with a pronounced, if indeterminate, East European accent. His attempts to correct and Americanize his stiff manner were fleeting and unsuccessful. ("Call me Irv.") I was sure he smoked pipes earlier in his career, before smoking was outlawed in the workplace. Of course, he was Jewish.

In our few sessions, I carefully went through the dilemmas I was facing. I explained my desire to take the job, followed by my hesitation. I described the destination, the opportunity, the career prospects, the family resistance, and the resulting paralysis and indecision.

He listened, nodded occasionally, smiled at the appropriate times, and frowned when that was called for.

He didn't really speak at length until our last session. I was on my way out the door when he dropped his professional demeanor and spoke to me with some vigor about the learned conclusions he had drawn:

"You're not crazy to be scared. You're crazy to go. Haven't you been watching the news? These people hate Jews. They're anti-Semites. I've dealt with these f'kakta Nazis all my life. Stay away from them. They'll never change. You're outta your mind if you think you're safe around them. You want to educate them? What kinda mishugana are you? They should all drop dead."

This went on for a while. (He was being paid by the hour.) But the thrust of his remarks was obvious. I had hoped for something beyond the Likudnik political rant I had already heard from my relatives at no charge. Dr. Strotz was, I concluded, not going to provide the needed therapy for calming my nerves as I faced this potentially fatal career move.

Fortunately, the solution was not far away. It arrived at the scheduled visit to my regular doctor, Dr. Walter Liu. Perhaps, being Chinese, he was more global, arguably more pragmatic and accepting in his outlook. When I went to see him for my predeparture checkup, he diagnosed me as anxious, which wasn't much of a stretch. His next move, however, bordered on brilliant in its simplicity: drugs. What could be more American? He wrote a prescription for antianxiety chemicals to enhance the neurotransmitters in my brain. For the next six weeks, I took a modest, daily dose of lorazepam.

Did these pharmaceuticals have any long-term health consequences? Did the pills resolve the underlying issues or merely conceal the symptoms? I had no idea. I changed none of my views about the dangers that lay ahead, didn't think any better of my Arab hosts and, when asked, still declared myself terrified about what I was doing.

I just didn't give a shit.

That's a deal I'll take anytime.

CHAPTER 2

Onward, Liberal Scholars: Georgetown Comes to Arabia

One spring morning, just as Doha's oppressive, humid heat was regaining its grip on the city, a recently graduated student stopped by my office. Dressed in a Qatari woman's fashionable black abaya and brushing strands of brown hair back under her hijab, she explained that she wanted to apply to graduate school in England. Any problem in writing a letter for her? No, she had gotten good grades in my class. But when discussing which studies she actually wanted to pursue, she became vague. I said it would be difficult to write a recommendation to a school if I wasn't sure why she wanted to attend.

An uncomfortable silence followed. Then she blurted out the truth. "I don't really want to go to graduate school but if I stay in Doha my family will make me get married. Going to London for grad school is acceptable to them. For me, it means I can put off getting married and not have to confront my parents."

I wrote the recommendation.

Once again, I was learning a lesson from a student. Clearly, her family valued education for their daughter. But what she learned was not supposed to be a platform from which she might make independent choices that undermined her role in the family. For her part, she was willing to use her American university degree to carve out some personal autonomy from the traditions and expectations of her family. Studying in London was unlikely to permanently resolve this tension; it might only delay an inevitable marriage. But maybe not. My Doha predictions had been wrong before.

Providing cover stories for young female students wanting to escape traditional family pressures was not exactly what Georgetown University intended when it brought faculty, administrators, and curriculum from Washington to the Middle East. In the multi-million-dollar contract the school signed with Qatar Foundation, Georgetown was obligated to establish an identical copy of its noted School of Foreign Service in Washington, presumably to educate and elevate the next generation of Qatari diplomats. But there was more to it than that.

Underlying this professional training in global affairs lay a set of values central to a liberal education. American universities, Georgetown among them, embraced a free marketplace of ideas. This required encouraging an individual's freedom of expression and a wide tolerance for others' choices and beliefs. In a flattening, twenty-first-century world, this ought to lead to respect for groups regardless of race, gender, ethnicity, religion, or political beliefs. Inevitably, American academics were teaching liberal values they hoped would be applied in a lifetime of acceptance for others, ethnic minorities and religious dissenters included.

The emirate of Qatar apparently saw the world a little differently. This was an Islamic kingdom, governed by a ruling family, the al-Thanis, following Sharia rules. It proudly followed the Wahhabi school of Islam, firmly in the fundamentalist wing, from which extremist groups like al Qaeda also sprang. Because of a more relaxed attitude toward dress, along with personal and women's rights, compared to its larger neighbor, Saudi Arabia, expats often referred to Qatar as "Wahhabi Lite." Patrick Theros, former American ambassador to Qatar, pointed to his Greek heritage to describe the traditional distinction between liberal sea powers such as Athens and Qatar and conservative land powers such as Sparta and Saudi Arabia. "Qatar, because of its openness toward trade and foreign cultures, reflects a classic coastal country," he told me. "This geography has made it less puritanical in its religion, politics, and culture than land-based countries, like its neighbor Saudi Arabia."

Though religious practices in Qatar weren't as strict as in Saudi Arabia, one wouldn't want to take the distinction too far. While the emir and the government were considered reform-minded, freedom of the press didn't extend to dissenters in the political realm, freedom of speech didn't include public commentary on regime spending, and freedom of religion only recently had allowed the first Christian church to be built. Most of the manual labor in the kingdom was done by Asian migrants who had few rights as workers and none as citizens. And, at least prior to the 2017 siege by its neighbors, Qatar's leaders faced far fewer threats to their regime than the Saudis did.

Despite academic freedom enjoyed by the university, there was clearly a rather large gap between the ideals of liberal education and this Arab society. Bridging this divide, as well as living with it, were the tasks facing Georgetown—America's oldest Catholic university with Qatar's first School of Foreign Service—and its Arab hosts. And I, a Jewish professor of American government, was somewhat anxious about my ability to navigate the distance between who I was, what and whom I taught, and this strange land in which I now dwelled.

Yet looking back, I can see I began my mission with a curious and far from fixed blend of apprehension and idealism. My apprehension centered on who I was and where I had landed. Beyond the recurring qualms about physical safety, often reinforced by the headline news reporting violent conflicts surrounding us in the region, there were the doubts about the distance that was yet to be bridged to reach unknown students with unfamiliar thoughts and aspirations. Why were these students here and what did they want? And could the barriers between us be breached? How much hostility could I stand? And why should I tolerate any?

Opposing these barriers was the force of my own idealism. I tightly gripped onto my belief that I had much to offer here—that so late in my life and career I had something to teach that might just transform those willing to listen. It embarrasses me even now to admit that I arrogantly embraced such a role. But the higher the imagined barriers, the more I was forced into a psychic rededication to the good my university and I were bringing. After all, we came as the bearer of the gifts of American democracy, Western liberalism, cultural tolerance, and intellectual honesty—while personally eviscerating racism and anti-Semitism wherever it surfaced. At my age, I had become, of all things, a missionary.

Clearly my apprehension and idealism collided with each other, like rams butting heads during mating season. My idealistic impulses helped overcome my fears about what I was doing; my anxieties served to quiet my naïve drives toward perfecting that part of humanity showing up to my classes. Counterbalancing each other, they produced the compromise of a get-along academic skeptic working for the lucre of wages and lifestyle. But my cynicism only covered the bubbles on the surface, derived from far deeper, much hotter conflicting forces that it concealed. I really did think I could change the world if I survived.

In time, I would find both my apprehension and ideals to be overdone.

But it would take time.

The Launch

"After September 11, I wondered what I could do. I no longer worked for the government. I was not in political military affairs any longer. I think the thing that came closest to satisfying this concern—in other words, that would scratch that particular itch—was working to establish this school in Qatar."—Dean Robert Gallucci, interview with Janet H. Moore, January 31, 2007

Jim Reardon-Anderson recalled the day in October 2002 when he was invited to come down to the office of the dean of Georgetown's School of Foreign Service in Washington "to meet some people from Doha." Reardon-Anderson, who would later serve as the first dean of the school in Qatar (2005–2010, 2016–2017), was surprised to find out that the group was interested in having Georgetown establish a branch of the Foreign Service School in Doha. His impression was that they apparently did not know much about Georgetown. They didn't know it was more than nominally Catholic and started by Jesuits. They thought it was a training institute for diplomats.

There was a backstory to the visit. Patrick Theros, who accompanied the Qataris, had been the American ambassador to Qatar (1996–1998). He was also a 1963 alumnus of the Foreign Service School and had served under the dean of the school, Robert Gallucci, when both were State Department foreign service officers. When Theros learned of the Qatari interest in training the country's diplomats for overseas service, he suggested they meet with Gallucci on a visit to the United States. A thin bundle of energy, Theros sang the praises of his alma mater as America's oldest and most prestigious school for international affairs. Buying the best brand of whatever product was being acquired was a recurring theme in Qatar's public policies.

The group from Doha envisioned a foreign service school fitting into the professional training provided by five other American universities on a campus they called Education City, a construction site that was on its way to becoming the largest overseas enclave of American colleges. Texas A&M University was training engineers to service Qatar's abundant natural gas fields offshore; Carnegie Mellon University was responsible for producing business and computer professionals; Virginia Commonwealth University offered art and fashion design; and Weill-Cornell Medical College prepared doctors. Later, in 2008, Northwestern University was brought in to turn out journalists and communication specialists. Qatar's leaders wanted excellence in each of these areas and they had decided that American institutions of higher education were the best in the world. Since the wealthy emirate could afford the best, it bought them.

"Unimaginable" was Dean Gallucci's initial response to the idea when he was approached earlier in 2002. In April of that year, Ambassador Theros had privately broached the topic in a chat with his old State Department colleague. At this point in the discussions, Georgetown's administrators were decidedly not interested. For starters, this initial conversation occurred only six months after 9/11, and that had to weigh on any consideration of relocating to the Arab world—and in a fundamentalist Islamic state at that. After a career in diplomacy, Gallucci was not exactly a naïve negotiator and this opening show of reluctance might have signaled an opening bid to the shrewd traders from the Persian Gulf. (Gallucci denies this interpretation.)

However hesitant the dean might have been, it was not enough to discourage another meeting a couple months later when the First Deputy Premier and Foreign Minister Sheikh Hamad bin Jassem bin Jabor Al-Thani was visiting Washington. This time, with Theros in attendance, the dean and minister met at the nearby Four Seasons Hotel, discreetly off campus. This initial meeting with a high-ranking Qatar official established the seriousness of the Gulf government in its pursuit of the School of Foreign Service. It was agreed that an official delegation from Doha would come in October to make a formal presentation.

The October Qatari delegation—the one with which Reardon-Anderson had met—was led by Sheikha Abdullah Al-Misnad, president of Qatar University and a prominent member of the ruling Al-Thani family. Accompanied by Qatar's ambassador to the United States as well as two members of Qatar's American law firm (Patton Boggs), Sheikha Al-Misnad made an impressive presentation. The Qataris had clearly talked to other schools, knew what they needed, and knew the proposal could work only if they reassured Georgetown administrators they would fully accept the University's freedom and autonomy in Doha.

Qatar's emir, Sheikh Hamad bin Khalifa Al Thani, had a reputation as a reformer who wanted to bring world-recognized education to his country. Sheikh Hamad was a high-energy monarch. He was a large man both in his bulk and his ambitions. In November 1996, he had launched and subsidized Al Jazeera, a respected global media network, and he soon expanded it to include an English-language channel paralleling the original Arabic one. He had tied Qatar closely to the United States first by building two military air bases and then by inviting American forces there after they had been asked to leave Saudi Arabia. The accumulating American universities in Doha added to Qatar's luster as a key American ally in the region. The tiny Gulf emirate was spoken of by many, in a mixture of awe and disdain, as "punching above its weight class."

The October meeting was followed by considerable back-and-forth. The Americans agreed to a site visit in Doha in January 2003. Deans Gallucci and Reardon-Anderson were accompanied by Jane McAuliffe, dean of Georgetown College, which, because of the way the university curriculum was structured, offered most of the classes that would have to be taught by the School of Foreign Service in Doha. The highlight of the trip was a presentation by Sheikha Mozah bint Nasser Al-Missad of Qatar about her plans for Georgetown and Education City. The three US visitors went home convinced that the project was worth pursuing.

Sheikha Mozah was the force behind Education City and Qatar Foundation's invitation to Georgetown. She was the third of the emir's wives, but as his consort was considered the first among equals as well as a powerful political player in Qatar. Many Qatari women, especially young, educated ones, held her up as an inspiration. One former student—clearly a fan—who worked for the sheikha described her as "a role model of female leadership and class":

Mozah bint Nasser is a symbol of modernity and female empowerment in the region. She has strong distinctly Middle Eastern features with tanned skin, sharp narrow nose and chiseled cheekbones. She has dark strong eyes often rimmed with black eyeliner, which is a symbol of beauty in traditional Qatari culture. She is tall and lean, often towering over her husband the emir, sporting colorful and glamorous belted floor length gowns with matching turban reflecting the modesty of the traditional Islamic dress with the modernity of today's Paris fashion houses. . . . Her carefully constructed outfits are a representation of her projected identity as a modern traditionalist.

Even a more detached Georgetown administrator who saw the sheikha speak in a number of different settings described her as "always being aware of her audience and of always projecting an intelligent, impressive persona." With an assured self-confidence, she gave no quarter in arguments, including any she may have had with her husband. Following one conversation between the two Foreign Service deans and the sheikha in 2003, ending with the Georgetown men enthusiastic about the prospects of coming, Jane McAuliffe said to her companions, "I am not going to leave you two alone with her again."

The Almighty Riyal

The Qataris brought considerable resources to bear in helping the sheikha overcome Georgetown's initial reluctance. Among these was the "Well of Knowledge" the sheikha had behind her. The story goes that one day she approached her husband about obtaining a secure funding source from the country's oil and gas reserves for Qatar Foundation's activities. As she recalled the conversation to a reporter: "I'm going to ask His Highness if he would dedicate a well to our programs. I'm going to call it a 'Well of Knowledge.' This is for a recycling of wealth from natural resources to human resources." The emir agreed to the plan. The deal was done in an afternoon. The sheikha added, "Anything related to education, he couldn't say no." Others concluded this covered most things related to the sheikha.

Qatar agreed to pay for all of Georgetown's expenses arising from the negotiations, travel, and proposal writing—at a cost of some $1.5 million. In addition, as a testament to good faith—that the university was "worthy of gifts" as one Georgetown administrator put it—there was an early understanding that Qatar would endow three faculty chairs at $5 million apiece for studies of the Middle East, an agreement signed in late 2005. While these chairs were named after the Al Thani royal family, the regime, as per normal university procedures, would have no role in selecting the professors who filled the chairs.

Subsequent criticism of Georgetown's involvement in Qatar focused to a considerable extent on the issue of money. The critique was essentially that the university sold its academic reputation and lowered its standards in order to reap the rewards of educating a privileged elite in an autocratic state. Georgetown was, as one staffer put it, "whorin' the brand."

But for those Georgetown administrators involved, money was more of a defensive protection than part of an acquisitive game plan. With Doha, offering "self-funding plus," there was no financial downside. When they had previously put out feelers for an overseas campus in China, the Chinese had been welcoming but they also made it clear the Hoyas had to bring their own dollars. One Georgetown department chair said the Qatar project would never have been approved on the main campus without the upfront costs being covered. He added that he thought the effort expended by Georgetown had been worth more than the money generated. Reardon-Anderson said, "No one thought we'd make money, but we wanted to be sure it wasn't a money loser." And Gallucci added, "We were not looking at it as a cash cow."

However, on a working level, the campus in Doha had to be made attractive enough for administrators, staff, and especially faculty to relocate to an unknown desert kingdom. To maintain the standards that were key to the project's success, there needed to be a "sell job" to get a permanent core of faculty. This required Georgetown to keep control of administration, curriculum, academic standards, and faculty recruitment. It also meant offering faculty some one-and-a-half times conventional salary, plus housing, a round-trip business ticket for home leave, a car allowance, private school education for the children, and the prospect of a glistening pot of research monies. Even then, reaction from the faculty on the main campus at the time could best be described as lukewarm. Beyond those already involved in Arab studies, few among Georgetown's faculty jumped at the chance of going to Doha. It was easier to recruit university staff for human resources, information technology, student affairs, and the library; they were more willing to take an excursion to an exotic land, all the while keeping their positions at Georgetown and adding income.

The dismissal of monetary motivations brings to mind H. L. Mencken's remark, "When somebody says it's not about the money, it's about the money." Clearly, the Doha deal checked off a few boxes in Georgetown's financial calculations.

Certainly, the Board of Trustees who made the final decision, after showing some initial reluctance, were aware that Georgetown's sterling academic reputation rested on a slender financial base. In 2003, Harvard ranked first in American university endowments with some $19 billion. Georgetown came in at seventy-sixth, with less than $591 million in its coffers. This put it at the same level as schools such as the University of Tennessee ($592 million) and less than St. Louis University ($645 million), a less-prestigious Catholic institution. Georgetown's annual operating revenues were $624 million that year. But it's fair to say that in 2003, Georgetown's financial resources did not match its scholarly aspirations.

Thus, the financial benefits to the university from exporting its education had to be welcomed. The ten-year deal as negotiated was cost free for Georgetown, with all compensations, buildings, and infrastructure paid for by Qatar.

The yearly budget was to range between $50 and $60 million with salaries and benefits making up 70 percent of the total. The main campus received an annual management fee of $5.8 million. But this underestimated the returns to Georgetown of their Gulf project. All its operations in Doha were cost free. The building and infrastructure (including maintenance and security personnel) were paid by Qatar Foundation, the nonprofit, government-owned agency running Education City. About 30 percent of the funds for compensation were sent to Washington to pay for the retirement, medical, and educational benefits of employees. This money went into university coffers and although the school in Qatar also benefited, the funds ended up in a pool for general use. The point is that beyond the almost $6 million in annual management fees, there were a few million more going back to Washington in indirect revenue. (This doesn't count the three chairs Doha funded on the Washington campus or any other contributions coming from the emirate.)

In its first ten years of operation (2005–2015), the School of Foreign Service in Qatar would go from 8 faculty members to 51.

At the end of that decade, total employees grew from 43 to 150, including faculty. The number of students in the first class—18—would grow by adding one class a year, cresting at 270 for all four years of college. (The school's target remains 300 students.) Meanwhile, the operating budget grew from $30 million to around $50 million.

The maintenance and service staff would be paid and managed directly by Qatar Foundation, which largely removed the school from the contentious issues surrounding migrant laborers: their treatment, rights, and compensations for their work in Qatar. Of course, the low-level salaries paid to these largely Asian migrants substantially lowered the costs of operating the school.

Negotiating the Mission

Checking off the financial boxes did not resolve all of Georgetown's doubts about the project or settle all the issues. The two and a half years of negotiating, from early 2003 to mid-2005, were used in part to answer questions that arose on Georgetown's side about undertaking a project unprecedented in its history.

Robert Gallucci put the central issue in terms of "mission." Is this what Georgetown does? Why would the university do it? On a summer day in 2015, he reminisced. When I interviewed him, he was sitting in the dining room of his Plains, Virginia, "place," a sprawling house in horse country thirty miles from Washington. Retired for a few years, he seemed settled following successful careers in the State Department, as a dean at Georgetown, and then as president of the MacArthur Foundation. He also considers the Qatar school to be one of his proudest accomplishments.

He answered his own questions appropriately for a career American diplomat with a practiced eye on the big picture.

"The Gulf is an important part of the world—important for the US. In these months after 9/11, the chance to shape the minds of rising elites in the Middle East was too great an opportunity to pass up. And isn't this what Georgetown as an international university should be doing? And wouldn't such a link with an Arab state, with an enlightened leadership, also enrich student and faculty life on the main campus?"

Issues arose. Georgetown's Board of Trustees wanted to make sure its connection to Qatar wouldn't weaken the School of Foreign Service, stretching its resources and faculty in unexpected ways. The Qataris' cost-plus contract and their resource wealth, as well as their close military ties to America, reassured the Trustees.

Some raised the question of whether this initiative might annoy the Saudis, Qatar's rivals in the Gulf. But Gallucci said the Saudis didn't seem to care. Endorsing an Arab state that hadn't formally accepted Israel's existence was raised as an objection. At the time, however, Qatar had commercial relations with Tel Aviv and fell into the more-or-less liberal camp compared to the rest of the Arab Middle East.

Strange as it seems, the prospect that Qatar's elite would use the school to educate their own children was never brought up or even foreseen by Georgetown's negotiators. One problem that *was* expected concerned Georgetown's identity as a Catholic university. For some Qatari leaders, Catholicism was arguably an attractive part of the package, presumably some faith and values being better than the "none of the above" found at more secular American colleges. Even teaching a required course on "The Problem of God" was not seen as offensive, at least after some explaining.

Qatari negotiators did object to Georgetown having a Jesuit chaplain on the Doha campus. Not unreasonably, they thought of Catholic missionaries trying to spread their faith and, worse yet, on the Arab state's dime. After considerable back and forth, the parties agreed that Georgetown could have a Jesuit on staff, he could give classes, counsel students, and say Mass, but he would not be called a chaplain. Georgetown's negotiators, having gained the substance of a Jesuit on campus, conceded on the title.

A small prayer room was allowed for Catholic Mass to be held once a week. Though it was open to them, Muslim students didn't use it. Sunday Mass was not to be advertised. Wine, while officially banned, would be smuggled into the building for the service. At the request of the Qataris, none of these understandings were put into writing.

Qatar's negotiators knew what they sought from the relationship: they wanted the best in undergraduate education in international affairs. From early in the discussions, the Arab leaders seemed convinced that Georgetown offered that. But the Georgetown negotiators didn't think the matter of "education" was quite so simple.

Recognizing the contrast between a modern American university and a traditional Arab nation, the Americans stressed that the package the Qataris were buying contained a liberal education. A career in modern international affairs rested on a broad study of the liberal arts. There was to be no shortcut in preparing undergraduates for diplomacy. Instead, there was a broad foundation in the social sciences, humanities, history, languages, and philosophy. That was essentially what Georgetown offered in its undergraduate curriculum. Curiously, courses in natural science were not included. But that was due to a peculiar myopia among the founders of the school, which had led to a long-standing student joke that "SFS" meant "Saved From Science." Gallucci wasn't sure the Qataris ever fully understood what they were buying. He recalled one Qatari saying, "You can persuade me there is a liberal education beneath this but I don't give a shit. I only want the best there is."

On this point, the two parties agreed to disagree. As one of the Qataris put it, in an off-the-record comment to the dean that hinted at future challenges, "You want liberal education. Fine, you can say it but don't say it too often."

Counting Down to Takeoff

On May 17, 2005, the agreement between Georgetown and Qatar Foundation was signed in New York City. The school was expected to open in the fall, mere months later. Surprisingly, it actually did.

Before the contract was even signed, Georgetown staff were in Doha planning for the new school. Junie Nathani, who was to serve as Chief Administrative Officer for the school, visited Doha in summer 2004 and again in February 2005. She moved to Doha three months later. She spoke with counterparts at Carnegie Mellon about their experiences and used their operations as a model. Not only did Nathani and her people have to hire everyone—faculty and staff—they also had to figure out residence permits, housing, expat allowances, taxes, health insurance, IT communications, recruitment of locals, and library resources. Looking back, she said, "It was crazy. We made it up as we went along."

Georgetown staffers were bolstered by a contagious, "all-hands-on-deck" enthusiasm arising from being part of a major start-up enterprise. Even the lack of Internet, television, or phones in their new housing compounds worked for them by encouraging the staff to spend evenings at school working. People were also startled by the resources Qatar was throwing their way. Their own building, architect included, was planned from the beginning. In the meantime, they were allotted ample space in the Liberal Arts and Sciences (LAS) building—affectionately called the LOST building for its complex office layouts—while Qatar Foundation handled the maintenance of infrastructure including managing the building workers, guards, and cleaners.

Relations with Qataris were proper if not close, a pattern that would endure. One administrator commented about "how little we interacted with Qataris." Curiously, there was no pressure to employ local Qataris. Georgetown's muted attempts to hire Qataris went nowhere. The Foundation sent over Qatari candidates who were either uninterested or unqualified. These candidates had government jobs available for the asking—positions notorious for requiring little effort or even much time in the office. One effect of this was that the staff and faculty, however diverse their background, soon got comfortable—socially and professionally—in expat circles. It may have been inevitable.

One bit of pressure from the Qatar side came from the desire to open the school sooner than some at Georgetown wanted. There was considerable doubt whether the university staff could manage the fall 2005 opening schedule. Most of this first class would be drawn from the offspring of local residents—including prominent Qatari officials, foreign diplomats, and wealthy businessmen. These sorts of families in Doha were anxiously waiting for the school to open. And no parent had more clout over the schedule than Sheikha Mozah. A mother's concern that her own child's education be completed on time may have been the most basic of motives behind the accelerated start. Her son, Mohammed, was ready to enter college that fall and would become an honors graduate in the first graduating class.

From early on, there was apprehension about the quality of the students who could be recruited. Reardon-Anderson told the Georgetown student newspaper, The *Hoya*, "The challenge will be to get a student body of the quality and caliber to sustain a Georgetown education." Despite some apprehension, recruiting students did not prove difficult. Since Georgetown staffers were trying to fill a freshman class of only twenty-five, the task was manageable. Staffers went as far as placing ads in the local papers soliciting students—a non-traditional, un-Hoya approach.

Freshman applicants and their parents were invited to gather at The Diplomatic Club, a venerable watering spot for the upper reaches of Doha's foreign community. The Club's ballroom lent a polished veneer to the proceedings. With its light blue-and-white décor, chandeliers, and doors opening to the waters of the Gulf, the setting embraced the two hundred people attending with a placid, refined elegance. It didn't last long.

Dean Reardon-Anderson was joined onstage by the Jesuit in residence, Father Ryan Maher, who asked the dean what he should say. The dean shrugged and said, "Whatever." Father Maher, in full priestly attire, proceeded to deliver what one attendee described as "a red-meat account of Catholicism." Without much calculation or planning, he described the school as committed to Christian ideals by delivering an education illuminated by Catholic values. He apparently went on for a while.

The audience sat quietly, clothed in the well-mannered silence of uncertain guests who had arrived late to someone else's party. But in the question-and-answer period that followed, one voluble local personality in full thobe and beard—a gentleman who would later and loudly infiltrate many of the school's events—let loose with a diatribe. "We don't need you here if what you're doing is bringing Christianity. We've already defeated you Crusaders once." And so on.

When he at last sat down, the dean searched the audience for any upraised hand that might still salvage an event that appeared to be flushing itself down a multicultural toilet. He pointed to a woman near the front who sincerely, if unintentionally, asked the most reassuring question the academics on the stage could have hoped for:

"What SAT score does my son need to get into your school?"

There were audible sighs of relief from the university staff on the stage. They were back in business. They could return to what passed for normal in college admissions. The dean remembers that session as the school's last major salvo on Christianity, outgoing or incoming.

The evening at The Diplomatic Club was a reminder, as Dean Reardon-Anderson ruefully put it, "We were not setting up a school in Belgium."

One curious trait of his Qatar hosts and benefactors was their hands-off approach to the school. In a sense, their self-restraint—if that's the proper characterization—was admirable. When it came to admitting students, even those from prominent families, there was notably little lobbying, much less than admissions officials had encountered on the main campus in Washington. Qatari students were given preference in admissions—along the lines of an informal affirmative action program. This was considered necessary to bring Qatari numbers up to around 30 percent of the student body. But the dean denied that academic standards were lowered. He pointed to the variation in the numbers of Qataris actually accepted, dropping as low as 20 percent of the total in one year.

One disappointing aspect of the hosts' detachment lay in the lack of Qatari involvement in the education Georgetown was providing. Despite the tens of millions of dollars that the school was costing each year, there seemed little interest in what was going on in the classrooms and administrators' suites and, even less, in the research undertaken outside of class. Qatar Foundation officials never visited the campus to see what their expensive hires were doing. Nor did they ever ask to meet with students or faculty.

This could be seen as admirable respect for the independence and autonomy of the scholarship they were underwriting. But other administrators pointed to the soon-to-be-opened art museum as a more relevant analogy. Like the collections for the expensive I. M. Pei-designed Museum of Islamic Art, education was another expensively wrapped commodity. Accumulating art or education didn't require engaging with either artists or educators. The process of creation was of secondary interest in both cases. Only the finished product seemed to matter. As one university administrator said about this Qatari attitude toward education, "It's just art on the wall."

On the Qatari Side

Which still leaves the question of Qatari motives for hosting Georgetown and the other American universities. Dean Gallucci, who probably spent more time with Qatari leaders than any other Georgetown official, summed up their thinking in a question: "What is Qatar going to be when the gas runs out?" The answer to diversifying the economy away from its dependence on a single resource inevitably went back to educating the people and ensuring that the next generations would have the skills to compete in a modern, globalizing world—what the leadership called "the Knowledge Economy." And by the way, keeping the ruling family in power with the foreign and domestic alliances that kept Qatar stable, independent, and prospering.

Some insight into Qatari thinking can be garnered from a speech given by Sheikha Mozah at the time her Foundation was in negotiations with Georgetown. On September 23, 2004, in Los Angeles at a Beverly Hills banquet, in front of eighty guests from the upper reaches of American business, politics, and entertainment, she spoke about her goals for higher education in Qatar. Calling Education City "an engine of change for Qatar," she continued, "In order to have effective citizens we need to have effective countries. And to achieve this we need to start with education. . . . We have the natural resources and we have to couple this with our human resources."

The sheikha held out hope that such education would lead to understanding and tolerance as well as providing building blocks to establishing a viable democracy. In speaking to a largely American business audience, the sheikha foresaw that there would be close relationships between global industrial giants and these world-class academic institutions. With some $40 billion of investments, mostly American, coming to Qatar in 2003 alone, partnerships with American universities and corporations in Doha seemed a reasonable prospect. By providing "the stability of economic freedom," such foreign involvement could, in turn, lead to establishing democracy, a somewhat happy notion probably pleasing to an American audience. In fact, during the years of Emir Hamad's rule, the public embrace of "democracy" became less and less of a priority for the ruling family.

A more conspicuous goal for the leadership was the hope that this education could overcome the economy's dependence on expatriate workers. As far back as 1935, Qatari leaders had signed agreements with foreign oil companies that allowed them to import technical employees, managers, and clerks where locals weren't available. This was always resented and in 1951 the emir at the time had demanded the expulsion of all foreign workers of Petroleum Development-Qatar. But the dependence on expats, even in education, only increased.

In 1977, Qatar's first and only indigenous university, Qatar University, was founded. Despite the money lavished on the school, Qatar University did not gain the international distinction that was hoped for. Put diplomatically, returns had generally been low. Attempts to reform the university or enter into cooperative ventures with overseas partners went nowhere. Scholarships were established for Qataris studying abroad and by 1985, some one thousand were enrolled in universities outside of Qatar.

By that same year, each of the Gulf States had established its own national university. The attempts at a single regional university serving all the states in the Gulf foundered on nationalism; each country wanted its own university as a mark of civilization and modernization. But their own national universities never quite lived up to the expectations of their founders. As Fathy Saoud, then higher-education adviser to Qatar Foundation, said in 2002, "Many of our region's higher-education institutions have been of average quality, and few, if any, have achieved international recognition. We want to encourage our top students to stay at home rather than going abroad."

Qatar saw the chance to gain leadership in the region through its promotion of quality higher education. Geoff Kelly, at the time Qatar Foundation Senior Media Officer, declared that the country wanted to become a hub for education and research in the region. "We want to produce a new generation of critical thinkers who are comfortable in the international marketplace—which is one of the reasons that Georgetown is a natural fit for us here." And he added, "Qatar's leaders don't feel that they have time to allow a university a century to mature, so we're building our own out of the best parts we can find—making a sort of university of universities."

The question facing Qatar's leaders remained how to provide quality, internationally recognized education for their students. The creation of Qatar Foundation in 1995 was intended in large part to recruit American universities to Qatar to achieve this goal. And in the words of Sheikh Abdullah Al-Thani, vice president for Education at Qatar Foundation, the problem was how to provide this education "right away, immediately."

Priority was given to finding a single foreign university that could offer top-quality education in three areas: medicine, engineering, and business. American universities were more receptive to collaborating with the Qataris than the Europeans who were approached. America's two long-established colleges in the Middle East—American University of Beirut (1866) and the American University of Cairo (1919)—contributed to the regional reputation of the United States for quality higher education. American universities since then had become the "gold standard" in global higher education and Qatar wanted one.

Bringing an overseas university to Qatar was a complex, multiyear task that was pursued at the highest levels of government. In early 1998, Sheikha Mozah had toured schools in the United States and

36

when she returned, she told an associate that "she had seen heaven." She was convinced American universities were the answer to providing Qataris with higher education. However, her approaches to two Ivy League schools, Harvard and Yale, were rebuffed. A visit to Georgetown University's president, Reverend Leo O'Donovan, SJ, was cordial but the president told the sheikha that his university was not the solution for Qatar; it did not have the capacity to create an entire university in the Middle East.

At the urging of Patrick Theros, Qatar began to seriously consider America's public state universities as overseas partners. Theros, who was then president of the US-Qatar Business Council, served as an advisor to the royal family and was closely involved in the education project. He argued that American public universities were generally larger and contained quality diversified professional schools. Ohio State University and the University of Illinois were approached but both negotiations eventually foundered because of faculty opposition. Other state universities were intrigued at first but abandoned the idea for one reason or another.

Laura D'Andrea Tyson, who had just left her position as chair of the President's Council of Economic Advisers in the Clinton Administration, was hired by the University of Virginia to help pitch a transplanted undergraduate curriculum to Education City. Operated by UVA, this established a model that would be emulated ten years later in Abu Dhabi by New York University. While negotiations with UVA went on for a while, by 1999 Virginia decided to forgo any deal. "We were very close to signing with Virginia," recalled Sheikha Mozah. But as a state university, the governing board may have been concerned about "selling" the school to an Arab "petrodollar" country. UVA's president at the time, John T. Casteen III, commented, "I remember being told it was just a long way from Virginia."

The University of North Carolina at Chapel Hill was interested enough to send a contingent of sixty faculty and staff in November 2001. But the business school that had taken the lead in the negotiations ultimately withdrew. Although there were reported disagreements over money, the challenge of faculty recruitment was the major reason cited by the dean of North Carolina's business school: "The number one area where we couldn't agree was on the number and duration of Chapel Hill faculty who would be in Qatar not for six or seven weeks, but for a year or two or more. It was something faculty were reluctant to do, particularly with the tensions building in the region."

The fear in Chapel Hill and elsewhere was that the difficulty of staffing would lead to hiring adjunct teachers and turning the overseas campus into a franchise operation. Partly this reflected the uncertain times everyone was operating under. As the *Chronicle of Higher Education* noted in 2002, "Qatar has become a much scarier place for Americans since the September 11 terrorist attacks and the buildup of US troops in Qatar in preparation for a possible invasion of Iraq."

Although faculty recruitment and terrorism were challenges, the issue of money lurked in the background—and foreground for that matter. One problem Qatar had was that its breakthrough in creating Education City was enticing Cornell's medical school to come to Doha. The price Qatar paid for this had set the bar pretty high for other schools' financial expectations.

For its Doha transplant, Cornell was receiving $750 million over eleven years plus an undisclosed gift that was to be kept secret. (Sources close to Qatar Foundation put it at $70 million.) North Carolina newspapers reported that UNC's business school wanted $35 million a year while Qatar offered $10 million. UNC claimed the larger sum was needed to provide incentives for its faculty to relocate. One UNC professor noted, "None of the other universities were offered anything near what Cornell was getting." There was a good reason for that.

Cornell's medical school's decision to locate a branch in Doha provided the needed kick start for launching Education City. It also took a uniquely positioned insider to bring it off. Sanford "Sandy" Weill was not only chief executive and chairman of Citigroup from 1998 to 2003 (the largest financial services company in the world at the time); he was also a member of the Qatar Foundation Board and a sufficiently large donor in 1998 to Cornell's medical school that it was renamed Weill-Cornell in his honor. A corporate executive of considerable ego, he suggested to the sheikha that the medical school would make a perfect fit for Doha. He then, in the words of one insider, "bludgeoned the school into it." Cornell signed on with Qatar Foundation in 2001.

Georgetown Arrives

From the Qatar side, the Georgetown venture began in earnest in early 2002. Patrick Theros remembered being invited to a meeting with the emir, the Sheikha Mozah, and Sheikh Jassim. At the meeting, Jassim announced that Qatar needed a "political" school. By this, he meant a school to train public servants for careers in diplomacy. They wanted the next generation of Qataris to be schooled in the arts of foreign affairs so they could fill positions to promote the country's hyperactive diplomacy. And they wanted the best.

Theros, ever the energetic, articulate Georgetown advocate, recalled the conversation this way:

Foreign Minister Jassim said they were only educating their youth in the sciences. This is not adequate. We need to expand into politics and public service, to produce a generation that can govern. Where can we get this?

The sheikha said she had heard of "Sauce" in Washington.

Theros: You mean SAIS Johns Hopkins School of Advanced International Studies. But that's not the best.

Sheikha: What's the best?

Theros: The best is the one that produced the best ambassador you ever had. Me. And my alma mater is Georgetown's School of Foreign Service.

The Qataris envisioned the school becoming a magnet for education in the Gulf, attracting students from their neighbors—much like in the 1950s when Qatar was known for having the best high school in the region and which drew in students from across the area.

Theros agreed to help by meeting with his friend and former boss who was now the dean of Georgetown's School of Foreign Service.

Shortly afterward, Theros held a series of meetings with Dean Gallucci that initially failed to engender much enthusiasm. When he first broached the idea, Gallucci asked if he had been drinking. Theros thought Gallucci's reluctance came less from thinking it was a bad idea than from not wanting to go to his boss because he feared rejection. The dean didn't think Jack DeGioia, who had become University President less than a year before, would go for it. When Gallucci finally went to DeGioia, he was surprised that DeGioia thought it was a great idea, well worth exploring. Word was sent back to Doha, the Qatari ambassador in Washington was brought into the discussions, and the negotiations commenced.

From Qatar's point of view, most of the issues were resolved fairly quickly but, as mentioned, the issue of Catholicism may have caused the negotiations to stall. On his initial visit to the sheikha, Dean Gallucci had declared that Georgetown's Catholic character was intrinsic to the school and couldn't be compromised. We come as a Catholic school or we don't come at all, the dean declared. Gallucci feared the religious issue might become a deal killer and would be better confronted early.

The sheikha hadn't batted an eye. She responded that she admired the university's ability to act as a critical school within the faith. They could encourage informed criticism under the roof of a Catholic university. Islam had lost that skill. She hoped they could learn how Catholics had adapted their own religion to allow liberal thinking and dissent at their schools while still retaining the core of their faith. It was an important lesson for Muslims to learn as well.

Whether everyone at Qatar Foundation was quite as tolerant of Catholicism is doubtful. Since most leading American private universities had religious origins and retained a loose affiliation with their faith—Yale was Congregationalist, for example—it would be easy for foreigners to confuse the importance of the school's origins with its current connection with religion. (In Georgetown's case, this included the central role of Jesuits in its administration— John DeGioia was Georgetown's first non-Jesuit president.) Theros thought the negotiations dragged on because Qatar Foundation administrators were worried about local conservative objections to a Christian college in Doha. After hearing about the delays, the sheikha called in the lead Qatari negotiator to ask what was holding things up. He said there were some unresolved issues. She told him to sign the agreement immediately; they would settle any outstanding issues afterward.

With Qatar hoping to attract Georgetown, it may have been a good thing that the sheikha had ordered a resolution of the negotiations. Reflecting the competition among Gulf countries, Gallucci recalled that during the negotiations with Doha he had been approached by high officials from the United Arab Emirates with an offer to host the school in Abu Dhabi. Gallucci, feeling obligated to the sheikha, had turned down a meeting with leaders of the emirates and kept it to himself.

The pattern of midlevel obstruction slowing down liberal reform from the top would be repeated in other dealings that Georgetown had with the Qatar government. (See chapter 9 on freedom as a teachable moment.) One Qatari administrator concluded that only a few people at the top in the emirate understood liberal education; others in the foundation and government simply didn't get it.

Given the substantial subsidies from Qatar to Georgetown and the other Education City universities (together estimated at more than $320 million a year), the major risk to the schools in coming to Doha was never financial. The risk was to their reputation. The challenge was that their "brands" would be weakened if the Qatar operations did not live up to their own standards for higher education. They would also inevitably be tarnished if the Qatar regime they were working for was publicly painted as corrupt or a violator of human rights.

The universities recognized this risk in deciding to open their Doha branches. Georgetown's president, John J. DeGioia, declared that his university had "carefully and exhaustively examined" whether it would be compromising its "core moral values" in going to Doha in 2005. Ten years later, in a *Washington Post* interview, he was convinced that Georgetown made the right decision: "Being engaged is better than not. We are contributing, I think, to building a common good in the region."

Of course, compromises were needed. Even though most faculty would later conclude that the students in Qatar were equal, or at least not notably inferior, to those at the Washington campus, the admissions rate varied considerably. In 2015, of 361 applicants to Qatar, 179 were accepted. This admission rate of 50 percent compared with 17 percent for Georgetown's main campus. Included in the Doha admissions were Qatari males who were generally considered the weakest academic group of the class. One dean called this a form of "affirmative action" needed to retain support—popular, political, and financial—in the host country.

CHAPTER 3

Qatar: A Brief History of a Brief Country

Why are you concerned with a country that wouldn't fill a second-rate hotel in Cairo?

—Hosni Mubarak

Starting with the basics: Qatar is small and rich. It's always been small; it has not always been rich.

About the size of the state of Connecticut, Qatar—at 4,416 square miles—is one of the smallest countries in the Middle East. If Saudi Arabia wanted to give the finger to Iran, geographically speaking, Qatar is **it**, sticking out into the Arab Gulf (known as the Persian Gulf to **most of** the world). Qatar is a land of non-arable desert; even today, it imports 90 percent of its food supply. The 559-mile coastline borders on the riches of the sea: the once-abundant pearl harvests that historically provided the tribes with much of their wealth, and more recently, oil and a vast natural gas reserve.

Qatar is hot. One Georgetown administrator, Maya Primorac, recalled that when she first arrived in Doha and exited her Qatar Airways flight, she thought the jet engines had been left on and she was being blasted by the exhaust. Most visitors who arrive between early April and late October have shared this introduction to the Gulf country. The other months of the year are quite dry and pleasant.

Qatar's population of almost 2.5 million is the second-smallest of the region. It shrinks even further when it's noted that expatriates make up 90 percent of that number, which leaves around 250,000 Qatari nationals, generally stated as one out of nine residents. Of these, no more than seven thousand are members of the extended ruling Al Thani family. The capital, Doha, has three-quarters of the country's population.

Qatar is, as my Georgetown colleague Mehran Kamrava puts it, "an inordinately wealthy country." According to Kamrava, its citizens are the wealthiest in the world with a per capita GDP of $450,000 in 2008. The reason for this wealth is pretty straightforward: it is the world's number one supplier of liquefied natural gas, sharing with Iran the world's largest gas field in the sea between the two countries (called the North Field by Qataris). Of the gas field's 9,700 square kilometers, 6,000 are in Qatari waters, while 3,700 are Iranian.

Hampered by sanctions and a political economy managed by religious zealots, Iran has only barely exploited the natural resource available to it. Priding itself as the leading power in the Gulf, Iran can be forgiven for resenting the uneven distribution of this interconnected resource. It extracts some 35,000 barrels per day, while Qatar takes 450,000 barrels daily. Iran must feel like a teenager who agrees to share a milk shake with a smaller neighbor, only to find the younger boy has the only straw that works.

Aided by massive investments from oil companies including ExxonMobil and Shell, Qatar has raised its liquid natural gas production from 23.7 billion cubic meters (bcm) in 2000 to 116.7 bcm in 2010. In a short period of time, Qatar has experienced a financial windfall; the 2011 *CIA World Factbook* cited it as the fastest-growing economy on earth with 19 percent growth.

This wealth has resulted in major benefits for ordinary Qataris. For starters, there is no need to tax citizens and thus no income tax. This arguably leads to a certain lack of ruler accountability on the part of citizens, who may reasonably conclude that it's not their money that's being spent.

What government can do is spread the largesse. And it does. Free medical care and education is provided from cradle to grave. Government contracts are spread among Qatari families. A generous wedding gift from the regime consists of a plot of land and an interest-free loan of $330,000 that enables Qatari newlyweds to build a house. Government employment for citizens is readily available with 87 percent of Qatari nationals ending up with jobs in the public sector. Qataris don't pay for water and electricity, and the price of gas is among the lowest in the world. As a result, the country has the highest per-capita water and electricity consumption rates in the world. And since non-Qataris are not allowed to own controlling shares in local businesses, most Qataris become silent (and inactive) partners in stores and shops of varying size throughout the country.

Qatar Emerges

I against my brother; my brothers and me against my cousins; my cousins and me against strangers.

—Old Bedouin saying

Qatar wasn't always like this.

In 1940, the British Political Resident described Doha as "a miserable fishing village" filled with fly-infested hovels, dusty roads, no electricity, and water that had to be carried from wells three miles from town. Surrounding the town was a barren desert filled with nomadic tribes in a relentless search for places to graze their herds. The sea held more promise. By the nineteenth century, at least half the population of Qatar was engaged in pearling. And the geography of a desert peninsula jutting into the Gulf encouraged overseas trade for importing needed food, for building dhows to ship valued pearls as far as Asia, and for piracy by those tribes without much else to exchange. What passed for an economy was marked by impermanent settlements in an impoverished land.

Authority in such a setting was fluid and loosely organized around different tribes, families, and sheiks. Unlike the strong hereditary monarchies in other parts of the Arab world, such as Morocco, there was no tradition of central rule in Qatar. Nor was there even a single tribe with a claim to power based, say, on descent from the Prophet or a greater source of wealth. When one tribe did rise to prominence it came from being centered on the pearling port of Doha and the skill of its leaders in forming alliances with other tribes. Even then this tribe, the Al-Thani, was no more than "first among equals."

This changed with an agreement with the British in 1868 that recognized the Al-Thani sheikh as in control of the peninsula. In effect, this move recognized Qatar as independent of its stronger neighbor, Bahrain. The "seemingly inescapable British," in Allen J. Fromherz's characterization, wanted to end the tribal conflicts in the area, stop piracy, and "find somebody to deal with in Qatar." The British interest was sea-based and focused on keeping the lines of trade open to India, meaning that Britain had to keep pesky Arab tribes subdued. Who actually ruled the territory was of secondary importance. But the Al-Thani "strategic manipulation" of stronger external powers to bolster its own authority over peoples and tribes would establish a pattern of rule in Qatar down to the present.

With the British fleet being at least symbolically behind the Al-Thani sheikh, Muhammad bin Thani, he could consolidate the power of his family over other rivals. But the process was hardly simple. Even before the sheikh's death in 1878, his son, Jassim, had aligned with the Ottoman Empire, which remained the dominant land power in the region and vigorously opposed British expansion. The jockeying for power within the family—and balancing the competing forces of larger external powers—continued with great fluidity. It culminated in the 1892 Battle of Wajbah when a group of tribes led by Sheikh Jassim repelled Turkish forces and asserted Qatar as a unified actor to be treated more as a respected ally than a colony. In 2007, this battle was elevated to National Day in a modern attempt to reinvigorate history and reinforce the unity of the country under Al-Thani leadership.

Well into the twentieth century, under the often-astute leadership of Al-Thani emirs, Qatar was able to keep itself from being absorbed by external powers. This balancing of rival, powerful interests required agile political and diplomatic skills. The establishment of Qatar as a British protectorate in the Anglo-Qatari Treaty of November 1916 was similar to earlier British agreements with Bahrain and Kuwait. For the United Kingdom, in the midst of the First World War, it formalized Arab cooperation against an Ottoman enemy. For Qatar's leaders, the treaty afforded protection against Ottoman and Saudi incursions as well as the internal family factions encouraged by these foreign powers. Al-Thani leaders became expert at using British worries about global rivals to consolidate their authority, and keep the ever-threatening Saudis from taking over the peninsula on the other side of uncertain borders.

British recognition encouraged Al-Thani strength. The British saw greater centralized power than in fact existed, mostly because it served to make their agreements with the emir cleaner. While the British agreement bolstered the emir, it didn't prevent the formation of a considerable number of family factions, coups and succession disputes, and frequently absentee rulers. The various sheikhs still had to negotiate within the family, and compromise with leaders of other tribes and clans on the peninsula. For their part, the British seemed relatively content with controlling Qatar's foreign policy and avoided too much meddling in the local economy and politics. That might be why, when ebbing British power caused its military protection in the Gulf to disappear in the late 1960s, the response of Qatar's royal family was more shock than pleasure.

Much of this imperial indifference can be attributed to the minor stakes involved. The pearl industry was in a long, slow decline, replaced by artificial gems from the East and producing years of hunger in Qatar between the World Wars. Oil profits still lay in the future. The 1916 Agreement had allowed Britain and its allied oil companies exclusive claims to potential deposits in Qatar. But it was not till the mid-1930s that actual oil concessions were signed, and that might have been motivated by a threat: the increasing reach of the Standard Oil Company, an American business, in nearby Saudi Arabia. The British and the Qataris shared an interest in defying Saudi claims to the oil on Qatari territory, hence deals were cut in 1935 for drilling by the British company that would be the predecessor to Qatar Petroleum. Actually, no significant amounts of oil would be exported until after World War II.

When oil was exported out, money flowed in. The British awakened to a greater interest in their protectorate and increasingly intervened in internal affairs. Their agents managed the bureaucracy and were key in deciding the frequent succession disputes over which factions of the Al-Thani family would control the office of the emir. An increasingly restless family demanded a larger share of the oil wealth. When combined with the rule of relatively weak emirs, the postwar decades reflected a sense of drift in leadership.

A bloodless coup in February 1972 replaced a disengaged ruler with a more dynamic emir, Sheikh Khalifa bin Abdulaziz, who would rule until he was deposed in a 1995 coup. The country entered a period of reform and adaptation to the British withdrawal from the Gulf. Sheikh Khalifa is credited with creating the foundations of the modern state. He certainly concentrated power in his own hands—to the point where checks for oil companies could not be signed when he was out of the country. Even before his coup, he had engineered Qatar's declaration of independence in 1971. He boldly ended the treaties that had linked Qatar to Britain as a protectorate. At the same time, he entered negotiations with the United States to replace the United Kingdom as the military protector of the country and its ruling family. The United States at the time wasn't interested, preferring to rely on the Saudis to play the role of regional policeman.

Sheikh Khalifa's efforts to promote economic growth had mixed results. Funds from oil exports were used in attempts to diversify the economy into industries like steel, cement, and fertilizer. But these plans were tripped up by the decline in oil prices in the late 1980s. Sheikh Khalifa himself had lost much of his youthful energy and involvement in government affairs. Soon Qatar would be suffering from tighter government budgets, decreased spending, and deficits.

By 1995, government funding, the main driver of the economy, fell by almost 20 percent. Not completely by coincidence, that was also the year that the emir was deposed by his son, Sheikh Hamad, in a bloodless coup.

The Hamad Era (1995–2013)

Under Sheikh Hamad bin Khalifa Al-Thani, economic development accelerated rapidly. While maintaining oil production, Qatar invested heavily in natural gas, becoming the world's fifth-largest exporter of all forms of natural gas and the largest exporter of liquefied natural gas. By 2011, it ranked third in the world in proven reserves behind only Russia and Iran. Natural gas was the driver of Qatar's fortune. Despite all the talk of the country running out of natural resources, Qatar's deposits of gas are expected to provide some two hundred years of production. Its oil reserves, a not-so-shabby thirteenth-largest in the world, will only last till 2020.

The man responsible for these developments—and under whose authority Georgetown would be invited to Qatar—came from a military background. Born in 1952, Sheikh Hamad graduated from the Royal Military Academy Sandhurst in the United Kingdom and later modernized Qatar's military as its supreme commander. He was hailed as a hero for his leadership of the Qatari forces that liberated the Saudi town of Khafji during the Gulf War (1990–1991). He had been named heir apparent in 1977 and had used his position as prime minister to overthrow his father. As head of the Supreme Planning Council, he had removed barriers to social and economic development and focused the country on the rapid growth of its petrochemical industry.

Under Sheik Hamad, a period of seemingly unlimited budgets began. Proposals were often scrapped not because they were too expensive but because they were not ambitious enough. Immediately after seizing power, Hamad sponsored the Al-Jazeera network that soon reached more than 35 million Arabic speakers. English-language broadcasting began a few years later with an even larger worldwide audience. Other major projects included spending on Qatar Railway ($26 billion), Doha International Airport ($2.8 billion), the new Doha Port ($7 billion), and the iconic real estate development project, The Pearl ($14 billion). In December 2010, Qatar won its bid for the 2022 FIFA World Cup, which will require further infrastructure spending, including twelve artificially cooled outdoor football stadiums and a high-speed rail and metro system, to the tune of well over $100 billion.

Promised reforms to the nation's economic and political systems were less apparent. Attempts to diversify the economy away from its dependence on petroleum products went nowhere. Hydrocarbon products composed 92 percent of exports in 2008 while oil and gas were responsible for almost 60 percent of GDP. Because of the strength of gas prices, Qatar was able to weather the global financial crisis pretty well with an estimated growth in its economy of 11 percent in 2009. Attempts to move the economy away from a dependence on nonnationals have not succeeded. Qatar's private sector with 78 percent of the labor force was more than 99 percent composed of expatriates.

Qatar remained a top-down monarchy dominated by the Al-Thani family. As former American ambassador Chase Untermeyer put it, "Qatar is a family business with a seat at the United Nations." It was classified as "not free" by Freedom House. Three municipal elections in 1999, 2003, and 2007 have not notably changed the authoritarian nature of the political system or weakened the emir's power. There appeared to be little popular demand for either greater participation in government or for weakening centralized power through popular elections or a representative assembly. Insiders described decision-making and policy changes as involving considerable negotiations and compromise within the Al-Thani family group. The Arab Spring seemed to have passed Qatar by without encouraging any widespread domestic call for reforms. If anything, conflicts elsewhere in the Arab world had reinforced a widespread belief that centralized rule was needed for national stability. The 2011 rise in government employee salaries and pensions of between 50 and 120 percent may have sweetened the icing on the cake served to the content citizens of Qatar.

Qatar's Ambitious Foreign Relations

Ruling a country notable for rapidly accumulating wealth, a small, comfortable citizenry, and a top-down, stable regime, the emir had the scope to act on his own political instincts in the region and world. Closely aligned with international capital, his coherent ruling group laid out its ambitious agenda for modernization and pursued it while increasing its own power through the government it dominated. Emir Hamad's self-confidence was reflected in the very lack of statues and portraits of him around Doha, unlike those of less-secure autocrats governing other states in the neighborhood. In the words of one associate who spent years with him, Sheikh Hamad was "the most radical pragmatist in the region."

This instinct to promote change in the Middle East and to align with popular movements was a fairly consistent goal of the emir's foreign policies, whether in opposing Mubarak in Egypt, in trying to overthrow the Assad regime in Syria, or in providing arms for insurgents in Libya. When Colonel Qaddafi's palace fell to rebels in Tripoli, the flag that was raised, temporarily, on the roof was Qatar's. The hoisting of its flag was a symbol of the rise of this small Gulf state and its success in identifying with the rebellious sentiment sweeping the Arab world.

These radical instincts contributed to the iciness that characterized Qatar's relations with Saudi Arabia during Hamad's reign. Not only didn't the Saudis support Hamad's successful coup against his father; they also backed attempts to overthrow him in 1996 and (perhaps) 2005. For his part, Hamad strongly resisted the Saudi domination that he had inherited. The rise of an independent Qatari foreign policy largely came at the expense of his larger neighbor. At various times, Al Jazeera's reporting of corruption within the Saudi royal family was a mark of the cold war between the two states. This cold war even affected Georgetown's education, as degrees granted in Doha to Saudi students were not recognized as legitimate by the regime in Riyadh.

Relations with Iran, the other major regional power, were ambiguous and conditional, though curiously not as conflicted as those with

Saudi Arabia. Qatar was on the Arab side of the divisions in the region that separated it from Iran by religion, geography, language, and history. Yet the Qataris remained more relaxed on religious differences, in part because, unlike the Saudis and Bahrainis, they lacked a substantial Shia minority. They maintained substantial commercial and trade ties, including with prominent Iranian merchant families residing in Doha, and a shared border through one of the world's great gas fields. The Qataris have managed relations with Iran that were somewhat independent of US interests. Yet a cynical realism pervaded their ties with their Persian neighbor. As the longtime prime minister, Hamad bin Jassim described the relationship with Iran to an American diplomat, "They lie to us and we lie to them."

However nuanced and assertive Qatar's foreign policies might be, they rested on the military security provided by the United States. This meant Qatar hosted two major US bases: the Al-Udeid air base, housing some 120 aircraft and ten thousand personnel, and Camp Al-Sayliyah, the army component of the US Central Command. They represented the two largest pre-positioning bases outside the United States. Qatar began building the Al-Udeid air base in 1992 in the hope that the United States would eventually occupy it, which didn't happen until the Americans left their Saudi bases after 9/11. While there was no explicit United States guarantee to defend Qatar from outside attack, the bases underlined an implicit promise of support.

Former US ambassador to Qatar Theros described Qatar as wanting to be America's best friend in the region both because of its preeminent military strength and because the emir saw the superpower as being the most compatible with his own interests. Although the United States had initially "walked away" from the Gulf in the early 1970s, the Iran-Iraq War had changed that policy of detachment. When Iraq invaded Kuwait in 1991, Qatar's soldiers aided in repelling them. The following year, Doha signed a defense cooperation agreement with the United States. Until Donald Trump began his improv foreign policy routines, Qatar was a close American ally in the Gulf. Yet this always required a certain "live and let live" tolerance from the superpower.

Although Qatar was willing to delegate its defense needs to the United States, this had not inhibited an independent foreign policy under this security umbrella. Being the "friend of everyone and enemy of no one" had at times meant taking positions far different from those of the United States. The US State Department described Qatar's counterterrorist activities as "the worst in the region" in a leaked WikiLeaks cable. This was not an accident.

Being too aligned with the United States opened the country to reprisals. Buying insurance from terrorist attacks may be one benefit of the covert funding from Qataris to radical movements. Osama bin Laden often released many of his video messages through Al-Jazeera. And some radical members of the Al-Thani family had shown sympathy toward jihadist beliefs. Before the post-Hamad warming of relations with Riyadh, Doha might not have been averse to the stern anti-Saudi posture of the Al-Qaeda/ISIS leadership. Nor was this independence necessarily averse to America. Arguably, maintaining a stable ally that was not a terrorist target, as well as retaining the local population's hospitality for its bases, was more supportive of American interests than would be a public rebuke of some of Qatar's stances. Having an Arab friend willing and able to engage one's enemies, arguably on its behalf, had to be seen as an asset by American policymakers.

Eventually, Qatar's independent path led to confrontations with Saudi Arabia in Egypt and Syria. In Egypt, Qatar's financial and political backing for the Muslim Brotherhood led to trouble when the Brotherhood government was overthrown in July 2013 in a military coup led by Abdel Fattah el-Sisi and supported by the Saudis. In Syria, Qatar and Saudi Arabia supported competing groups rebelling against the Assad regime. This divided the opposition and empowered jihadist groups, some of whom were supported by both Gulf powers.

The Qatar attempt to pick winners in the region after the Arab Spring was plagued by miscalculations and international pressure, as well as an intensification of its rivalry with Saudi Arabia. By 2014, it was clear these policies were not working. Both external and domestic pressure led Qatar to swing back into the Saudi orbit. Its independence diminished and its revenues reduced by the decline in oil prices, Qatar under a new emir began to focus more on internal problems and less on daring foreign policy initiatives.

Sheikh Hamad's sudden abdication in June 2013 and the installation of the heir apparent, his thirty-three-year-old son Sheikh Tamim, as emir, was very much in keeping with the style of the now former emir. It removed him and his prime minister but in a way that underlined continuity with the old regime. Unlike his predecessors, who were overthrown by their sons, he did it on his own terms and timing. The World Cup remained scheduled for 2022 along with the massive development projects it required. Qatar Foundation and its educational and charitable programs were continued as well, if at decreasing levels.

There was a notable reduction in the intensity and visibility shown by the new ruler's policies. The previous emir's flair for the dramatic was muted, notably in foreign policies. Relations with Saudi Arabia were initially improved to the point of deferring to Saudi leadership. Funding was cut to numerous agencies—including the budgets of the Education City universities—in line with the decline in world oil prices. Clearly, a new emir was consolidating himself in power and moving cautiously in his father's footsteps. Confidence in the regime remained high with little apparent public interest in democratic change. Sheikh Tamim seemed more content than his father with managing the old regime's initiatives and winning over conservative public opinion, in part by stressing administrative competence and a bit less spending. In effect, the new sheikh slowed down the liberal changes initiated by his father.

But backing away from the ambitious policies of his father was not enough to prevent the crisis that confronted Qatar in the summer of 2017. The young sheikh's attempt to both moderate and continue an independent foreign policy came to a crashing halt when surrounding Arab states, led by Saudi Arabia, initiated a harsh travel and diplomatic boycott. Encouraged by an impulsive new American president eager to act against terrorism, the Saudi group suddenly declared that Qatar's support for the Muslim Brotherhood, moderate ties with Iran, and financing for Al Jazeera TV were intolerable to its Gulf neighbors. Qatar's leaders responded by reorienting food imports away from Saudi Arabia, adding Turkish troops to their own forces, and looking to friends in America and Europe for support.

Qatar had ample resources to withstand the economic isolation indefinitely. But whether its ability to undertake a foreign policy that thumbed its nose at its larger neighbor could be continued seemed dubious at best. The Americans might keep the crisis under control. They seemed less likely to resolve it in Qatar's favor. Despite Sheikh Tamim's popularity as a result of these attacks, Qatar seemed destined for less autonomy from the wishes of powerful states in the future. And this had ominous, uncertain consequences for all concerned. As a former student wrote me: "By throwing Qatar under the bus, the Americans have upset the Gulf—the one pocket of stability in a region of great instability."

The Importance of Branding

Branding—becoming important to others and acquiring a positive reputation in the world—continued as a survival strategy for this rich, vulnerable state. Branding was one component of state power that wealthy Qatar could harness to enhance its own security in a troubled region. This positive image, both in general and in specific tasks, has created a "brand state" in varied arenas of politics, culture, sports, media, and education.

Qatar's branding was most apparent where it was most visible. Establishing the TV network Al Jazeera—a credible source of news, openness, and debate in the Arab world—gave Qatar a reputation as an important regional and global media player. Expanding to a 24-hour satellite channel in English and Arabic, Al Jazeera was by 2010 the main source of international news for three-quarters of the Arab world. Its success rested on the emir's subsidies to the network's operating budget. With the coming of the Arab Spring in 2011, Al Jazeera solidified its role as an indispensable source of news about, and encouragement for, the rebellions spreading across the region.

The emirate has not been reluctant to put its name on other global activities. These ranged from advertisements for Qatar Airways as "the world's five-star airline" to I. M. Pei's iconic world-class Museum of Islamic Art to Qatar Foundation's proclamation that it would "help the world think." In sports, "Qatar Airways" was emblazoned on the shirts of Barcelona's football team; the country hosted the 2011 Asian Cup in football, bid for the 2016 Summer Olympics, and audaciously became the host for the 2022 FIFA World Cup. Generous charitable efforts included a personal visit by the emir to New Orleans, where he wrote a check for $100 million to victims of Hurricane Katrina. In 2012, Sheikha Mozah collaborated with the United Nations in the effort to educate the world's 61 million children with no access to schools.

Mediation has traditionally been held in high regard in Arab culture. In recent years, Qatar has actively pursued the role of mediator resolving regional and global conflicts. In fact, Qatar has succeeded in helping end a number of bloody disputes. These included the Sudanese civil war, the border dispute between Djibouti and Eritrea and, most notably, a resolution of the crisis in Lebanon in 2008. With less success, Qatar brought its mediation experience to talks between Fatah and Hamas in Palestine and between rebels and the government of Yemen in 2010. Qatari leaders have not been reluctant to publicly highlight their peace efforts in a region overflowing with conflicts. This image of an honest broker has enhanced its brand as a nation promoting stability.

Not quite as disinterested as mediation was the financial clout flowing from Doha. Qatar has been more aggressive than other Gulf states in its investments, especially those focused on Europe. While aiming for profits, its Sovereign Wealth Fund (Qatar Investment Authority), with some $100 billion in assets, has broadly supported the country's branding goals. Qatar owned properties in thirty-two countries, making it one of the world's largest overseas investors. It had opportunistically sought assets in Europe, becoming the biggest buyer of European property in 2012, with 80 percent of its purchases in London and Paris. These highly visible deals included the London Olympic Village, a shopping mall on Paris's Champs-Élysées and Harrods elegant department store, as well as stakes in Barclays and the London Stock Exchange.

Nor was Washington left out. *Washington Post* reporter Marc Fisher could report in late 2013: "Qatar is suddenly investing heavily in the US, bankrolling DC's City Center and other projects." The

Times of London resentfully editorialized that because of its investments in England, Qatar now called the shots in dealings with the British: "The Government pays homage to Qatar, peers fly there, royals seek the emir's favour." In a more reserved conclusion, one scholar observed that Qatar had become a "highly consequential player in the world of global finance and diplomacy."

Promoting Qatar as a center for excellence in education in the Gulf certainly fit within the overall strategy of branding. At least as important was that Sheikh Hamad and his wife, Sheikha Mozah, took a personal interest in higher education and made the state's investments in a "knowledge economy" one of their most important initiatives. By 2008, Qatar was spending some $4 billion on education. Yet whether this was an instrument for mobilizing and employing the young in a modernizing economy or just another consumer subsidy like health care or wedding gifts that Qataris had come to expect, remained unanswered.

Negotiating a Cruise

The Qatari leadership's personal involvement in the universities they had invited to Doha surfaced in the summer of 2008 on a cruise off the French Riviera. Those few days also pulled back a curtain on the personalities and interests engaged in bringing American higher education to the Arab Gulf. Certainly, the Qataris had the will and the wallet to charm their guests and, as seen in a relaxed gathering on a large yacht in the Mediterranean Sea, they largely succeeded.

Robert Galluci and his wife Jennifer Sims showed up unfashionably early on the dock at 7:30 a.m.— arguably appropriate for visiting Americans outside their comfort zone. The Côte d'Azur sun was only beginning to break up the cloud cover, revealing the large, modern ship they were being ushered aboard. Stretching 408 feet long with a gross tonnage of 7,922 tons, the *Katara* was the fourteenth-largest yacht in the world. As they boarded, they caught a glimpse of the outdoor swimming pool and the helicopter pad. Five sailors, clad in white naval shorts and shirts, stood stiffly in a line that led them to a smiling officer. He greeted them in a clipped South African accent and escorted them to their suite. They were the first to arrive.

Neither of the Galluccis were quite sure why they were there. The invitation to lunch with the emir of Qatar had come earlier that summer. It had been delivered by the foreign minister, Abdul Rahman, in an offhanded way. In fact, Gallucci first thought the invite meant the emir was going to be visiting Washington. No, this lunch was to be served in the south of France. Understandably, the dean hesitated. The initial reason for pause was resolved by the minister's reassurance that the emir was paying for two first-class airfares to France along with any expenses. Another cause of hesitation involved the question of whether any university interest was involved. Robert checked with Jack DeGioia, Georgetown University president, who agreed that although the cruise would hardly be a scholarly confab, the university could envision something to be gained from shmoozing with a multimillion-dollar donor.

As befitted guests of one of the world's wealthiest men, the Galluccis were met at the airport by a gleaming Mercedes and a well-dressed gentleman who introduced himself as their escort. He offered not only to take them to their lavish suite in one of the Riviera's top hotels but also wherever else they wanted to go. Somewhat jet-lagged, they were content with the hotel's luxuries until their Sunday brunch the following day at the emir's place in the hills overlooking Nice.

Gallucci recalled the brunch as a blur of kids running around on a beautiful hillside, casually dressed guests relaxing in the warm sun, and an abundance of gossip about the politics of the region and its leaders. When the conversation turned toward America, Gallucci and his wife—a former State Department official—were impressed by the Qatari's inside-the-beltway knowledge. The Qataris were big fans of ex-CIA director George Tenet, who they thought should run for president.

The one minor spat that broke out was over whose boat would be used the following day for their cruise. The debate—between the emir and his prime minister, Hamad bin Jassim—was resolved, not unexpectedly, in the boss's favor. This, despite the fact that Sheikh Jassim's yacht, the *Al Mirqab*, which he had only just acquired, was at 436 feet slightly longer than the emir's. At some level of affluence, perhaps size doesn't matter. Both ships ranked among the largest motor yachts in the world.

Both Americans expressed concern that they hadn't brought the right clothes to wear for the cruise. But the sheikha insisted that it wasn't important. This reassurance of informality was underlined in the morning as they waited on the boat for the others to arrive. In the distance, they heard a putt-putt sound. Qatar's emir, Sheikh Hamad bin Khalifa Al Thani and Sheikha Mozah Bint Nasser Al-Missned, were arriving. The emir, a massively built man, arrived driving his scooter down from the hills above the dock. Holding on to the emir, perched on the seat behind, was the sheikha riding sidesaddle. They were both smiling.

Gallucci recalled the three-day cruise as relaxed and fun. The boat headed west along the Riviera with little security in evidence. Three couples were there the whole time: the emir and sheikha, Jassim and his wife, and Robert and Jennifer. The emir strolled around with his shirt outside his beachwear. The Qataris didn't drink, but fine wine was available to the guests as well as Cuban cigars. Another bow to custom occurred when the men went swimming and the women disappeared to another part of the boat. When Jennifer Sims, forgetting the traditional gender separation, said she preferred to stay where she was reading, she was politely but insistently urged by the sheikha to join the women and give the men the privacy of their swim.

The shore visits seemed unplanned; on one, the Galluccis were asked what they wanted to eat. Taken by surprise, their response ("pizza") received boisterous acclaim and the Qataris set about finding a suitable restaurant in the neighborhood. Discreet conversations were held with the owner, and the emir's men cleared out half the restaurant, which the party then occupied. It is good to be king. Afterward, ice cream was nominated as the dessert of choice. The sheikha took names and flavors, and then charged off down the street to fill the requests.

The most serious discussion that came up was over what looked to be—and was—the coming market crash of fall 2008. "Which banks will go? What do we do with Qatar's sovereign wealth fund?" Gallucci, recognizing the limits of his experience, replied that he didn't know, adding that the emir should ask his financial advisers. The emir responded, recognizing the limits of his forecasters: "We already have advice from the experts."

In his informal talks with the Qatari leaders, Gallucci was getting a picture of how this elite group thought and what lay behind their invitations to American universities. The emir himself had declared publicly that the "hopelessness of youth" was the root cause of terrorism. But immediate counterinsurgency tactics hardly justified their huge investments in education.

The emir would later demonstrate his own sympathy for the sentiments behind the Arab Spring. The Arab world had stagnated. Its regimes, corrupt and ineffective, had blocked the societies they ruled from the progress the rest of the world was enjoying. Horrible wrongs had been done to their own citizens by Arab governments harshly denying their people democratic participation. Creating Al Jazeera as a reliable news source throughout the Arab world was a deliberate attempt to spread ferment, to give the Arab street a reliable means of communication, among Arabs themselves and with the outside world. The emir would later be delighted by the overthrow of Mubarak in Egypt and he would pour billions into a failed attempt to consolidate that brief revolution.

Education reform fit easily into this worldview and the emir's vision for his country. In baseball terms, Qatar was playing "a long game and not small ball." Its leaders embraced the values of education, health care, and even "democracy with filters." They would open up their countries to Western influence, not to become dependent on these foreign powers but because they wanted to develop their own identity. What this identity would look like was to be left to future generations.

In casual conversation, references to sixteenth-century Spain had arisen. The Spanish monarchy of that day had managed to use its discovery of gold from the New World to make itself into a global superpower. But it had not managed to employ its wealth to transform its tradition-bound autocratic society. When the gold ran out, so did Spanish power. It became a backward state, overwhelmed by the rise of modernizing European states to its north. Qatar's dilemma was similar: how to turn its natural wealth (oil and gas) into human resources (education and health) that could sustain the nation when its mineral wealth ran out. Georgetown, then, was in Qatar not to transform a traditional society but to preserve it in the modern world by giving the Qataris the skills and energy they needed when their natural bounty had been exhausted.

Perhaps there were aspects of the Arab rejectionists' antagonism toward Western dominance of the region with which Qatari leaders sympathized. But their solution radically differed. The issue was not to push the West out but to take advantage of it. Adopt and adapt what they needed to equal and surpass the developed world. They wanted the best of the West and they were willing to pay for the highest quality in corporations and clothes, universities and yachts.

But this buying up of what the West had to offer had a bizarre side to it; nothing seemed too grand or too insignificant. So, on one of the last evenings of the cruise, Robert Gallucci found himself with a high Qatari official on the upper deck of the $300 million superyacht with its fourteen ample suites, swimming pool and Jacuzzi, cinema, helicopter pad, and all the luxury services the crew of sixty could provide.

As they were looking at the coast of the French Riviera, Gallucci recalled, this wealthy gentleman looked at the travel jacket the dean was wearing. He asked him what kind it was. When he found out, the Qatari turned to an aide telling him to write down "L.L.Bean." He would buy it.

International brands meant something.

CHAPTER 4

Learning and Teaching in Qatar

During fall orientation, the Student Affairs Office staged a reading of autobiographical essays written by students. The new freshman class of around seventy filled about a quarter of the school's new auditorium. Three students read portions from some of the papers that freshmen had written as part of their admission requirements. I thought the essays gave an arresting picture of how these students saw themselves. To my surprise, many were mavericks—not quite fitting in to the societies that raised them or the schools they attended. Some samples:

D.: In high school, I never fit under a certain label. . . . That is the problem with high school, though: so much of it is all about labels and once you get your label, it follows you around and limits you to that one definition, when in reality, we are each our own person with a little bit of everything and a little bit of everyone in us.

E.: (Talking about the impact of the Arab Spring in his country): We demanded that the country's fortune went to making everyone's life easier. We wanted to break through the ugly and seemingly eternal cycle of poverty, illiteracy, and backwardness. . . . My country needs change, and change comes with education. . . . I have been in the middle of demonstrations. My house received some stray bullets while our neighbor's house was completely destroyed. . . . Life is the cruelest teacher because it gives us the test before the lesson. However, I believe we had passed the test. The youth and I, as young as we are, have made a difference and participated in changing the course of history in my country.

I.: Growing up in a closed community of religious people, traditions, and empty political rhetoric, I felt as if my creativity and open-mindedness was being eaten piece-by-piece by school, teachers, and friends. As a student in a religious school, I had a terribly hard time fitting in. . . . One day when I was sitting in an Islamic Studies class, my teacher started talking about politics: how everyone is our enemy, how every other religion is nonsense, and everyone would go to hell. . . . "Every single one of them will go to hell but not the pure-hearted among us," my teacher said. . . . To my surprise, most students agreed with what he had said. . . . In the final marking period when we were assigned a presentation of our choice, I felt that this was my chance to stand up for what I believe in. . . . I showed how other religions are not as bad as my teacher had talked about. That day I got an F in my presentation. At the end of the day, I felt the satisfaction of standing up for what I believe in.

As successful as these students had been in high school—to be admitted to Georgetown—many didn't see themselves as accepted members of their communities. They were idealistic, smart, and disruptive graduates of their secondary schools. While most seemed close to their families, they were hardly accepting of the political, economic, or religious authorities they confronted in their communities. With care and learning and luck, they may still turn out to be leaders of their generation. Or they could be lost in the mess that many of their countries have become.

Either way, I was reminded that these students were not living up to—or down to—the stereotypes I had arrived with. They were neither rooted in tradition, enamored with ideology, passively apathetic, nor committed to the vision of modern consumerism they saw around them. They were very much minds in motion. They would likely approach college with the same skepticism they showed the familiar, conventional authorities back home.

*

The early days of teaching were a bit of a blur. Perhaps it was because, counter to all my anxieties, the initial experiences in the classroom were not that exceptional.

The temptation in a discussion of teaching in a foreign land is to stress the contrasts, to elevate the exotic to an undeserved prominence. As illustrated by my ill-fated lesson on that first day of teaching American politics, there were differences. Yet what passed for acts of education committed each day in Doha were similar to what happens on most American campuses. The professor dispenses wisdom, answers questions, and occasionally allows for debate and disagreement. From both ledges of the canyon between teaching and learning, the participants arrive expecting a conventional university education; that's what the students are paying for, that's why the faculty has been hired. There's little incentive to disappoint either party.

Students enrolled in the first years of the school were a small, ambitious group that was lavished with attention, including overseas travel and foreign visitors. One student from the first-year class described that initial time as being in a fishbowl and becoming, not unwillingly, "a poster child" for Georgetown. She felt this initial class had bonded in a unique way, if only because they were "always together." She thought the school had become more corporate as it added new classes and staff in subsequent years. She agreed that neither Doha nor the school were as exotic as one might think before getting there.

Still, allowances needed to be made. English was a second language, often a third, in most classes. English proficiency was probably the biggest obstacle to foreign students seeking admission. Slang was misunderstood; understandably, any background in, or familiarity with, subjects such as American politics could not be presumed.

Humor didn't translate well, which never kept me from trying. My attempts generally provoked smiles only when some of the more attentive students noticed that their professor thought he had said something amusing. And that may be due more to Arabs' good manners and the usual deference to authority than any heartfelt recognition of a joke.

By way of illustration, I talked about Bill Clinton's attempt while running for president to position himself as a moderate Democrat, which meant in his first race appearing tough on crime. This led to support of the death penalty, a position that distanced him from past liberal candidates. At that time, he was still governor of Arkansas and was being petitioned for clemency for a black man named Ricky Ray Rector who stood convicted of murder and was scheduled to be executed. Ricky had issues.

In the aftermath of a robbery in which he had killed one person, Ricky had fatally shot a police officer who had been a friend of Rector's family in their rural town. Ricky then tried to kill himself and had the same measure of success as in everything else he'd attempted. The bullet left him brain damaged. It didn't help. Clinton interrupted his presidential campaign to return to Arkansas to preside over Ricky's execution with all the publicity that went with it. However, there was some doubt whether the prisoner even knew what was going on. Witnesses noted that when he ate his final meal just before his lethal injection, the convict put aside his dessert of pecan pie because, as Ricky said, he "wanted to save it for later."

Here I paused to let the grim impact sink in, including the cold calculation of presidential ambition that allowed Clinton to preside over the execution of this handicapped black man. Dark humor though it was, I thought it deserved at least a snicker of acknowledgment. I could see the word spread back from the front rows that the professor expected this to be noted. At last, always polite if not quite getting it, the class relented with the slightest of chuckling.

Who knows, maybe it was an actual case of not-very-funny gallows humor.

First Sightings

Authority was deferred to in the broader Arab societies as well as in the classrooms of our transplanted schools. My liberal colleagues, even when questioning societies' conventional power structures in their professional writings and political leanings, were content to see them fortified in their own classes. Given my baggage of vulnerabilities, I lined up in strict support of the hierarchy of power offered to teachers—especially older, foreign, male ones.

Student deference was shown even when an alien authority figure imposed peculiar practices contrary to regional customs. Patricia O'Connor taught English in Georgetown's early days in Doha. A no-nonsense West Virginian, Patricia had spent much of her career working with prisoners in Baltimore programs she created and ran. She pointed out to me how local women adapted to the university's coed classes—a novel experience for many of them.

Initially, these students were reluctant to sit next to men. They would bunch up with one another in the classroom. Only if the teacher directed them to sit interspersed regardless of gender would they leave their group. They needed higher approval in order to sit, or be seen sitting, next to a guy, Professor O'Connor thought. As time went on, students became more accepting of coed education. But in the early years, they passively accepted direction and then probably reported their edgy behavior to their parents.

Needless to add, like all generalizations, this deference to authority had to be modified with exceptions.

Jeremy was a bright, underachieving, often-rebellious student in a few of my classes. He had a perpetually wry smile on his handsome face under a mop of black hair. His favorite way to begin a sentence seemed to be, "Yes, but . . ." He was far from an easy student to teach but we got along. The eldest son of a Palestinian doctor and a Polish nurse, he was a product of a globalized concept of mixed marriage. His background didn't make his politics any easier to predict.

A young historian described her first day in class with Jeremy. A freshly minted PhD from an Ivy League graduate school, my colleague was eager to demonstrate her progressive sympathies for the region. Not surprisingly, this meant a lecture critical of US foreign policy. She initially felt pretty good about the well-rehearsed tour d'horizon of American misadventures she had delivered. It hadn't lasted long. Perhaps because her scholarly bubble had been pricked or her expectations of students confounded, she had come to my office afterward to complain about Jeremy.

After class, he had approached her with what Jeremy at least would consider a legitimate question: "Is this course going to be typical anti-imperialist, anti-American drivel?" Jeremy, in the throes of a neoconservative online insurgency, dropped her class.

Who Gets In

Of 336 applicants for the 2013 school year, 139 were admitted and 73 were actually enrolled in the Class of 2017. The students admitted in the class represented twenty-nine nations ranging from Australia to Yemen. Their homelands tended to cluster around the Arab countries of the Middle East from Tunisia to Iraq. The Annual Report for the 2012–2013 year boasted of the school's 40 percent increase in Qatari male enrollment in fall 2013. Given these young men's reputation for being wealthy slackers, this was a sensitive issue for the university and its host.

Around 30 percent of each class were Qataris, a percentage that varied from year to year. They were overwhelmingly girls. Qatari boys were generally less ready for college and performed less well as students. In a recent year, some fifteen boys applied, five were admitted, and three ultimately enrolled. As one director of admissions said about young male Qataris, "Why should they work hard and earn mostly the same as they would without working hard?"

Georgetown attempts to recruit in a number of high schools but the counseling within regional high schools is generally poor or at least not up to American standards. That means relatively few students come from the public schools because few apply. Most are from well-tended private schools in Doha—such as Qatar Academy, the American School of Doha, and Doha College. These selective schools offer an education for selective students in the British curriculum (Doha College), the American system (American School), and international standards as overseen by Qatar Foundation (Qatar Academy). Those students who show promise but lack the required language skills find themselves channeled into the Academic Bridge Program for a year. This program operates on campus and focuses on improving English language proficiency, as well as the math and science skills needed for admission to the colleges of Education City.

Another one-third of students are non-Qatari residents of Doha. They are Arabs and non-Arabs; they are certainly from the professional classes. That doesn't mean that the united front these students appeared to present to their new professor existed in reality. One non-Qatari of Indian descent wrote me later about the shock he felt in attempting to scale social barriers encountered at Georgetown:

> I was born in Qatar and lived there my entire life. However, it was only during my New Student Orientation in 2007 at the age of 19, that I was able to interact directly with a Qatari peer. I now actually knew a Qatari by name, and we were actually in the same classroom together. It was quite surreal, and the first several months were extremely complicated for me to try and interact with this other person who was someone I had always been intimidated by. It did not matter that this was an illegitimate fear, because all the conversations we had as children growing up was how we should be careful around Qataris as they all had the power to deport anyone who rubbed them the wrong way.

Other divisions in Qatari society were not bridged in the classroom. In the words of one dean, "there are very few children of laborers" at Georgetown in Qatar. This was despite the fact that most of the students—international and local—received financial aid from an expansive Qatari government. Most were on need-based aid, and most of them received loans that were both interest free and forgiven if the graduate worked for a few years in Qatar after graduating. Even when this employment requirement wasn't fulfilled, the Doha regime was not known for tracking down those students who didn't pay off their loans. The American government's fastidiousness toward student loans was not replicated in Qatar. However, in the last couple of years, the tightening budgets in Doha led to cutbacks in financial aid and a number of foreign students who were admitted were unable to attend.

The financial aid available to international students from outside Doha, a group comprising the final third of an average class, was generous and necessary. Its generosity was consistent with the Qatari leadership's vision of Education City as a place to bring a wide range of young people together as well as to establish Qatar as a recognized center of international learning. The largesse was necessary to keep the standards of education up to the level of its prestigious American university collaborators. The quality of the classroom could not be maintained without these international students, who generally came from the Muslim world, from Bosnia to Bangladesh. Many faculty thought their Pakistani students were the best prepared.

War Refugees

One striking feature in a student body drawn largely from the Middle East: a number of students—unfortunately ever-increasing—grew up in the midst of war and violence. Political conflict was less abstract for them than it might be for most Americans. Some of them had parents who had gone through violent upheaval with consequences that reminded me of friends I had grown up with whose parents were Holocaust survivors. They too were guarded, fearful, even paranoid toward outsiders. Memories had been buried, kept from the children, and the kids then suffered with the silence their parents imposed on them. I wondered how many of my students were survivors of violence, scarred by the dangers and unrest all around us.

Over time, some of their stories came out.

One Syrian student wrote me a couple of years after she had graduated. I had asked her how her education changed her life, particularly her career, since graduating. Though she mentioned trying to balance attending college with taking care of her baby, that was not what had stuck with her. College, almost accidentally, had given her the opportunity to talk with her father for the first time about his life and the traumas of war he had endured.

In her sophomore year, she had begun talking with her father about her class in Middle East history. This had prompted him to speak for the first time about his life under the Assad regime in Syria, his imprisonment, and being forced to flee afterward. Gradually, she learned details of his life he had never before revealed—that he had survived the massacre in the city of Hama in 1982. She heard about the barbaric methods of the regime and shared concrete details of this dictatorship in class.

It gave her a new understanding of her father. "My dad's experience has taught him to keep everything to himself and not to burden us with political issues of the past," she wrote. "This event was so important in his life and it's the reason why there's never a place we can call home." Curiously, it was during a Georgetown-sponsored visit to Auschwitz when she had realized a life lesson about the similarity of tragedies that are thought of as distant and unique. Because of what her father had been through and what he had shared with her, she could identify with those who suffered there in ways not unlike what her father had suffered. Her understanding of his pain opened her to the pain of others, no matter how different and far removed they seemed to be.

In its early years in Doha, Georgetown sponsored "reach out" events. These were encounters with people of different religions, nations, and races, reflecting groups students wouldn't ordinarily get to know. The school undertook them bravely, a bit naïvely and, to my mind, all too frequently.

These were part of a liberal quest to overcome political barriers and religious biases, to get our newly discovered Arab friends and protégés to join hands with us in singing "Kumbaya" around the campfire of Yankee-sponsored brotherhood. In later years, perhaps as experience overcame hope, and fewer faculty came from America and more came from the region, such undertakings were less and less common. Or maybe we all became more "practical," less hopeful.

Near the end of spring semester of my first year, a group of public policy graduate students from Tel Aviv arrived for an afternoon tea. This was not exactly an everyday event for a kingdom noted for its Wahhabi fundamentalism and for financing the militant Hamas movement in Gaza. Gathered in the student lounge, a dozen Israelis met a dozen of our undergraduates. A couple of Egyptian faculty members had, as was their custom, encouraged their students to boycott the event. In the lounge, both sides gamely tried not to be too defensive, appearing polite if detached. I introduced a couple of separate groups of students that were circling each other and left as the gathering faded into semi-cordial mumbles.

Afterward, Aisha came to my office. A student in my media class, she demanded to know what I had expected when I introduced her to the visitors. She seemed upset and I asked why. She said the Israelis had said the same old stuff. "You hate us, don't you?" one guy had asked her without much nuance. Aisha's eyes moistened.

Now I recalled she was from southern Lebanon. She said her family had been trapped in her aunt's house during the Israeli invasion the summer before. She told me of her fears from the weeks she spent in her aunt's basement listening to jets screaming overhead and bombs exploding nearby. Even today, the sound of jets at airports paralyzes her. She had to leave her family in the war zone when school started. Her face flashed fear, anger, guilt, and bewilderment as she relived the time.

I said little. I told her there was no way I could fully appreciate what her family had gone through. We were part of a university that provided a place to think and talk. And while this didn't seem like much now, it was really all we had to offer. I felt inadequate and sad.

Later, as I got to know her better, she recalled that while being evacuated, she'd watched a CBS news report on the war in Lebanon. Sounding like a cynical California valley girl reflecting on how stupid adults are, she remembered the coverage was "followed by a story on diet pills." For a while, she became "fiercely Lebanese." This feeling faded in the months that followed as she heard Hezbollah proclaim a glorious victory from the war. But she had seen for herself the devastation, including some of the twelve hundred dead Lebanese. Her grief melded into an interest in the media and how they communicated news and messages about the region to the public. These reactions led her to study international affairs to prepare for a career in broadcasting. Now, several years after she graduated, she is working in a distant European capital for an international TV network.

Different Folks, Different Strokes

A dizzying range of beliefs, abilities, and motivations animated most classrooms. Some of the students hailed from wealthy local families, descendants of Bedouin desert tribes that now shared in the bounty of gas and oil just offshore. Georgetown largely ran a commuter school. When school let out, the freshly cleaned Mercedes SUVs with drivers at the wheel would be waiting to take their young scholars home to their families. No Qatari that I know of has ever slept in a school dorm.

However large and chauffeured the vehicles many Qataris arrive at school in, they also show up without much of a tradition of book learning. The Gulf Arabs in Doha reminded me of southern Californians with their dearth of bookstores and lack of a reading culture. On the lengthy flights I took, the women would talk, the kids would play electronic games, and the men would watch movies—or just sit lost in thought. Pulling out a book or magazine to read was rare. Other colleagues confirmed this unscientific observation.

One non-Qatari wrote me later of his reaction to witnessing the privileges of wealthy locals carrying on a lifestyle that passed for ordinary:

A pet peeve some students had was seeing many students being dropped off at the university by drivers and being walked all the way up to the stairs of the building with their maid in uniform carrying their books. It was quite unnecessary, at best, and terribly debauched at worst. These students were perfectly capable of carrying their notebooks and files and we were all allocated lockers to put any other material we may need. . . . Needless to say, I do not remember anyone calling them out on these behaviors, lest we get into trouble for interference. There were fabulously wealthy students who were our classmates, but then again Georgetown in Qatar was nothing more than a microcosm of the society our campus was in.

Such students can be spoiled and uninterested in the life of the mind. Some from affluent Qatari families, however, were among our best students. Regardless of ability, most students expected more direction than I had been used to rendering. Consequently I, the authority, had to give the classes structure. If I didn't take attendance, a good number of students didn't show up. If I didn't punish tardiness, some showed up late. And if I didn't give frequent quizzes, students didn't keep up with the readings. They didn't seem to do well with too much uncertainty. My own preference for hang-loose laissez-faire instruction, which I had followed in the United States, was overtaken by on-the-ground teaching experiences. These students liked to know what to expect with no surprises.

This reliance on rules extended to their relations with one another. Students had their own ways of dealing with classmates who didn't fit in. Many of the Qataris were products of a few elite private schools in Doha. Friends and cliques acquired in high school were apparently retained into the college years. As I found out, these sometimes took on vigilante functions, overseeing classmates' behavior.

Asma was not a very good student in the Media and Foreign Policy seminar I taught in my second year in Doha. While bright enough, she was indifferent to her studies. As a Qatari, she wore the customary abaya; like many young Arab girls, she compensated for her concealed body by directing attention to her riveting face. She was tall and attractive to start with but she made herself more striking with darkly lined eyes and heavy makeup. She was not beyond flirting, a coquettishness reinforced when one day she showed up to class in novel attire. She was dressed to the nines, abaya-less, in what looked—to a professor considerably out of his depth—like the latest Paris fashions. In our class of fifteen students, it did not go unnoticed.

I am still not sure whether her change in dress had anything to do with what followed a few weeks later. Some two-thirds of the class, about nine students, trooped into my office: a solemn and unusual delegation with a serious agenda. They had come to complain about Asma. They said she had gotten help from her father in writing her class seminar paper. The proof: she had told a few of them. They urged that she be punished.

Since this was a seminar, the paper was half of the grade. The problem was that the first draft of Asma's paper, comparing news coverage by Al Jazeera Arabic with that of its sister network Al Jazeera English, wasn't very good. The organization was poor, the writing abysmal, the logic nonexistent. In short, it looked like her own work. She appeared to have done the half-assed job I'd expected from her. Should I have blamed her dad for helping or for not helping enough?

That the majority of the class—some very good students and some from leading Qatari families—would turn in a fellow student for cheating on her paper, left me confused. Cheating was not exactly unknown on campus with rumors afoot that some wealthy students hired foreign graduate students online to write their papers. The Honor System that Georgetown later established wasn't yet in place so I was left to make my own Solomonic judgment.

Perplexed, I went to the Assistant Dean of Students, Brendan Hill, who was familiar with all the students involved and had a street savvy that I lacked. He told me to forget about it. Brendan saw this as the workings of high school cliques, their gossip, and backbiting. Asma, for any number of reasons, was now on the outs with the "in crowd." Peer group social sanctions were strong and I, as an authority, was expected to back the dominant groups, to sew on the scarlet letter in this case.

I didn't relish the role. I see teaching, especially lessons of values such as this case, as more important than punishing. So instead, I spoke to Asma after class about the seriousness of plagiarism and the importance of doing her own work. I hoped the adult-being-formed could learn something in the process.

Asma nodded in agreement with my admonitions and denied everything else. She passed the class with a "D."

Years later, I spoke about the incident with a much better student, Maria, who was in the class. She recalled it differently. Asma was resented, not for no longer wearing her abaya, but for not taking the class seriously. The rumor was that she had hired someone to do her media paper. The group—of which this honors Georgetown graduate was a part—waxed indignant that Asma was "getting away with it." The bonds unifying these pioneering students, Maria concluded, were less rooted in local tradition and more reflective of an intense group of overachievers resenting a cheater blemishing the first class in their new school.

Teachers

My teaching colleagues were more connected to the students than I could claim. Many of them had ties to the people, language, culture, and religion of the region. Most were at the end or the beginning of their careers—half hadn't yet learned to teach and half had forgotten, one friend joked. An overseas post for a few years was viewed as a short-term boost to their plans for the future. Mid-careerists tended to stay at home because of teenagers in high school, wives with stable jobs and professional aspirations in the mother country. For those who did come, the added income—when combined with free housing, rent received from a now-empty house back home, and other perks—could double one's previous salary. Chances for travel—always by air— were not only abundant but also necessary in an isolated, hot, bleak, and very small country.

Whatever the motives for being in Doha, family issues were always present. Single people had to handle the isolation of living in a city and an unfamiliar culture that frowned on alcohol and public displays of affection between the sexes. Married couples had problems when teachers' spouses had difficulty getting a job or keeping busy if they didn't work. Many simply missed family back home. Parents with children had to find places for them in private schools where admission could be limited and expensive.

But to paraphrase friends from Alcoholics Anonymous, if you have a problem money can solve, you don't have a problem. With the availability of inexpensive housekeeping and child care, stipends for education, and subsidies for transportation, as well as large houses and SUVs, expats can overcome most of the challenges. And most seem to stay longer than they planned when they arrived.

Our mandate at Georgetown was to reproduce the same standards and content as existed at the main campus in Washington. Academic freedom might not be up for debate but what we were doing—and whether we were succeeding—certainly was, among a faculty prone to overthinking and overrating its mission. Was the education appropriate? How much was it shaping the next generation of Arab leaders? Were we allowing students to retain traditional values while modernizing the habits of the heart that had held back a great people? Both the questions and any answers overflowed with ambivalence.

In the middle of my third year in Doha, I wrote an article for the *Chronicle of Higher Education*. It ended in this somewhat ambiguous way:

The worst part of teaching in Qatar may actually occur before arrival: in the worried expectations of friends and family when they first hear of your pending departure. Arabs have a bad press in America and that filters down to sincere concerns about physical security and intolerance. While generalizations about an admittedly volatile region should be minimized, the surprises in being here for three years are almost all on the positive side. And for a faculty that includes priests, Jews, and other nonconformists, the response has been welcoming and, premising a degree of discretion, accepting. People of this region seem to want what we have to offer and are willing to put up with the eccentric baggage that Westerners inevitably bring with them. It's not a bad deal for either side, so far.

What Are We Doing?

One recurring question among teachers, especially in the early years of the school, was what exactly they and their students were doing in Doha. For expatriate faculty, motives were usually adapted from the old British imperial credo of "God, gold, and glory" to suit the more secular goals of liberal scholars. Promoting interest in intellectual inquiry, religious tolerance, and an openness for dissent and debate—all while making a comfortable living in an exotic setting—covered quite a few of the likely motives.

For the students, the debate was summed up by one philosophy colleague, a European, who thought the students' secular Western loyalties were only an inch thick on the surface while their Muslim and Arab cultural traditions comprised the deeper underlying soil. Another colleague, a Muslim, thought the exact opposite: that the religious rituals and ethnic dress and behavior were the inch-thick, superficial parts. The Western consumption, cultural amusements, and rational thinking patterns were the more profound, the more likely to last. When I posed these alternative divisions to a Qatari student, one of the best of the school's graduates, he agreed with my Muslim colleague that the globalist, consumer parts were the deeper, more embedded in his generation.

Although I often engage in the argument, I usually throw up my hands in the end. I have no idea.

Qataris have, on occasion, been heard to admonish casually dressed European women in malls with the phrase: "You must respect our values." When questions were asked what this meant, the responses usually related to dress, drinking, and other ritualized behaviors such as refraining from eating in public during Ramadan daylight hours. More than one foreign Arab pointed out that many Qatari traditions were recently created or at least embellished. An Egyptian member of one of the school's first classes remembered that when a visiting professor asked about the essence of Qatari heritage, a member of the Qatari royal family in the class answered, "The thobe." Hearing men's robes touted as a central tradition suggested to the Egyptian student—a proud descendant of an ancient civilization of pharaohs and pyramids—that he had come to a largely invented country.

Outsiders frequently take the rise of fundamentalism in the Arab world as a given. What this meant for some students—other than a rejection of Western ways and a commitment to certain traditional practices and beliefs—was never clear to me. A fleeting attempt to introduce Islamic religious rituals into the life of students at Georgetown went nowhere. After I left Doha, a group of students circulated a petition to have the call to prayer broadcast the usual five times a day throughout the school. The faculty opposed the idea and only a handful of faith-based students supported the move. The idea was dropped.

Wahhabism, the predominant and conservative school of Islam in Saudi Arabia and in less-intense form in Qatar, was a response to modern influences in the region during the nineteenth century. As such, as my more knowledgeable colleagues told me, it too was a form of adaptation to the modern world by Arab thinkers. Some students upset by the numbers of expats in Doha as well as the perceived dominance of Western products and culture felt threatened by this foreign incursion. But exactly what the threat was and what the response should be got muddled whenever I heard it expressed.

An academic dean at the school pointed out that the students generally, including those from the Gulf, lacked much knowledge of Islam. What they knew were practices: don't eat pork, don't drink liquor, dress modestly, and pray five times a day. But the values that guide a good life were not articulated by most of them, if they were known at all.

Clyde Wilcox, a professor of comparative politics from the main campus who took my place in Doha when I left, taught a course on religion and politics. He raised the issue of the influence of religion on politics. He found most of the class didn't understand the question. In a religion that stressed behavioral norms, any underlying ethics was difficult to grasp. Wilcox probed the students by asking whether their religious beliefs might affect how they treated migrant workers. One said he thought the frequent harassment of divorced women who were working shouldn't be allowed. A Saudi student, referring to the harsh working conditions of immigrant labor in Doha, said, "We should not be treating Sunnis this way." Students seemed to be befuddled by how their religious beliefs could be applied as universal values in relations with those outside their group or religion.

CHAPTER 5

On Women and Girls and Abayas

In Doha, the public display of gender and sex was often fraught with tension. One example came in the form of an artistic mini-crisis, brought about by the highly regarded British artist Damien Hirst, whose statues were—or were not—on display in front of the Sidra Medical and Research Center. These large, outdoor bronze sculptures—fourteen of them—boldly showed the gestation of a fetus inside a uterus, from conception—depicting the male sperm affixed to the female egg—to birth. They ended with a naked, forty-six-foot-tall baby boy in all his exposed glory.

At least, I've read this is what they look like. They were erected across the street from my office but I've never actually seen them. Explaining why is an interesting tale.

Commissioned in secrecy by Sheikha al Mayassa, the head of the Qatar Museums Authority and sister of the current emir, they reportedly cost north of $20 million. The sculptures were designed to artistically reflect the work of the newly constructed medical center, which specialized in female and child medical treatment. They were placed out front. Called the "Miraculous Journey," the statues were unveiled on October 7, 2013. Briefly.

One can only imagine the criticism—all privately voiced—that was directed at this very visible display of private matters along one of Doha's major highways—and sited across the road from

Georgetown's classrooms. In defending this edgy display of public art, the thirty-year-old chairwoman cited a verse in the Koran praising the miracle of birth, adding, "To have something like this is less daring than having a lot of nudity." It probably didn't help much but the sculptures were supported by American pro-life groups affiliated with the Catholic Church. They endorsed them as a reminder of the sacredness of the fetus.

Within a few weeks of being unwrapped, the statues were rewrapped under large cloth tarpaulins. A few stories circulated. One suggested that these tarps aimed to protect the statues from the construction dust generated at the yet-to-be-completed hospital site. Then there was the story that the statues were unfinished. Another stated that they were to be moved. Staff at the hospital's information booth claimed, without great conviction, that they would be unveiled on Opening Day.

As the years passed, the statues remained covered. Drivers sped past, the fourteen windblown, camouflaged, and very expensive blobs standing as mute testimony to another unresolved tension within Qatar. Suspended between elite art tastes and conservative public dismay, they were neither removed nor uncovered. By the beginning of 2017, the cover-up seemed permanent with wooden scaffolding boxing in the sculptures and dark fencing the color of an abaya blocking the view from the highway. Most spectators willing to comment agreed with a faculty colleague's conclusion: "The statues will never be unwrapped to be publicly displayed."

*

Parents in Doha wanted American educators in their city partly because they didn't want their daughters educated in America. Their hope for this "home-delivery college" was that one could deconstruct a modern university, expose students to the good stuff, and keep them away from the bad. And they especially wanted to shield their daughters from the downsides of Western culture. Learning was fine, acquiring job skills was great, and familiarity with the world at large

81

was okay if necessary. But the other foibles of youth that American campuses contained—social rebellion, sexual experimentation, drug and alcohol abuse, a debased online culture, and secular questioning of religious beliefs—not so good. Admittedly, this parental fantasy of separating the positive from the negative in their kids' college years is a familiar one outside the Middle East. But in Doha, there's at least the possibility of paying for the dream.

Has it worked? Has moving Georgetown to Doha removed the perils and produced graduates who can seamlessly fill their expected places in this society? Disentangling the impact of a university on its women graduates is as muddled as unpacking their actual educational experiences. From the women students, much is expected, much is feared. Educated women offer a unique catalyst for changing what are largely patriarchal societies. What these women—now composing 70 percent of the student body—do when they graduate is a key test of whether this type of education can actually transform these societies. Or are women graduates compelled to leave their countries to fully use what they've learned, what they've become? I spent time listening to educated women, both graduates and faculty, wrestle with their time in and out of school.

Amira

Amira took several of my classes and I got to know her as well as any of my students. I watched her develop from a shy, bright, but awkward girl into a socially adept young woman. She entered college with a cynicism that I thought came from living in a society where young girls were expected to listen to older, usually male, adults. Because she was usually smarter than the people she was listening to, she got comfortable quietly disregarding others' opinions, especially those of us in authority.

I never saw Amira wearing an abaya; she preferred the contemporary casual dress—jeans and long-sleeved blouses—of a globalized teenager with a hint of restraint inherited from her conservative Syrian family. She would not be called conventionally pretty—too many angles on her long, Semitic face—but her large eyes stood out beneath her rimless glasses. She was a diligent student, seldom assertive in class. But her papers reflected someone who took her studies seriously.

She took my question about how a university education affected women like her and gave me a thoughtful response: "Education in the Middle East is a way to get a job, not to change the way you think. For women from families that can afford it, the norm is now education. A university degree no longer takes away your chances of getting married. Most of the women from my graduating class in 2009 are in fact married."

But there was a price she paid for her education. University had changed her. Even worse for family tranquility, it had affected the way she thought.

"Believe me, my parents didn't send me to Georgetown to widen my horizons or liberate my mind. But it often does change the way students think." She paused and gave me a half smile. "After Georgetown, I have become more curious and less certain."

She had become sadder, perhaps more realistic, about her hopes for the region and others' grand schemes to improve life there.

And yet when she stopped to think about her classmates, she said that even before the Arab Spring, "Everyone has gotten good at playing the victim."

Although Amira had passed on the student trip to Israel ("What was the point of it?"), she had signed on to the following year's visit to Rwanda. It had changed her. Under the rubric "Zones of Conflict, Zones of Peace," the Office of Student Affairs had organized a series of overseas trips each year. In spring 2009, they had visited the sites of the 1994 genocide of Tutsis by Hutus. They went to memorials for victims and talked to people who had lived through the mass murders of some six hundred thousand people. The most meaningful experience for Amira was sitting in on the operations of grassroots courts, called Gaccaca, where people who had killed their neighbors with machetes were confronted by the families of the victims. Amira was especially struck by children who, though they had no memories of the horror, were made to attend the trials. She recalls how impassively they watched.

Not only had the trials emphasized forgiveness, they also de-emphasized the country's tribal divisions. Indeed, the terms "Hutu" and "Tutsi" were never used. What struck Amira was how the memories of the violence were channeled into the courts and schools, and so the searing topic of genocide was in the main kept out of family discussions and social engagements. She compared this with her own experiences among Palestinian refugees and how their memories of war were never institutionalized but were left to the families with all the harsh, personal baggage that parents added to them.

She had not lost her cold-eyed view of the Arab world. She mentioned a story her father told her in explaining the spate of violence afflicting the region, following the Arab Spring. "When you lock people in a dark room and deprive them of a lot of things, including freedom, they may appear calm and adjusted. Then someone comes along and suddenly opens the door. No one files out in an orderly, single line. Instead, they rush out to the light, trampling each other on the way. In their desperation to fit through the narrow opening, they harm themselves and each other. It's a shame but understandable."

*

Rogaia was having none of it.

Professor Rogaia Abusharaf, a Sudanese-born anthropologist teaching at our school, clad in black slacks and colorful wedged shoes, brought up a point that often gets raised among women in Qatar when they gather to "talk gender." What's wrong with the men? The women of Doha—those from elsewhere as well as Qataris—hardly struck one as a weak, downcast social group. Rogaia endorsed the consensus view of her colleagues that our women students were better at their studies than the men. "Our Qatari women students are driven. They take pride in their work. And they have a strong sense of urgency toward their studies. No wonder. They worry about depending on men."

She quoted a friend who said, "Men are cheap." It is the women who are populating the government agencies. It was the best of our graduates, often women, who were allowing the Islamic world to compete in a global economy. And their families were behind this change, celebrating their success quite as much as that of their men. "Confidence is not an issue for our women students," Rogaia added. "They have come to us with their family supports already in place. There are few clear-cut boundaries restraining them in their lives."

Rogaia's point is that Westerners' preconceived notions of traditional societies have blinded many to the diversity and complexity of male-female relations. Women traditionally played a strong, if not dominant, role in villages while the men were off partying and hanging out with their buddies. This left the women central to financial, child-rearing, and housekeeping decisions made in the family. The myth of a harem and men with multiple wives is just that, she says: a myth. Qatari men seldom took more than one wife, even in the old days.

The truth in many Arab families is that "the women call the shots." Rogaia recounted the story of an Arab professor in the social sciences—she wouldn't tell me his name—whom she was recruiting to work on a project during the summer break. He apparently wanted to join the research but said he couldn't. He said his wife wouldn't allow him to travel during the summer. She wanted him at home. He stayed put.

In another story reinforcing the same theme, Rogaia spoke of an Egyptian housepainter who complained to her that a Qatari man he worked for couldn't make a decision on the color of paint to use for rooms in his house. The Qatari man said he couldn't decide without his wife present. She was apparently in another of their homes. The painter asked his employer to invite her to the house to decide. No, he responded, I tried but she won't come. The project was put on hold, indefinitely.

The painter's conclusion, shared by Rogaia, was that behind the appearance of patriarchy and male dominance, Qatari couples operated "like everyone else." Where wives are the stronger personality, they will be in charge.

Rogaia disputed the dichotomy between modern and traditional in discussing the roles of women. She concluded bluntly, "I don't subscribe to the idea of tradition making women subservient or holding them back."

Boys and Girls Together

Most of the young men and women in our school would be easily recognizable in a middle-tier American liberal arts college. Some were bright, some weren't; some worked hard, some didn't. They had the customary range of abilities and interests and identities. Many were mature and motivated. Others were just occupying space. And why not? Education for their children was one of many benefits Qataris and their families expected from the state. Students were fulfilling expectations that they reflect the family's position among a status-conscious people. Georgetown offered another expensive import: a prestigious university degree.

Girls seemed better prepared, more focused on getting good grades, sometimes just smarter. Figuring out why was not beyond faculty speculation. Many of the boys we were teaching, especially those from the Gulf, were already familiar with the material pleasures of life: Porsches, summers on the Riviera, fast catamarans, drivers, servants. They came from closely knit, wealthy families in which they had inherited an elevated position. If they were Qatari, they were guaranteed a well-paying, not-very-demanding government job if they wanted, supplemented by financial grants from the regime that allowed them to live a very comfortable life. Bottom line: Gulf men did not have to do well in school to do well in life. Unsurprisingly, teachers who voiced an opinion thought Qatari male students were less motivated than the women. The president of Qatar University, Sheikha Missad, might concur: "This country doesn't have a woman problem," she was often quoted as saying, "it has a man problem."

None of which is to say that girls didn't engage equally with the material benefits that came with affluence. A graduate of Georgetown's first class, Katrina Quirolgico, thought the discrimination facing Qatari women depended on their social class. The higher your standing in the social strata, the less likely you were to face adversity because of gender. The less affluent confronted more social restrictions. As for upper-class Qatari women, observed Ms. Quirolgico, "They do what they want to do."

But for those not quite as privileged, a university education promised an elevation at home and within their female-subordinated society. It might even provide a path to a lifestyle that could take them out of traditional home-and-hearth roles. Wealthy, educated women did not have to give up their families to have a profession. Education for women was prized in traditional societies as long as the consequences of that education didn't undermine the family, the male-dominated hierarchy, and the faith.

Those women who made it to Georgetown had already proven themselves outstanding students. One Egyptian colleague described her female students as "strong, confident, and assertive." If they were intimidated by men or a male-dominated culture, I never noticed it in the classroom. Doing their best in college increased their options, including grad school and delaying marriage. In short, Georgetown opened the possibility of following the Western female models portrayed in the global media.

Mixing with men in academia was a daring step for many of them. After an unsteady first year, most of the women adapted fairly easily. But that doesn't mean the broader cultures did the same. It was not uncommon to hear that Georgetown women were considered "sluts" for mixing with men by their peers at gender-separated, less-prestigious Qatar University across town. One graduate of our "University of Kafirs" told of a prospective husband closely questioning her over the phone about having gone to college with men and then never calling again.

Social mixing between unmarried women and men was still *haram* in most Gulf families. When it did occur, the results could in some cases be dire. A colleague told the harrowing story of a female student who had a boyfriend at school. As did others, they would sometimes meet and hold hands in inconspicuous corners of the school building. My colleague thought it rather sweet and innocent. Unfortunately, the female student sent an email intended for her boyfriend to her father by accident. The father, who hadn't known of the boyfriend, confronted her at home, stripped the girl to the waist, and lashed her with a belt. The girl knew enough to take photos of her injuries at the school clinic and to give an account there of what had happened. Her mother supported her daughter and they both moved out of the compound where they lived; from there, they went into hiding.

The father, with the girl's brother, came looking for them. My colleague was sure they meant to punish the girl, likely with another beating, perhaps worse. At this point, the police intervened to protect the women. It was now plain, however, that it was too dangerous for the girl and her mother to stay in Qatar. The women had stepped outside of customary boundaries and the males in the family were unforgiving. The women fled to another country in the Gulf where the girl continued her education.

A clash of cultures, which could have had a tragic outcome, seemed to resolve well enough for the girl involved, in part because of her own ability to use the resources that our school made available to her.

Gender in the Streets

Most expat men arrived in Qatar forearmed with warnings about how to deal with women. If you were an expat woman, you were briefed by friends or employers on how to dress and act. These preparations didn't always help.

A student development officer and recent graduate of Georgetown's Washington campus was initially entranced by Arabs and Qatar. She worked in student affairs in the early years of the school. As an Egyptian student—a friend of hers—told the tale, she studied Arabic and learned about Islam. She made friends easily and was active in groups that taught English to low-income migrants. She was also pretty and liked to run for exercise on weekends on the Corniche along the waterfront. She would wear jogging gear that would be considered normal in her native California, but she and her outfit attracted unwanted attention in the new neighborhood. She was harassed with comments, whistles, stares, and worse. Soon she was giving these groups of men the finger. She increasingly kept to herself, felt isolated from the larger society, and became disillusioned about Qatar. She left after a year.

Foreign men also had their gender issues. "Don't talk to Qatari women—they'll have you deported," a Lebanese tech staffer heard upon his arrival. Of course, for those of us who were teachers, this suggestion was inoperative. At the same time, colleagues noted that Qatari females in their first year never came to faculty offices alone. By junior year, they would show up by themselves but office doors were almost always left ajar. Shaking hands with a woman was a close call and only to be initiated by the woman: if she extended her hand you could shake it, I was told; otherwise keep your hands to yourself.

And the females in class were "girls," not "women"; the latter phrase was reserved for those with husband and family. (That took some doing on my part: I had raised a modern American daughter who, starting at age nine, thought being called a "girl" was a sexist putdown.)

Problems still arose; not every encounter was clearly explained in advance. The son of Dan Stoll, the former academic dean, was working at a government ministry when he entered an elevator already occupied by two Qatari women. After exiting on his floor, he was bawled out by a local for being alone in an elevator with two women. He should have let the elevator pass, he was told. Well, that was a clear boundary. Except when it wasn't. The dean relayed this story to a Qatari friend; this gentleman shook his head, expressing dismay that any countryman would even raise such an issue.

In expatriate compounds, Western cultural norms usually prevailed, which meant nobody complained about drinking alcohol and women could generally wear whatever they wanted. But not always. In a couple of incidents in two different compounds, women voiced objections to men exercising with them in the gym. In another case, an Egyptian brought his Russian girlfriend with him to work out. They were both asked to leave by other men when they arrived to exercise. Though malls were generally treated as a mixing bowl of cultures, a number of Western women complained later that they were approached by men in thobes and told they could not wear the casual T-shirts or shorts they had put on. In general, exposure of arms and legs by women was a risky proposition, mostly frowned on, sometimes in verbal confrontations.

Confusing the picture further was that these same ultramodern malls featured advertisements of alluring, half-dressed, sexy women trying to get locals to buy Benetton perfume, Dansko shoes, Nike sportswear, and Polo undergarments. At least once a year, in February when the professional tennis tour came to Doha, posters of scantily clad, attractive young tennis players would spring up all around the city. One clear advantage that these very exposed female bodies had over those of any women pedestrians below was that they were about thirty feet in height and positioned to be stared at.

Azra

Azra was one of the most striking graduates of the school's first decade. Faculty colleagues, some of whom probably shouldn't remember, still bring up her graduation march. Not only did she monopolize the honors ceremony that Georgetown—ever in love with its rituals—insisted on transferring to Doha; she also wore a miniskirt visible on each of her several walks across the stage to receive these honors. The long, athletic legs of this six-footer served as a not-so-subtle parting act of defiance toward the assembled, mostly robed, mostly conservative senior Gulf Arabs seated in the honored front rows of the auditorium. In the United States, it might resemble a coed throwing a wet farewell kiss to that crotchety uncle who just finished paying her college tuition.

Not that Azra could ever be called a rebel; she was too driven and ambitious a student for that. But until I spoke to her in a Washington coffee house several years after she had graduated, I didn't realize how alienated this bright Turkish girl had been during her years in Qatar.

"Doha was the strangest place in the world," she said, opening our conversation and shaking a head of ringlets that looked like a Turkish version of an Afro.

Student life at Georgetown provided a social bubble for Qatari women. Azra talked about her Qatari girlfriend who was friendly with a boy from high school but couldn't be seen with him in public, even as part of a group. "Even though there was nothing romantic going on, she was reluctant to be seen with him outside of the university. Hanging out at the uni was okay, but outside of campus our group had to go to a restaurant where they wouldn't be seen."

Azra reminisced about her Qatari girlfriend. "Five years after graduating, she had gotten a 'just okay' job with the government. She had spent a year at the London School of Economics. She has turned down two offers of marriage to Qatari men presented by her parents. The men's lack of an education equivalent to hers figured in both rejections. She felt a gap in communicating with both guys.

"She fantasizes about living in the West. But is frankly unwilling to give up the many advantages that come from being in a wealthy Qatari family, from jewelry to servants. Her dilemma could be resolved by the 'right' marriage—a man willing to tolerate the lifestyle of a Western woman. But that hasn't happened yet."

Though Azra now lives abroad as a graduate student in an American city and dates non-Arab, non-Islamic men, the issues of family and tradition remained. She considers herself a Muslim, though she doesn't fast during Ramadan and, since she took the "Problem of God" class at Georgetown, has found atheism an understandable option. She accepted that if she were to choose a husband from a different background than hers, she probably could not move back home or be fully accepted by her family. This meant that in her own mind a non-Muslim suitor had a higher threshold to pass before she would consider a serious relationship. She thought her parents—her father is a journalist, her mother a teacher—would understand and eventually allow her to make her own choice. However, she added, "The consequences of certain choices would be painful for my family and for me."

To Abaya or Not to Abaya

Even the most obvious symbol of tradition in Doha, a woman's appearance, reflects neither compulsion nor subordination, according to Rogaia.

Women wear abayas in Qatar, and elsewhere, for many reasons. They wear these loose-fitting black robes to embrace their national culture, to reflect their loyalty to their culture and people. They may just wear them for privacy. Rogaia told about her girlfriend who wore an abaya but also covered her face with a niqab when she drove her car so she could move about unseen. When she arrived, she removed it, revealing her contemporary outfit. (Doha is a small place and there are frequent stories told, bordering on legend, about Gulf women covering so that they could not be identified as they rendezvous with gentlemen for secret liaisons.) As a non-covered woman, Rogaia has never felt discriminated against because she didn't wear an abaya. She admitted that back in her native Sudan, where the abaya has become politicized, she was more likely to be harassed by men when not wearing a traditional women's covering.

Few Qatari women dress traditionally when they are abroad. The lack of pressure to wear an abaya overseas always seemed strange to me. After all, wouldn't most believers view their women as more vulnerable in crime-filled, sex-obsessed, non-Islamic, anonymous, Western cities? Yet many Muslim women seem to enjoy the freedom of wearing a variety of clothes for different occasions. Women spending money on expensive clothes is not an activity that has national boundaries and the Qataris have the means to indulge. Of the dozens of Qatari women who studied at the Washington campus, very few wore abayas. Professor Patricia O'Connor, with typical West Virginian realism, put the Qatari logic simply: "If you don't want unwanted attention in Qatar, you wear an abaya. If you don't want unwanted attention in the US, you don't wear an abaya."

Abayas are, of course, a clothing fashion as well as a cultural statement and they can be expected to wax and wane in popularity over time. Some Qatari students pointed out that in photos of Doha from the 1960s and 1970s, there are very few women in abayas or men in thobes. One recalled her grandmother going to the beach in a two-piece bathing suit. The 1970s brought independence, a rise in nationalism, and a popular desire to imitate a leadership that dressed traditionally. Enhancing this sentiment, the Iranian Revolution in

1979 brought the ascent of religious orthodoxy, which echoed across the Gulf. And now, most Qatari students agree, they would be upbraided by family and friends for not dressing in the traditional manner.

Which is not to say there isn't a range of motivations behind a woman's choice of traditional dress, from outside pressure to self-expression. Women frequently cite the convenience, allowing them to throw on an abaya while wearing whatever they want underneath, including pajamas. Abayas also conceal extra pounds, which are easy to gain given the Gulf's meat-protein and wheat/rice-carbo diet.

Amina Husain, the wife of an economics teacher at our school, focused on religious self-expression to explain the abaya she wore. Husain, whose family was from India, was raised in the United States, where she taught biology and met her husband, Ganesh Seshan. When she returned to the United States, she wore her abaya, as did Miriam, the oldest of her three children. How Amina dressed was rooted in religious teachings. Her abaya was a convenient, comfortable way for a Muslim woman to conform to the modesty called for by her faith. With the creative use of fabrics, crepe, silk, rayon, and chiffon, it was breathable and allowed a variety of clothes underneath. The new styles appearing in Qatar—abayas shaped like blouses and skirts, even blazers—allowed modern Muslim women to put their personality on display.

Amina cited an example of cultural coercion: an American-educated friend confessed to urging her daughter to wear an abaya because, in the friend's words, "I don't want her to forget she's Qatari." Amina thought many women who cover—but then wear makeup and tight clothes—are being pressured by their families to dress traditionally and are rebelling by adding a provocative spin to their appearance. Her own daughter chose to wear an abaya at age ten even though she didn't need to begin until puberty. Although Amina admits that she would have been disappointed if Miriam hadn't covered, she insists it was her daughter's own choice.

This issue of individual choice was paramount for Amina. When I pointed out this was a very American approach with very unusual outcomes, she nodded in agreement. "My dress is that of an individual in relation to God, not in relation to society. If people choose to dress alike, that's their problem." And she counseled me not to assume mindless conformity because of the similarity of dress. She was following a social code, shaped by her religious beliefs. And one could add—though Amina didn't—that dressing in an abaya in 2017 America was not the easiest way of blending into this society's acceptable customs unnoticed and unbothered.

A friend, a retired professor of Middle Eastern history, pointed to a variety of motives behind college students' decision to wear abayas or hijabs in a city like Cairo where he taught. One reason was to demonstrate to their family that they could still be traditional, modest women while pursuing higher education. Second was that it made social interaction with authorities and classmates easier—these young women were spoken for and had to be treated respectfully. Closely related to this was the sad reality that walking on the streets of Cairo in an abaya meant avoiding some of the harassment and outright groping from ill-mannered Egyptian men, an increasingly frequent experience for uncovered women.

My friend was struck by how many different styles could be incorporated in the variety of dress that Arab women manage to customize in interpreting the demands of tradition. A case in point was one young woman he saw in Berlin with her head covered. So far, so good. Below her covering, she had on a miniskirt, fishnet stockings, high heels, and a skintight upper body garment. This seemed a rather brazen updating of traditional apparel.

Clearly, there was a range of behavior within what outsiders characterized as "traditional." This, of course, doesn't mean there weren't real dilemmas facing women brought up in families that followed a conservative patriarchy limiting their roles and dress, and steering them toward fulfilling expectations of being the wives and mothers that kept home and hearth. Women who challenged these inherited norms had a fight on their hands, as a former student discovered.

Aatikah

I'd only seen Aatikah a couple times in the five years since she had graduated. She had come to my office—for some combination of advice/letters of recommendations—always wearing the abaya expected of a Qatari girl from one of the country's prominent families. When we met in a Chinese restaurant near Harvard Square in Boston where she had gone for graduate studies, I was somewhat surprised to see a young lady in an expensive black T-shirt and faded jeans. Her longish, dark hair and caramel complexion would not have made a Spanish accent seem out of place.

While Aatikah had always been direct and no-nonsense in our conversations, I still was taken aback by how quickly she got to the point she wanted to make.

"For the first time in my life, I have stopped trying to convince my parents and gain their approval for what I want to do. Now I am getting on with my life. I am not going to worry about trying to manipulate them. I've come to the end of my rope with that."

Aatikah painted a picture of struggle over what was expected of a girl in the Arab Gulf. Her parents wanted to protect her; she wanted to explore. She was the oldest of six sisters and brothers. She recalls this tension when she was a child of ten.

"How come Ahmad (her younger brother) can go out on his bike and I can't?"

"Because you're a girl."

She knew this was wrong but couldn't say why at the time. As she puts it, "I hadn't learned the language of resistance yet."

Her parents didn't understand gender inequality. Their unexamined argument that she was a girl ignored her strong will. As she grew up, they told her she worked too hard, that she didn't have to go to conferences or take up leadership in school clubs. And yet, though she doesn't admit it, there may have been a grudging admiration for her ambition. They wanted to be supportive within limits. Her mother pushed her to wear an abaya. Aatikah, not wanting to deal with the conflicts of not wearing one, complied. She never felt authentic in it. And she took off her abaya as soon as she went overseas.

Georgetown hadn't seemed to drastically change the direction she was headed in; instead, it supported her in her growth already underway. Her courses gave her more confidence in her thinking, as well as shaping her ideas of individualism and providing a glimpse of women's lives in the rest of the world. Curiously, she didn't find much support from other girls at school who might have been confronting similar questions. Her experience was that Qatari girls didn't speak to one another about feminine issues.

She did get help from the counseling that the school provided. Psychiatric care remains rare in the Arab world. Aatikah found a safe place with Georgetown's counselors to talk about the issues she was confronting at home. And she learned to trust strangers outside of the family, a notion alien to her traditions. Later, in America, she would continue this counseling with a Palestinian-American therapist who offered her guidance from her own life experiences. Her independence of mind and emotional stability in defying her parents were cemented by these contemporary professional supports.

Continuing her education meant leaving her country. And that meant more fights with her parents. Ultimately, they agreed she could earn her master's abroad. But part of the compromise was that her younger brother, also studying in the United States, would live with her. Although his lifestyle was not restricted, she was monitored by him. She grins, "He was on the other team."

When she had finished her master's, she pushed for getting a PhD. Her parents resisted. It was time for her to return home, live with the family, look for a husband. Their financial arguments didn't work because she had been offered a scholarship from an American school. And Aatikah realized that returning to Doha meant putting her abaya back on; no casual coffees with mixed groups at the Villagio Mall near school; no vacations in Italy with girlfriends; and living a gender-segregated social life at home.

She understood she was no longer the traditional person she had been raised to be. She saw the freedom that women in the West had: free to dress as they wanted, to travel, to hang out with friends of either gender, to pursue their career dreams; free to experience life on their own terms.

Aatikah didn't know what came next. She kept in touch with her folks and looked forward to them visiting the following year. At twenty-eight, she said she was not interested in marriage and her parents didn't seem to be pushing it—one of the advantages of having five brothers and sisters following traditional ways, she added. She ended on a decidedly ambivalent note:

"Maybe in a few months I'll want my parents more involved in my life. I may go back to Doha to teach someday or I may stay in the West—and become a global citizen. I date, including non-Arab guys, and I've learned to trust people outside my tribe and faith. My friends here call me 'the Arab Princess' because they think I am fabulously wealthy. And it's tough giving up the servants and stuff I could have back in Qatar. I live here in a small apartment."

Here she stopped and shrugged.

"Those privileges are a distraction. For the first time, I am doing what I want."

Where Do They Go Next?

An independent-minded Pakistani coed who graduated with honors from Georgetown and went to graduate school in California remarked, "My family has both given up on me and is proud of me."

Outside the classroom, many women confront the binding traditions they have temporarily left. They have increased their value in the marriage market, yet they may intimidate the less-educated men available. The women, too, might have gotten a little bit pickier, less amenable to the pressures put on them by their parents, who have selected partners for them. One former Georgetown student insisted that her husband-to-be had to be a college graduate. Needing to live up to his new wife's expectations, after their wedding he went back to college to get his degree. Georgetown's former dean Gerd Nonneman called this a "reinvention of traditional elements" by women graduates. While these women still might be socially constrained, many were insisting on rights in their marriage contract that included continuing their education and having a separate house to live in.

Marriages arranged by parents still occur but in the cases I heard about, those pairing off had a say—often a veto—over any parental choice. As one said, we are not forced into marriage but we are pressured. With gender separation in force, it became somewhat difficult for prospective partners in Qatar to make an independent selection. Often the mothers were key in making the choice for their offspring.

My wife, Ann, saw this at a Qatar wedding she was invited to. There were two celebrations held miles apart: one for men, one for women. At the female gathering, an interesting fashion show occurred. Young women, dressed in very revealing clothes, paraded on a stage in front of an audience consisting mainly of older women, most of whom were described to Ann as being the mothers of eligible sons. This was apparently an opportunity for the mothers to "inspect the goods." The ones passing this initial physical review would presumably merit a recommendation for their sons and a pass to the next level of selection.

Careers for women in Doha were possible, indeed sometimes easier than in other parts of the world. Becoming a mother in Doha was not a career killer as it could be in the United States. With plenty of servants and extended families, day care was not an issue. But the quality of jobs could be a challenge. Two Georgetown graduates spoke about taking their guaranteed jobs in the Ministry of Foreign Affairs. The Ministry had a poor reputation among students as an uncreative place to work and these grads' story illustrated why. Apparently, the women were assigned to the fourth floor of the Ministry, where female employees gathered mostly to gossip and do their nails. When they were invited to hear visiting speakers, they were seated in the back and given pro forma questions to ask. They complained that in their time at the Ministry they were not assigned anything significant to do. They both quit after six months.

There was a debate in the corridors of our school about whether female graduates of Western universities could ever fulfill their professional ambitions if they remained in Doha. Many recent grads stayed in Doha, if only because they were required to remain for a couple years if they wanted their financial aid from Qatar to be forgiven. Most found jobs in multinational corporations, nonprofits, or government agencies, courtesy of a still-expanding, prosperous economy. Sheikha Mozah was a model for many Qatari women seeking positions in Qatar society. Female students often pointed with pride to the three Qatari women who had become ambassadors. Some added knowingly that none of the three was married.

On the other side of the debate was a realpolitik appraisal that we were educating women for a world that didn't quite exist in the Arab Gulf. Georgetown's first and, later, interim dean, Jim Reardon-Anderson, put it this way: "Success of women lies with those who take our education into the global marketplace. Those who don't are stuck." In reality, the women grads of Georgetown in Doha were not doing what women who gained a degree from the main campus had available to them. The non-Qatari women educated here have taken wing, the dean added. For the others, they might have to wait for the next generation.

And of course, there was the other side. An Arab friend criticized America for letting its women wander the streets at all hours of the night, vulnerable and unprotected. He pointed to crimes against women and how many were victimized by predators or trapped raising children on their own without the support of a husband or strong family. But women in America have collectively decided they don't want men's protection; they want tasks and careers equal to those of men. Pressuring or steering women toward subordinate roles in the family or workplace was no longer acceptable for increasing numbers of them. Justifying this practice because of their "weaker" feminine inclinations or inherited customs was equally unacceptable. If the women themselves rejected these identities, men were unlikely to be able to impose them for long.

Creating choices for individual women was what many Georgetown administrators, faculty, and families recognized and supported. One Georgetown graduate and feminist leader, Melanne Verveer, put the point well: "An educated girl was the single most important develop-ment story."

Many in the Muslim world and elsewhere do not allow women to make their own choices or honor them when made. This will not likely halt the increasing number of women who want to travel their own paths and live with the consequences. Arguing that there were no differences between how women were treated in "traditional" and "modern" societies was not consistent with the experiences of these students. This doesn't mean there wasn't considerable variation in both types of society.

Amira

My last meeting with Amira was in a Washington coffee house—one of those modern, mostly glass affairs on a downtown corner but nearly empty on the late Friday afternoon when we sat down to talk. It had just rained, a sudden summer downpour. I was wet and late. She had arrived on time, which was not like her.

Amira seemed unusually upbeat. She proudly declared that she had given up cigarettes. She was working for an English non-profit that campaigned to expand press freedoms and online access throughout the world.

I turned the conversation to her life. She said she had a serious boyfriend.

"He's a Catholic, an American, working as an international consultant."

"What do your parents think?"

"Actually, he was traveling through Doha and he stopped by to meet the family. He stayed for dinner and it went well."

She said this with a bit of can-you-believe-this in her voice.

"My mother was surprisingly accepting. My father didn't seem concerned; he worries more about my safety living in the West. He doesn't understand my living so far away from the family with no rel-atives to depend on. He doesn't quite get the concept of roommates."

"What happened?"

"I just turned twenty-seven. That's quite old in our family for an unmarried woman. They just want to see me get married. And they don't seem to care to whom."

We said good-bye on the corner outside the café. In keeping with my Gulf training, I waited for her to reach out her hand to shake mine, knowing that in Qatar only a few Arab women were willing to indulge this seemingly daring courtesy.

Instead, she grinned and gave me a hug. Yet another step away from Doha.

Walking away, I wondered about her parents and their acceptance of her boyfriend. I thought of my mom when, in my late thirties, I brought home a divorced woman, not Jewish of course, with her six-year-old boy. I told Mom we wanted to get married. She never objected to Ann. Indeed, she welcomed Daniel as if he were already a grandson and seemed quite happy. I was pretty impressed with this late-in-life flexibility. Afterward, other family members mentioned, offhandedly, that despite having witnessed a series of my girlfriends, Mom worried that I was gay. She may have been joking, which didn't mean she—a woman of stern traditions—wasn't worried.

Who knows what fears, spoken and unspoken, caused Amira's parents to accept her changes and choices. Perhaps the prospects she presented them were a vast improvement on the disasters they were witnessing in their own part of the world, not to mention other fears of what they could imagine harming their precious daughter. Maybe her parents were not that different from mine. One can almost hear them all reciting the oft-spoken oath of parents—from many different lands and faiths, of times ancient and current, who—when presented with an offer they can't refuse from children they can't control—bravely if halfheartedly respond:

"As long as you're happy, dear."

CHAPTER 6

On America: My Country 'Tis of This

Iwas not shocked that a number of students walked out of Georgetown with many of the same ideas they walked in with. Sometimes this was only accidentally revealed. For instance: Ella was an attractive, lively Syrian girl, dressed in the latest European fashions, a step up from the jeans and blouses worn by her more casually clothed classmates. I never saw her in an abaya or with her hair or arms covered.

Ella graduated near the top of her class and shortly thereafter was one of several voices featured in a Doha newspaper article. She was asked her opinion of the 2012 American presidential campaign, which was then nearing an end. Her answer, as I recall, was that it really didn't matter because the Zionists controlled the banks, the media, and both political parties and wouldn't let anything change in America. Ella had spent a semester at Georgetown in DC and, even more depressing for me, had been a good student in my American government course. Whether she was playing to the folks back home or, as I fear, really spoke her mind might not matter much. Her interview response was yet another reminder to me of the uncertain impact of the classroom experience.

After a short while, my students lost most of the traditional deference for teachers I had initially taken advantage of, and readily questioned the messages I delivered in class. One young lady objected to a phrase in my American government textbook after I, piqued by curiosity, asked if the class had any criticism of the book. She asked why I had characterized the 9/11 terrorists who had attacked New York and Washington as belonging to a "radical Arab" group. The question, essentially, was whether their ethnic identity was a defining aspect of who they were and what they did. Joined by a few class-mates, she objected to the "Arab" connection that seemed relevant to most Americans, including me. But she had a point.

Later, I noticed that when Al Jazeera TV covered the 2014 shooting spree that killed a Canadian soldier at the Parliament building in Ottawa, it left out the fact that the lone gunman was a recent Muslim convert. This had been central to the narrative in North American networks' coverage of the event. For Al Jazeera, it was enough to say this individual was deranged; for them, his religion had little to do with his criminal actions.

Although I didn't agree with the Al Jazeera deletion, I understood the sensitivity of the faithful in seeing their beliefs cited as the key motivation behind horrors committed by people of their religion. In the next edition of my text, I changed my description of the 9/11 terrorists to "radical Islamists." Their convictions were central to what they did; their ethnicity was less relevant. In reflecting on this characterization, I recalled that fifteen of the nineteen hijackers were citizens of Saudi Arabia. Nationality may have been at least as important to the acts they committed as ethnic identity. Yet, it was rarely the default identification ("Saudi terrorists?") used in American media coverage. Choosing an identity meant selecting a motivation, with someone—an important, wealthy ally in this case—bound to take offense.

Inside the Belly of the Beast, or American Government Today

For most of my years in Doha, I headed up our school's American Studies program, which gave me a light supervisory role in directing the cross-disciplinary studies of American literature, history, economics, and politics. Students taking enough classes in these areas and then writing a lengthy essay on a relevant topic were awarded a certificate in American Studies when they graduated. As the one full professor in an American field, the dean asked me to oversee the program, which I did. The study of America was included as one of the deliverables in the contract with Qatar that Georgetown was committed to provide. Alas, in this part of the world, there wasn't a huge amount of interest in scholarly approaches to my homeland.

Part of this can be blamed on a faculty that identified strongly with neither American culture nor its politics and was understandably reluctant to be cast as a representative of either. Being a missionary for the mother country was not part of the job description our teachers signed. Many of my colleagues came to Qatar because of their interest in this region, not the one some of them left. (At any one time, more than half the faculty was probably foreign-born, though many were American citizens.) The students bolstered these sentiments with their own lack of curiosity in the underpinnings of current and commercial America. While they might be eager consumers of Americana, from clothes and computers to music and movies, there was a certain indifference to more cerebral concepts applying to government, economics, foreign policy, and political thought. That scholarly ideas about these arenas might help organize and make sense of the deluge of American stuff raining down on them outside of the classroom seldom motivated further study into the United States. Admittedly, they resembled their American peers in this way.

In my year teaching graduate students in Nanjing, China, I had been on the receiving end of a far greater number of questions from students as to how, for example, Americans balanced government power with individual liberties, or how federalism worked in dividing authority between Washington and the states, or whether Americans really knew enough to make a choice in voting for different candidates. Chinese students considered such issues important to China's own political evolution and they seemed to want to draw lessons they could improve on and apply at home. They showed more curiosity than Doha students—or most American students, for that matter—in trying to figure out what made Americans and their government tick.

In the Gulf, I had the impression that many students remained uncertain that they could ever apply these lessons to their own nations or that the American example had any relevance in their lives. There might also have been a sneaking suspicion that American ideas were somewhat subversive to their own societies, if not reflective of a decadent, impious country on its last legs—a perspective not completely alien to Chinese students as well. I wondered whether Doha students' lack of curiosity might reflect a certainty derived from living in nations that followed a single set of beliefs and punished dissent, thus discouraging the search for conflicting ideas.

The prospect of "knowing the enemy" didn't seem to attract interest in American Studies either. Uncovering the truth from within the belly of the beast wasn't necessary if you already knew as much as you needed.

This is not to say there weren't opinions on the United States. There were lots of them. Students' views toward America reflected a usually muddled attempt to derive certainties from the constant stream of data reaching them. On the benevolent side, America seemed to be a lot of fun. To retreat to the lifestyle of the sixties—sex, drugs, and rock 'n' roll or their twenty-first-century echoes—might still sum up the personal freedoms that America represented to the young and eager of the Middle East. While some might take refuge in their religious beliefs to avoid this contamination, most seemed to find this culture attractive and didn't need to be educated in its whys and wherefores to want to indulge in a taste of the good life.

Those who had visited or studied in the United States generally returned having enjoyed the experience. One of my not-so-diligent students—a tall, good-looking Qatari, clean shaven in his white thobe—talked fondly about his summers in southern California among the surfers and blondes. "Ah, America is cool," he concluded with a broad, knowing grin.

For all its surface charms, the United States also appeared from the outside to be dangerous. This view was influenced in part by

American policies within the Middle East, which in recent decades had shown an inclination for killing people. It was evident that the world's only superpower could project violence into this neighborhood. The bases, ships, troops, jets, and drones in the Gulf reflected American dominance—a force of arms both respected and feared. This was not to say that the United States was always seen as wrong in its use and support of military power, though its support of Israel clearly was a long-standing irritant. It was to say that a certain apprehension trailed any conversation about American policies—the anxiety of "unleashing the giant" with unpredictable, frequently damaging, results.

In accepting that America had *great* power, students often went further in thinking the United States had *unlimited* power. When unexpected events occurred in the region, the default explanation, at least initially, was that America had something to do with it. This was often accompanied by some convoluted logic that differed markedly from the public narrative around the flow of events. Professor Clyde Wilcox described a discussion in his class in which a student asserted that America had started and funded ISIS. His proof was that in a movie—unnamed—he had seen an ISIS recruit wearing a CIA bracelet (whatever that was). The counterargument that the United States was publicly attacking, sending troops, and funding the fight against ISIS provoked a strange response from the student. See, he argued, this demonstrated the prevailing American strategy: keep the countries of the region weak by encouraging them to fight each other. Look at the Iraq-Iran War. Arm both sides and keep the wars going. Divide and conquer; Arabia loses, America wins.

This was a recurrent complaint about America: its strength came from Arab weakness. Students believed in a conscious policy to keep the Arab/Muslim world divided. They believed this was an offshoot of the alleged US plan to dominate the region. The weak, corrupt, undemocratic regimes dominating the Middle East would toady up to the West while selling out their own peoples' interests. This, of course, was less a perspective on America than a political critique and call to arms for Arabia. At the extremes, this view slid into support for the radical jihadist movements with their emphasis on unity as a means of regaining the lost power of the Arab world. This search for a resurgent, powerful Middle East was a much more prevalent vision for the future than any religious dream about recreating a medieval "one true Islamic faith" throughout the region. As one student declared, "Religious unity enables us to regain political unity."

Given the importance of the Middle East to these students, it was difficult for them to realize it wasn't quite as important to America.

Even my best students had some problems appreciating the limits the mightiest of imperial powers faced in the real world. One day after class, I spoke with Muammar, a bright Saudi student. At the time, in early 2011, Hosni Mubarak was still hanging onto power in Cairo during the early stages of the Arab Spring. Our dialogue went something like this:

Muammar: Egypt is dominated by America through its money to the military, its aid, and trade. Right?

Me: Okay.

Muammar: Mubarak is a client and friend of the US who has kept peace with your major ally, Israel, for some thirty years.

Me: Agreed.

Muammar: Then why isn't this great imperial power intervening to keep Mubarak in power?

Me: Well, partly because after the Iraq invasion, US leaders are more aware of the limits and costs of any US military intervention in the region. And partly because we're not sure that a more democratic, popular regime wouldn't be better for Egypt than this aging autocrat. But mainly because you just can't get away with doing that stuff in a large, complicated state like Egypt.

Muammar: What's the point of America being an imperial power if it can't control its clients?

Me: I am not sure.

In my opinion, students' fears of "stranger danger" were not primarily a critique of US foreign policy. America was not just dangerous to other countries; it was hazardous to its own people. My homeland was a violent place. (More violent, one could add, than the amazingly crime-free states of the Arab Gulf.) Media presentations—from news reports to cinematic blockbusters—highlighted a land of gangs, uncontrolled automatic weapons, racial tension, psychotic serial killers, and sporadic breakdowns in law and order. America, as seen on the overseas airwaves, was scary.

Several women grads studying in the United States complained to me about their parents' real worry when their daughters brought up going to America: not that they would convert from Islam or marry someone without their parents' consent but that they would get hurt. Those crime headlines again. I repeatedly heard about Arab fathers who were educated in America but insisted their daughters not go to school there. It might have reflected memories, perhaps embellished by time, of their own wild undergraduate days there, and wanting to avoid picturing their daughters being treated as they had acted with coeds. Or it might have been their fear that the America they had known had been replaced by a far more dangerous replicant.

Anyway, every fall, I addressed the incoming freshman class on the virtues of supplementing their college career with American studies. I reminded them that they were, if luck and pluck held true, eventually to be awarded a degree from an American university. It turned out that "What will my degree say?" was the most often-repeated question that Dean of Admissions Joe Hernandez was asked by incoming freshmen. They worried that somehow their diploma would be of lesser value than the one granted in the United States. Hernandez reassured them that it was exactly the same. However, since it was written in Latin, no one knew what it said. Later, I would tell my students the Latin on their degree was the well-known Christian benediction: "Jesus Hates Losers." That seemed to put an end to the questions.

I continued my spiel. Earning this degree, I said, will bring burdensome inference from coworkers, friends, and families, who will assume you know something about America and thus are able to answer questions about the latest political idiocy arising in the United States. (And this was years before Trump.) They, however, wouldn't necessarily know much about America just from having a Georgetown education—a program of studies, I noted, that didn't require a course in American government. (This was a peculiar effort by our school to avoid looking too parochial but leading to criticism from Congress that American diplomats knew more about the foreign country they were sent to than the one they represented.) If one wanted such familiarity this could, I argued, be garnered from our American Studies program. About a half-dozen students, say 10 percent of the class, would sign up, though fewer completed the program.

America in the Classroom

In class, I taught American politics with two somewhat contradictory goals. One was for students to become familiar with how American politics functioned, how the government was structured, and which constitutional values underpinned the whole structure. All well and good; sometimes it worked, often it didn't.

My other goal was to confuse students. None of them walked into class without a host of ideas, impressions, and delusions about the United States. Although some were reasonable, many were close to slander. This reflected poor education, the anti-American sentiments of political elites in their own countries, and a flood of lies and distortions online. If I could make them a little less certain of the pieties concerning America with which they entered, I considered it time well spent.

I was usually battling conspiracy theories that premised a degree of control and manipulation that was simply beyond any group in the muddled mess of American politics. My own bias was that power was hopelessly, not equally, divided: among the states, between them and the federal government, among the branches of the federal government, among the agencies of the executive, on top of competing groups in the media, political parties, corporations and interest groups, all resting on a continent-wide public of varying regions, religions, incomes, genders, races, age groups, and political beliefs. And almost all of these entities thought one or more of the others had too much power, exercised corruptly and to their own group's disadvantage. The result—and I might have gone too far in attempting to undermine simplistic power elite theories—was neither coherency nor conspiracy. It was paralysis and incomprehensible compromises.

This was not a very happy state of affairs, either in practice or theory. It was an especially difficult message to deliver to students who already thought they had the answers regarding American behavior and wanted them confirmed. And their own answers, although incorrect, had the advantage of being simple, easily understood, and entertaining. This was even harder to communicate to youths who had grown up with their own nations' politics, which were often managed by a few thuggish elites who manipulated the press and public, and killed opponents. Believing ill about a foreign superpower that had inflicted great harm in the neighborhood was not a difficult leap of faith. And like a stopped watch telling time correctly twice a day, sometimes they were proven right.

These biases and insights needed to be tested and analyzed in classes on American politics. Since I taught a variety of courses on this general subject—e.g., Introduction to American Government, Media and Foreign Policy, Political Parties and Elections, and Interest Groups and Lobbies—I had the opportunity to discuss the ideas and practices that undergirded American politics. In the classroom, I had the opportunity to explore some current national issues and find out what my students thought. It had its moments.

The Israel Lobby, in Fact and in Class

Because of my previously voiced fears of exhibiting my tribal scars—and because I was not an expert on the region—I avoided discussions on Israel. But the opportunity to discuss the pro-Israel lobby (a topic I had written about) in a class on lobbying and interest groups was too enticing to pass up. It was the one lobby my students had heard about and the one they frequently considered the power behind any and all US policies. To leave the topic unmentioned in a class on American lobbies would be to desert this battlefield of ideas without firing a shot.

I devoted a week toward the end of the term to the pro-Israel lobby, specifically the American Israel Public Affairs Committee (AIPAC). Students read the scholarly attack on the Israel lobby by two international relations professors, John Mearsheimer and Stephen Walt (*The Israel Lobby and U.S. Foreign Policy*, 2007) as well as several critiques of their work. In the first class of the week, I gave a lecture on the history of the lobby and my assessment of its influence. The second class was turned over to the students, who staged a debate on the topic, "Resolved: The American pro-Israel lobby has a negative and overwhelming influence over US policies toward the Middle East."

The debate focused the discussion on two aspects of the lobby's influence on US policies. One was that the lobby distorted what were America's real interests in the region, i.e., friendship with Arab states and access to oil. The second was that the very power of the lobby led American leaders to do what they wouldn't otherwise do. Money and votes, chiefly from Jews, changed how policymakers saw the region and what they were able to do. The results were numerous conflicts and virulent anti-American sentiments. The debates were spirited with students eager to extol whatever side they had chosen to argue for.

The debate over the power of the lobby often focused on the American decision to invade Iraq in 2003. Mearsheimer and Walt made the point that the pro-Israel forces lobbied for the invasion and mobilized liberal voices for the war. They claimed the war would not have happened without this pressure, notably because it brought democratic and liberal opinion behind the plans for war. The problem with this argument was that none of the principals involved in the decision to invade—Bush, Cheney, Powell, etc.—even mentioned the lobby or the Israelis as being a factor in their discussions. In addition, Israeli government representatives were actually lobbying the Bush administration for action against Iran. They worried that invading Iraq was a distraction from actions against their major enemy, Iran.

In my lecture, I tried to leave the class with a simple point: the power of the pro-Israel lobby had been inflated by supporters and opponents alike for their own reasons. Although clearly a powerful player in foreign policy, AIPAC was only narrowly influential and constrained by other public and political interests. Its power varied depending both on who was in power in Washington and on whether Israel was seen as a strategic ally by those policymakers.

I presented the lobby's history beginning in the modern era with the guilt that American Jews felt over their own and their country's neglect of the millions of European Jews exterminated by Hitler's Germany. Afraid of being accused of dual loyalties, American Jews had held back from pushing their government to protect European Jews or even admit them as refugees. Embarrassed about this sorry history, after World War II, Jews organized to help the fledging state of Israel. But for the first twenty years of Israel's existence, the United States was not its leading supplier of arms—that was France—and the United States had a weapons embargo on the Jewish state at the start of the 1967 Six-Day War.

Reminding students of policies that AIPAC had lobbied and lost—the sale of AWACs planes to Saudi Arabia in the early eighties, backing for West Bank settlements, and (usually behind closed doors) the most advanced weapons systems to most Arab states—the case could be made that the lobby had dominance in certain areas, such as foreign assistance to Israel, but less in other areas, such as broad American policies toward the Middle East. When Carter pushed human rights or Obama wanted a nuclear deal with Iran, Jewish financing of the Democratic party hadn't halted the moves. Nor did George W. Bush's unwavering support for Israel reflect Jewish votes that had overwhelmingly gone to his Democratic opponents. (The adage in electoral politics was that Jews lived like Episcopalians and voted like Puerto Ricans.)

Congressional members generally found foreign policy issues to be irrelevant to winning reelection. Therefore, any domestic group interested in foreign policy that could inject funds and lobbying into congressional campaigns could make the issue of Israel an easy "yes" for representatives to support. There was simply no countervailing force. (On my final exam, I asked students to create a strategy for an

American lobby for Palestinians, helping them understand the difficulties of such an opposition.) But it was also true that the Jewish community was more divided than AIPAC leaders acknowledged. Even the central role of Jewish donors in funding the Democratic party hadn't necessarily equated with support for the pro-Israel lobby. George Soros, who was John Kerry's leading fund-raiser in 2004, strongly opposed AIPAC and had helped create J Street, a liberal group dedicated to countering the lobby. I also disputed the much-ballyhooed charge that the lobby had "stifled public debate" about Israeli policy in the United States. I noted that Mearsheimer and Walt—who made this point—had received an advance of $600,000 from a leading publisher and the book had become a bestseller. Since my own manuscript on the arrest and prosecution of two AIPAC lobbyists had not found a publisher, there might have been some sour grapes in my observation.

The issue of Jewish power in America complicated things for me in Doha. I never saw it as an issue in my study of American politics or much of a personal concern prior to arriving in Qatar. I didn't think my tribal membership had actually given me much political power. If there were a secret handshake for *landsman* loyalists that would give me a leg up in attaining a high position, I would have loved to learn it. Any network of support from friends and colleagues that had helped me in my career was not limited to Jews nor had much to do with their issues. The politics of my Jewish friends ran from anarchist anti-Zionism to right-wing Likudism. I didn't see much coherence or agreed-upon goals. Most politically ambitious Americans, members of the Tribe included, seemed to be in the game for themselves.

Arriving in Doha, I was confronted with a very different attitude. The autonomy, coherence and power of American Jews was assumed. Some of this might echo the long history of anti-Semitism, from early Christianity to the *Protocols of the Learned Elders of Zion* to the biases of Henry Ford and other powerful men. But American Jews did seem organized and powerful from the perspective of those who saw themselves as victimized by the establishment and expansion of Israel. If one fixated on Israel, it was an easy connection to the political actions of anyone who was Jewish and supportive of the Jewish state. Since US policies were the consequences of domestic political activities, blaming the Jews allowed one to excuse the government and people of America. And Israel did give the American Jewish community a coherence it otherwise lacked.

Coherence, alas, does not a conspiracy make. A generally shared outlook toward preserving a Jewish homeland in Israel could be taken to unreasonable lengths by critics. I had heard a Doha colleague argue that Jewish financial backing for Martin Luther King Jr., the civil rights movement, and, later, Barack Obama, was connected to turning the black population away from Palestinian rights. The problem with this, like much of the foreign/Arab analysis of American politics, was that it transferred the foreigners' priorities onto American domestic groups. Jewish liberals backed civil rights because they supported this progressive movement, largely because of their own history and values. Period. If there was another agenda, I haven't come across it in my readings of the histories of civil rights.

Similarly, Jewish donors to partisan political causes might or might not point to Israel as the reason for their contributions. Those from Wall Street with whom I dealt in my career in Washington certainly had explicit financial priorities motivating their lobbying activities. There was also enough written about so-called "Jewish-led" institutions—e.g., national newspapers and Hollywood movie studios—whose leaders were later called to account for avoiding positions that might cause others to attribute their actions to religious loyalties. The *New York Times'* sparse coverage of the persecution of European Jews during the Second World War has been attributed to their Jewish publisher's reluctance to be seen as using his paper in a self-serving way. If anything, the charge of "dual loyalties" might have been taken too much to heart by Jews and led to a reversal of loyalties.

Not all those who overstated Jewish power—and assigned Jews a monopoly over Israeli policies—deserved to be branded anti-Semites. It was admittedly a slippery slope, especially in the Middle

East. In discussions of American politics, I would accept a fairly dark critique of the United States without viewing it as fringe lunacy. People, including friends, could disagree with just about everything the American hegemon had done abroad since World War II and still consider themselves patriots. I didn't for a moment argue the point. But in my own mind, something changed when they crossed over into dark conspiracies about small groups, controlling the government in their own interest, who edged into traitors who sold out the American people.

Similarly, with Israel, I understood disagreements with Israeli policies, including the expanding boundaries of that state. The competing claims of different groups for the same land was not unique to this conflict and was a cause for accommodation, not the eradication of either side. Wanting to see the world's only Jewish state destroyed put this disagreement on a different plane. Then the argument over politics became something that made this state unique and its disappearance uniquely harsh. It was the difference between wanting to see America withdraw from its interventionist and military roles in the Middle East and wanting to see the American nation dismembered.

America in the Headlines

Katrina Quirolgico, a member of Georgetown's 2009 graduating class in Doha, was an honor student and a talented singer from a Filipino family in Los Angeles. She put it well when commenting on students' interests in the rest of the world. "Students talk the headlines," she declared. As issues arose—be they women's rights, terrorist violence, the Arab Spring, or American elections—discussions in the halls would reflect the agenda set by international media and the events they were reporting. This led to a certain Ping-Pong effect on what was discussed, when, and exactly what students or anyone else thought about the topic. Consistency was only occasionally maintained.

I often tried to get students' minds off the passing news events to reflect on somewhat longer-term interests and values. Sometimes it worked. During my second year of teaching, Colin Powell came through Doha (on a mission for some financial conglomerate that was employing him in his golden years) and dropped by to speak to the students. Confronting George W. Bush's Secretary of State, not to mention an architect and UN mouthpiece for the Iraq debacle, was tempting. Students were looking forward to slinging denunciations, masquerading as questions, at him. Just before the general's talk, I urged them not "to play journalists" but to try to learn something about him personally; see what he had to teach them. Ask him what he was like as a student; ask him personal questions about being the only black man in a room full of generals; ask how he prepared and won arguments in the White House. Since he didn't allow faculty into his talk, I am not sure how much good my briefing did. But years later, one of my students remembered the advice I had given.

Barack Obama's election was met by a great deal of hope by students and others in the Muslim world. Given the seemingly universal despair and resentment that trailed the Bush administration by the time I arrived in Qatar in 2006, any change in administration was seen as welcome. Obama—an eloquent and populist-sounding black man—couldn't fail to connect with foreign students who retained a smidgen of hope for the United States. The reaction to his election was almost unanimous relief, accompanied by unrealistic expectations for American policy in the Middle East.

There were the cynics. I recalled an ongoing dialogue I had with a Lebanese political analyst who worked for Al Jazeera. During the American election season, I was being called by Al Jazeera pretty regularly for interviews. A senior commentator, Marwan Bishara, would pass me in the hall during the primaries in early 2008, nod, refer to my generally positive commentary on Obama and say, smiling, "He'll never get the nomination." After the Democratic Convention of that summer, we would run into each other again, exchange pleasantries, argue briefly about Obama's chances, with Bishara concluding, "He'll never win. They won't allow it." After the November elections, I remember once again meeting in the studios and he remarked, "No

The skyline of downtown Doha around 2008 with the Diplomatic Club in the foreground and cranes everywhere else.
Credit: Kai-Henrik Barth

A profile of a younger, smaller Doha taken by the British Air Force in 1947.
Credit: Hunting Aerosurvey Ltd./CGIS/Rob Carter

Barzan 2, #52, the author's home for eight years.
Credit: Ann Wasserman

Georgetown's dining room and three-story atrium, the center of the University's impressive new building.
Credit: Kai–Henrik Barth

The author, at far left, continuing his lecture in the hall.
Credit: Georgetown University in Qatar

Typical rush-hour traffic in downtown Doha.
Credit: Alexey Sergeev

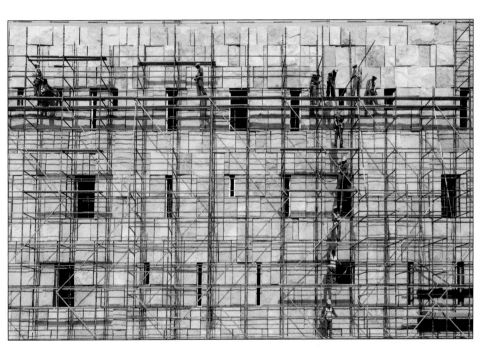

Workers blend into the scaffolding at Northwestern University's building under construction in Education City.
Credit: Kai-Henrik Barth

Women now make up a majority of students at Georgetown in Qatar.
Credit: Georgetown University

way he'll serve out his term. They'll shoot him." Bishara was nothing if not consistent.

On the whole, Obama elevated expectations of people in the region. Unrealistically. Not surprisingly, because of who he was—a young black man with a Muslim name—and the slogan on which he ran ("Hope and Change"), promises of a sparkling future were inflated. His own soaring rhetoric and devastating critique of the Bush Administration's foreign policies, especially toward Iraq, led many to envision a new dawn. Beneath a certain surface cynicism, people were happy with the Democrat's victory and hopeful for the future. I did my best to remind students and the Al Jazeera TV audiences of the limits of presidential power, the incremental nature of change in large democracies, and the tendency of candidates "to campaign in poetry and govern in prose."

Despite my warnings and my own muted expectations, I was soon labeled an apologist for the Administration, a charge that had some truth to it. In the years that followed, it became clear that changing policies toward the Middle East was not a high priority for the team in Washington. Other than partially withdrawing from two losing conflicts and not getting involved in any further ones, little seemed to change. My students and others soon seemed perplexed that the United States didn't assert itself in the region. Even the liberals in Doha appreciated the realpolitik insight in Napoleon's advice: "You can do anything with bayonets except sit on them."

The result was somewhat schizophrenic discussions. Students went from stridently opposing the brutish promotion of American power by President Bush to a quieter concern about Obama's diminishing interest in the region. Confusion reigned over whether the United States supported, opposed, or was indifferent to the progressive movements of the Arab Spring. To me, the United States seemed to adopt a fairly consistent noninvolvement, with a partial and disastrous exception in Libya. I could not always defend a president for the worthwhile initiatives he *failed* to support, such as offering air strikes to keep Mubarak in power; intervening in Syria, in light of Russian intrusion; supporting air strikes on Iranian nuclear facilities;

urging human rights proclamations about Turkey, Bahrain, or Iraq; and offering support for Netanyahu's expanding settlement plans. In truth, Obama was destined to disappoint the Middle East and others while living down to my own expectations.

America in the Air: Al Jazeera

For our news of America, the Middle East, and the world, Ann and I watched Al Jazeera. The Qatar TV network covered far more than American networks did and in far more depth. Whether it was stories of Zimbabwean refugees in South Africa, child trafficking in India, right-wing settler politics on the West Bank, or Shia demonstrations in Bahrain, its correspondents were not only professional and thorough; they were also given enough airtime to do lengthy reports. Advocacy was evident especially as regional conflicts got longer and bloodier. Whether it was Palestinians demonstrating in Nablus, Muslim Brotherhood members being arrested in Cairo, or Hamas teenagers building tunnels in Gaza, it was usually clear who were the progressives standing up for "the people" and therefore which side the reporters were backing. But this was pretty much the case for correspondents in any overseas war. And I was surprised that when it came to the ongoing conflicts with Israel, I found more balance in Al Jazeera's coverage than in that of the BBC, which alternately slammed and ignored the Israeli side of most disputes.

Al Jazeera—the name refers to the Arabian Peninsula—was born in 1996 with $137 million from the new emir, Sheikh Hamad Khalifa. Annual subsidies from the regime have kept the network afloat since then. Qatar inherited the BBC's Arab-language TV station that had been supported by the Saudis but failed after Riyadh had tried to censor the news coverage. The opportunity to create a relatively impartial news source for the Arab world while succeeding where his old Saudi nemesis had failed proved irresistible to the reforming emir. Al Jazeera presented news and programs that had not been seen before by Arab audiences—controversial talk shows, Israelis arguing their case, and reports that antagonized the Egyptian, Algerian, and Saudi Arabian governments as well as the

US forces in Iraq and Afghanistan. (The United States bombed Al Jazeera's Baghdad bureau "by mistake" in April 2003.) It soon gained the most viewers in the Arab world and was cited by scholars for its role in helping spread the Arab Spring from country to country. Its English-language channel began in November 2006, ten years after Al Jazeera had started. Despite budget cutbacks and an unsuccessful venture into the American market, the network remained the go-to media for the region. Not surprisingly, eliminating Al Jazeera was a central demand by the Saudi coalition seeking to weaken Qatar in their 2017 confrontation.

As one of Doha's two American professors of American politics, I was regularly asked by Al Jazeera to do TV interviews. The studios were not that far a drive from my compound, I enjoyed talking about American politics, and there was the opportunity of being heard by an audience of, oh, say, 100 million people. I loved it.

The main obstacle to the Al Jazeera interviews was getting into the fenced, barren campus that housed its studios. The gate where all cars were stopped had a guardhouse that was manned by Arab guards who actually looked like guards. Unlike the small, unarmed Nepalese at our compound, these were mostly unshaven, mostly unsmiling, large Yemenis. I recalled a rifle propped up in the corner. Here's how my entrance was supposed to go: the producer who had asked me to appear would send a pass to the guardhouse, giving them my name and car license with instructions to let me through after showing my ID. It never worked. The guard, speaking hardly any English, would look up from the appointment book and declare I wasn't listed.

Then I'd ask them to call the studio. I would park my car, sit on the wooden chair in the guardhouse reserved for this purpose, and wait for some sweating, pasty-faced, young, English-speaking female associate-something to hurriedly walk the hundred yards from the studios, tell the guards her boss had sent over the slip, sign me in, and then rush me back. All of this usually occurred within ten minutes of airtime. No one ever figured out what happened to the pass; everyone thanked everyone else for their "help." The guards went back to reading Arabic comic books and I got made-up for the interview. This scene repeated itself nearly every time I went. It never improved; perhaps it never had to. Everyone kept their job, no one lost face, and after a short while I built an extra fifteen minutes into my schedule to compensate.

Todd Kent was the other professor of American politics in Doha. He was a Texas conservative who had worked his way up the state's Republican ladder, including a stint with a pre-Bush Karl Rove. Later, Todd taught US politics courses in Doha at Texas A&M. This was harder than my job because he was trying to kindle sparks of interest from Arab engineering majors. He was younger than I, was more of a numbers guy in the discipline, had a few more pounds on his bones, wore a crew cut, and handily beat me in tennis. Although we differed in our political loyalties, we shared a professional cynicism about policy outcomes and candidates' integrity. Our compatibility meant we depended on each other to hold "pro and con" debates when we ran out of ideas for after-class panels on American politics.

This "Doha duopoly" in American politics meant our paths often crossed at Al Jazeera. Whenever elections loomed, high officials visited, crises blossomed, or updates were required, the call would go out to one or both of us. It was usually at the last minute with a vague mandate. Once it was determined we weren't going to be an on-air embarrassment and we could be at the studios in a couple of hours, these requests expanded, extending to topics way outside our expertise, from forestry to boundary disputes. Al Jazeera Arabic called me once to offer an American's reaction to Osama bin Laden's latest statement on Israel. I declined. What would I say: "Good sound bite, lose the beard?" Some residual professional modesty led me to avoid commenting on fields beyond my knowledge. Looking back, I probably shouldn't have worried.

From my dozens of appearances on Al Jazeera, I concluded that most of the audience spent very little time listening to what I said. On one hand, I was impressed by the global audience that my producers claimed they could reach. Speaking from a dark studio to uncounted millions certainly seemed to be an advance over lectures aimed at the relatively few undergraduates sporadically taking notes in my classes. Yet whenever I alerted friends to my upcoming appearance on global TV, they would dutifully watch and seemed to appreciate the apparent savoir faire with which I handled whatever topic was being thrown my way. Their near-universal reactions were along the lines of, "Hey, you looked great." But that was because, even under questioning, they could barely remember anything I actually said. The visuals were all that seemed to leave any lasting impression and, let me tell you, they were being gentle on those close-ups of my face. It was a jarring personal reminder of the dominance of appearance over substance on television.

A partial exception occurred when two friends from Berkeley, John and Pat Rea, were vacationing in Turkey. They had come down to breakfast at their bed-and-breakfast in Cappadocia, a cavernous resort a few hundred miles east of Istanbul. The TV was tuned to Al Jazeera and as John began to ask about breakfast, one of the guests shushed him, saying he wanted to hear this interview—it was about Obama visiting Europe. John looked up and saw his old buddy Gary on the screen. John later told me his initial reaction was mild outrage, informing the other guest that he knew this guy and they didn't really have to keep silent while I spoke. (John must have thought we were having breakfast together.) Anyway, the Reas emailed me later, said I did fine—a little vague on content—and congratulated me on my global reach. I considered being seen by friends on TV in a far-off land the pinnacle of my broadcasting career.

Anyway, in fairness to the Al Jazeera staff, they seemed to understand that content was a secondary part of their product. Premising that last-minute, fast-breaking news needed expert simplifying, they'd amiably give you a rushed greeting upon arrival. Then you'd quickly slap some makeup on in the backroom and rush out to meet the anchor-interviewer—always better looking and calmer than the guest. There was no time for any pregame briefings or warm-ups, just perhaps a few indifferent questions as the mike was adjusted, with eye contact reserved for the cameras. Afterward, not even a cigarette or a "how was it for you?" Instead, a hurried good-bye, sometimes a small check, and an escort to the door. No feedback was offered. The airtime was filled, professionalism maintained, and a worldwide audience briefly enlightened.

A Somewhat Traditional Thanksgiving

A number of faculty, staff, and students were first-generation Americans with all the ambivalence and affection of immigrants for their adopted country. They exhibited a range of ideas as to what being an American meant. On one end was the Lebanese staffer who used his Georgetown employment to fly his pregnant wife to the United States so that their baby would be an American citizen. He had no intention of immigrating but could see the advantages in the wider choices his child would have. A few years later, he did the same for a second child.

Greater emotional ties to the United States were shown in a Thanksgiving celebration held by the American Studies faculty in 2007. The affair was jerry-rigged—folding chairs, paper table-cloths over metal tables, a movie screen in front—at the juncture of halls that met at the large entrance inside the Liberal Arts and Sciences building. As successful as we might have felt it was, by the following year, larger forces within the school pushed for a potluck Thanksgiving that would include all staff and their families. Our one-off celebration was confined by budget, haphazard planning, and the limits of our own creative ideas. Quite by accident, it turned into a moment that I still remember.

We were always in a quandary about celebrating US holidays—what to emphasize, what to talk about, and whether anyone would show up. Left-wing colleagues objected to the "cultural imperial-ism" or "Orientalism" of indulging in our national holidays. Still, a few of us pushed the educational value of an American university-sponsored Thanksgiving festival. Ultimately, we did, with some compromises.

The moderates among the faculty were assigned the responsibil-ity of preparing the food—a traditional meal of turkey, stuffing, rolls, apple cider, green beans, sweet potatoes, and pumpkin pie.

The progressives controlled the movie selection and accompanying commentary. In their hands, the celebration placed due emphasis on graphic examples of Native Americans massacred by white guys.

The actual event began at five in the evening with a surprisingly good and very diverse turnout. Those of us inclined to communicate a more benevolent view of American history were saved by technology—make that the lack of technology. Like many home movie projectors of childhood memory, ours didn't work. Something went wrong either with the video or the delivery system. The lack of media left us speechless, temporarily.

Attempting to compensate for the blank movie screen as well as the yawning depths of a silenced holiday, a brave young faculty communard rose up to address the crowd from the ramparts. She pointed to the establishment of the holiday as an effort to recreate a history that never existed. This peaceful, communal meal between the settler colonizers and Native Americans was fabricated by subsequent generations. (She added, in a personal attempt to identify with the oppressed, that because of her dark complexion she had been repeatedly anointed to play the part of an Indian squaw in her elementary school's Thanksgiving pageant.) America's actual legacy, she proclaimed, was littered with genocide, broken treaties, burning villages, concentration camps, racism, etc.

She did, of course, have a point. I, for one, was not going to argue that American history had nothing to do with white foreigners invading a continent, murdering the darker residents, stealing their land, and locking them up in wasteland reservations—all of which took place, I assumed, prior to the modern emergence of civil rights advocates, student activists, and, presumably, progressive feminist historians. The problem with this history wasn't so much with the accuracy of the presentation—leaving aside any attempt at balance—as with the largely Middle Eastern audience.

Trying to horrify a group from this region with the sins of seventeenth- and eighteenth-centur America was a tough sell. Here were people already introduced to government by, for, and of the predators: thugs who killed, imprisoned, robbed, and tortured men, women, and children because of ethnic or religious or regional or political differences. And, of course, stole their lands and raped their wives and daughters in the process. The critical, unspoken distinction was that these were current events—neighborhood regimes that had committed their crimes in real time on some of those in the audience and their families and friends. Many of those listening had gone or hoped to go to America to rid themselves of these contemporary afflictions. For them, the history of two centuries ago only reminded them of what they had already survived and wanted to be rid of in the century in which they lived.

Such sentiments were only quietly and privately expressed, some of which I heard because I was sitting in the back. This was not a crowd that had come to engage in public debate. Instead, when people were invited to speak, they were encouraged to share personal memories of their own Thanksgivings. This had been inspired by necessity—to fill the time left by the unavailable movie. Purely by accident, the event turned into something unusual.

In the customary order of these affairs, the least shy went first. In this case, the most articulate, highest ranking, whitest, usually male, native-born Americans started. One staffer from Boston remembered a particular Thanksgiving that was his first visit home during his freshman year of college. That dinner marked the moment he felt acknowledged as an adult and welcomed back in his family as a man who had his own presence in the world.

Dean Brendan Hill recounted the mixed customs, food, and conversations around the table of his half-Japanese, half-Irish family in Wahiawa, Hawaii. There was chicken chow mein and sushi, along with turkey ("nothing that went with anything else," he recalled). This uniquely unharmonious cacophony of divided cultures provided an instance of togetherness for a family that hadn't always been that close.

Brendan's heartfelt recollections loosened up other recent immigrants who had hesitated to speak of their own not-quite-American memories. It became an unexpectedly patriotic occasion.

An Egyptian bookkeeper spoke movingly of his family's difficulty fitting into his New Jersey neighborhood. They were aliens with a different language, religion, and customs. For them, holidays like the Fourth of July and Christmas seemed strange and difficult to embrace wholeheartedly. A Libyan staffer remembered Independence Day as smacking of boisterous, breast-beating patriotism, screaming fireworks, and smelly, drunk barbecues. Others noted that Christmas, the holiest of Christian holidays, with crosses, mangers, and carols, was not exactly a "y'all c'mon down" welcome for those of other faiths. Admittedly, there is something spectacularly parochial in much of my countrymen's eagerness to claim, with a straight face, that Christmas in America has become a secular holiday.

Thanksgiving, a librarian from Iran recounted, was different. Religion was invisible. Symbols of nationalism faded into the background. Family and food came to the fore. Here were two true universals, recognizable and comforting. Captured by this most American holiday, family and feasting were two warm constants that really did transcend cultures, religions, and national origins.

Family at Thanksgiving showed Americans at their most welcoming. The distant relatives, cousins, neighbors, friends, singles, and students from abroad who are rarely included in the secularists' nuclear family are embraced as equal to kin on this holiday. And immigrants related their eagerness to greet at Thanksgiving as many as could fit around their tables. Now they could play the host, welcoming to their home new friends and others who lacked a place for the holidays. Thanksgiving became their tradition.

The holiday was the meal; the meal was the holiday. The Cairo-born husband of a woman in the admissions office remembered the warm feeling of having Egyptian dishes of kashari and fatta being cooked in his kitchen for the American holiday. This moved formerly quiet women to stand and speak.

Preparing a family meal was something mothers from anywhere knew how to do. Get the men out of the kitchen, let them waste time talking politics, smoking, watching sports on TV, or other harmless pastimes. And let the womenfolk get on with the serious preparation of the goats, sheep, chicken, fish, or even this large, strange, American fowl shown in the newspaper advertisements. They might not understand how to get on escalators or boot up computers or say what they meant in English but they sure as hell knew how to cook for their families.

Toward the end of what had become a long afternoon, an ageless Yemeni woman stood up. In her abaya with a scarf over her hair, she emotionally told about cooking a turkey mandi, a dish that mixed two cultures in the kitchen. She said it was the first time she felt that, yes, she too could be an American.

CHAPTER 7

Teaching While Jewish

I have my religion and you have your religion.
—Qur'an (109:6)

porting an unusually wide grin, Hussein, one of my best and most serious students, came up to me after our Introduction to International Relations class. He asked if he could touch me. Turning to his friend with something approaching a twinkle in his eye, he explained he had never touched a Jew before. With a shrug, I obliged. His provincialism toward this racy topic illustrated a simple fact: few of these students knew any Jews.

Later, Hussein would tell me what little background knowledge he had acquired in his exclusive private school in Saudi Arabia. Beyond the surprising revelation that Al Gore was a Jew, there was his Islamic studies teacher's assertion that Israel's Mossad was behind 9/11. This was followed by the curious bias—heard elsewhere from students—that Arabs were incapable of planning such a complex, successful operation and that the United States had it coming anyway. I asked how his teacher could support the attack on 9/11 yet see it as some mammoth Zionist conspiracy, presumably serving Israeli interests. He looked at me for a moment, resigned that yet another naïve foreigner failed to appreciate how holding two contradictory opinions at the same time was consistent with the political views permeating the region.

The conversation with Hussein took place several years into my teaching experience in Doha, in fall 2009. I am sure of this, because when I first arrived, I followed the advice to keep my faith to myself. A Georgetown colleague in Washington, who was an expert on the region, had described becoming "a private Jew" when he lived in Arab countries. This meant not revealing your religion and avoiding public debates on contentious topics such as Israel. His advice was that casual socializing was easier when not broadcasting your faith, whatever you might share with close friends. The parallel dilemma facing gays in these conservative societies came to mind. Gay friends in Qatar generally kept their homosexuality undeclared and discreet. And they faced the added burden of being outside the law and in theory faced jail or—more likely for expats—expulsion.

To this I added my own reasons (or excuses?) for keeping my Judaism to myself. One was that I didn't want to be "the Jewish professor"—and for almost all of my time in Doha, I was Georgetown's only one. That wasn't what I was doing, wasn't how I saw myself, wasn't how I wanted to be identified. I was a professor of American politics. To this could be appended a montage of labels: male, old, grumpy, tough, liberal, American, stupid, etc. But not primarily Jewish.

My concern was that, if only for its novelty in the Arab world, the "Jewish" label would dominate. I didn't want the burden of representing the other 16 million Jews in the world whom my students hadn't met. It was too easy to imagine their unspoken responses: "Y'know, he's Jewish." "Yeah, I could tell." Or "So that's what those horns are." Or "No wonder he flunked me." I might have overthought this. One student later said to me, after she had graduated, that the only student discussion she recalls about my religion was the worry that I might feel isolated and out of place.

The other aspect of my concern had to do with tribal identity, one of the great banes of the Middle East. For this region, tribal loyalty, broadly defined, determined how people identified, thought, and acted. For my students, this translated into the simple questions: "Who are they?" and "Who are we?" Given that Frenchmen I have encountered have thought Jews (and Arabs for that matter) couldn't truly be members of the French nation, then Arab tribal attitudes could be easily understood as well.

My goals were limited. I was trying to avoid having students interpret conclusions I reached in lectures on the basis of who I was. The intensity surrounding the politics of the region seemed to come more from tribal loyalty and less from ideology or economic interests. Loyalties to tribe, clan, and religion explained the public's motivations for political activity. Nor was this likely to be mitigated in the short run by logic, debate, or study. It was why political coalitions, pluralist governments, and moderation toward adversaries by those in power in the Middle East appeared so fleeting.

The Gulf was hardly the only region exhibiting the strength of blood loyalties. No practicing politician in any modern Western democracy would hold office for long without recognizing the power of ethnic identities and the political alliances that reinforced them. Big city politics, from Boston to Chicago to San Francisco, was about coalitions and rivalries among the Irish, Poles, Jews, Hispanics, and blacks. Reason was a weak rejoinder to the strength of family and tribe and race. The British historian H. V. Hudson, discussing colonial politics, partially summed up the point: "Man is a political animal only by education; he is a racial animal by birth."

But I was not walking the boroughs of New York City looking for votes by presenting myself as one of the folks—a homey from the hood. I was in a university classroom, committing acts of education on political issues about which most of my non-American students already have opinions. The readings, lectures, and discussions were intended to encourage them to reexamine the conclusions they had when entering the class and to subject them to new facts, contrary opinions, scholars' thoughts, and the historical record. As a teacher, I was trying to offer insights on power, poverty, wealth, wars and government policies—aspects of which might be novel to them. Without sounding either too self-righteous or too wonky, we teachers were making an effort to get students to look closely at inherited truths, consensus thoughts and unexamined conclusions. At the least, I'd like them to question the political beliefs with which they entered the class and depart somewhat confused.

I adopted the role of arbiter of reason in the classroom on the subjects under discussion. I told them—and half-believed—that I didn't care what their politics were or what conclusions they reached on the issues before us. But I wanted them to learn the value of research, rigorous debate, and logical conclusions and, at least as important, to respect and listen to one another. Also, I wanted them to have enough confidence in me that I was not selling them a bill of goods. And that I was open to their own conclusions and struggles to uncover the approximate truths of politics.

This was not meant to be smug. Quite the opposite. (One Egyptian student reminded me that my favorite phrase was, "What do *I* know?" He took this as my admission that it was all a big mystery.) I intended to convey a certain tentativeness regarding almost all the conclusions reached in modern politics. Looking at recent history and the sketchy beliefs and ideologies that have temporarily enraptured groups and individuals, some modesty ought to inform our conclusions. Communicating this to students in a region where they were surrounded by true believers, extremists, and group thinkers did not seem an unreasonable goal for a liberal outsider.

There were limits. When a Tunisian student, with more balls than brains, brought the Arab street to the classroom by raising the idea that the US Air Force was behind the 9/11 attacks on New York and Washington, I told him to take it back to the barber shop where he heard it. Admittedly, I was rejecting this conspiracy theory as absurd. Why the United States would inflict immense damage on itself just to take revenge on the Arab world for some imagined harm reflected both hysteria and self-absorption overcoming reasoned analysis. I was trying to convey that in the university we were operating within a canon of scholarship, writing, research, and facts, and that I hadn't read anything on the attacks that came anywhere near offering evidence for this conclusion. Although my students were welcome to research and investigate their hypotheses, they weren't going to lower the level of debate in an academic setting by introducing rabble-rousing nonsense.

The Jewish Question: Who Asked?

The option of being "a private Jew" was, as they say, overtaken by events. One Student Affairs staffer, when asked by a sophomore, declared me to be Jewish. I took umbrage at this—it was none of his business. He replied that he thought it was general knowledge. I noted it obviously wasn't for the student who asked him. He frowned. I asked him if he identified other faculty members by their religions. More uncomfortable frowns.

Not that much was being concealed for long. Doha was a small place.

There was no one moment when I "came out." Native-born Americans on the faculty mostly assumed my ethnicity; others might have but were too polite to inquire. Some asked where I was from and, when I said I had been born in Washington, replied that they thought I was from New York (like most Jews?). Sometimes this topic was even awkward with other Jews.

One day in the early spring of 2010, a man I didn't know, David Fichner, called to ask if he could come by my office. He was a just-arrived engineering professor at Carnegie Mellon and said someone had recommended he talk with me. He didn't say why.

David and Grace Fichner seemed nervous when they came to the office. After some preliminary chitchat, they asked a question I had never heard before: "Do you know any rabbis in Doha?" I knitted my brow and looked closely to see if they were serious. Their expressions were sufficiently uncomfortable to indicate that no irony was intended. I responded that I didn't know any and doubted if there were any. There was a pause.

"You two are Jewish, right?"

Quiet nods greeted my question.

"Me, too."

Sighs of relief all around.

The backstory was that they had approached another professor at Carnegie Mellon—left unidentified—who, they were told, was Jewish. Either he wasn't or he wasn't willing to admit it. Either way, this was obviously not a warm and fuzzy moment. Having been bitten once, they were twice shy about asking who was a member of the Tribe. (My wife once asked a woman if she was pregnant when she wasn't. Answering "Are you Jewish?" with a negative created a similar awkward moment. It was hard to come back with a suitable riposte.)

Roger Bensky taught public speaking and theater in Doha in 2009–2010. European-born and multilingual with considerable erudition and familiarity with different cultures, Roger was trim, dapper, and in his midsixties with longish hair combed straight back. Although he claimed not to speak Arabic well, Saudi poets had selected him to translate their work into English. Unlike many expatriates, he had great affection for Arab culture and boasted of having a number of Arab friends. He was also Jewish.

Roger generally didn't reveal this to the Arabs he met. He explained to me that he didn't want to set up barriers to learning about them. He told me, "Once I've set up a pleasant relationship with Arab scholars I've met, they are so pleased to be explaining and talking about their culture that they seldom ask me much about myself." They were not curious about him. Perhaps they saw this as respecting his privacy. Yet he told me a story that offered an exception to the rule:

"I told a Jordanian friend who was driving me in his car that I was Jewish. It was spontaneous and only somewhat relevant to our discussion. He met my revelation with a long silence. When he resumed talking it was about a completely different subject.

"The next time we were together, my friend brought the subject up. 'You said you were Jewish. What is your opinion of Israel?'"

Roger answered that he was a man of peace. That he favored a two-state solution under which the sides could retain their land and live in some harmony together.

This seemed to reassure his friend. "You are the first Jew I have ever known," said the Jordanian, who was in his midthirties.

Roger added, "The conversation continued where it had left off before the awkward turn. Doha's spring was offering a lovely sunny day. Some hint of rain and clouds appeared in the sky but then the sun came out again. We carried on as before."

As my public identity emerged, I made a few discoveries about local attitudes toward Jews. As mentioned, no one knew any. My students couldn't identify Jewish names or distinguish who was Jewish among overseas visitors. I never encountered any racial stereotyping—dark skin, black beards, prominent noses—traits that would have been shared by a number of Arabs as well. Jews, in theory, were accepted as members of the same ancient Abrahamic faith, making them—along with Christians—People of the Book. This gave Jews a leg up on Hindus and Buddhists, whose appreciation of multifaceted deities put them considerably lower on the Muslim food chain of acceptable religions.

Jews were adversaries of the Prophet and precursors of his mission. Present-day Israelis were clearly the Zionist enemy, Western colonizers cruelly occupying Arab lands. But Jews from Europe and America fell between the poles of an acceptable Abrahamic faith and a detested, anti-Arab, colonizing force. Since Jews as individuals were seldom encountered in the Gulf states, they remained concealed, an ambivalent mystery.

The lack of observable evidence didn't stop local diatribes. Yusuf al-Qaradawi, a prominent Egyptian sheik based in Doha, could be seen online praising Hitler's treatment of Jews as "divine judgment" and calling them "Allah's enemies." He refused to attend the annual conference of the Doha International Center for Interfaith Dialogue because of the participation of Jews and he had referred to them as "vermin." The aging anti-Semite's weekly sermons were regularly reprinted in the local English-language newspapers.

But I never got any hint of such sentiments from students; indeed, the surprise was their attribution to Jews of extraordinary levels of intelligence and power. This view gave Jews a rather distinctive aura. To lend credence to the conspiracy theories embodied in the notorious Czarist fable, the *Protocols of the Learned Elders of Zion* (available in Doha bookstores), was to credit a tiny minority for much of world history—including depressions and world wars. But on occasion my students seemed to invert the myth. If this small group was guilty of so many world-changing events, they were clearly an impressive group—one that included their teacher.

In deference to my origins, some students assumed that whatever I said about the workings of Washington had the added luster of being "inside dope." Supposedly, being Jewish gave me access to the inner circles of the American elite. Perhaps they assumed I was privy to dark plans hatched among power brokers such as Kissinger during our weekly confabs at the local synagogue. Presumably this was where the plots were drawn up, the policies decided, the presidents made and unmade.

Somewhat hesitantly, I tried to dissent. Adopting what my students probably interpreted as modesty, I disavowed any personal access to the top of the American power pyramid. It wasn't how I understood American politics to operate and even if it were, I wasn't part of it. But my attempt to humble myself was, I confess, half-hearted. Why should I discredit my own opinions? Perhaps I did offer valuable insights on how "the powerful" thought. In any event, my denials were taken as part of how the game was played. After all, my students reasoned, conspiracies couldn't be conspiracies unless they were kept secret.

A Qatari student recalled my telling a joke that I had hoped spoke to this inflated notion of Jewish omnipotence. It featured a guy reciting a list of tragedies caused by Jews including the sinking of the *Titanic*. When it was pointed out that the *Titanic* was sunk by an iceberg, he retorted: "Iceberg, Rosenberg, Goldberg, what difference does it make which one did it?" My student, with the politeness of a well-bred young man from a culture of respect, recalled hesitating to laugh, not knowing whether it was appropriate.

A Growing Unease

Early 2010 was a time of growing unease about the direction the school and faculty were heading. Being Jewish made me aware, arguably hyperaware, of certain changes. Dean Jim Reardon-Anderson had launched the school, shaped its beginning and reigned as a soft-spoken, "Midwestern nice," American strongman. A China scholar, he had stuck to practices and values honed at Georgetown's Washington campus to administer an evolving, growing, and often intemperate overseas faculty. He had left at the end of the previous school year after fights with Washington over which part of the university would oversee the profitable branch in Qatar. The new interim dean, Mehran Kamrava, was a prolific scholar of international relations, Iranian-born, and now a resident of California. His hands-on style annoyed some in the faculty who, typically, preferred to be left alone. But Mehran understood the need to get beyond the start-up phase by raising the academic level and numbers of our student body. As an Iranian, he had in the past resisted the push by some faculty to exclude non-Arab states—Turkey, Iran, and Israel—from Middle Eastern studies. He seemed able to navigate the tensions between the main campus in Washington and the regional pull of local forces.

The school and faculty were changing. Much of this was the more-or-less natural growth of a small start-up evolving into something larger and more complex. Qatar's abundant resources set few limits on the rapid expansion of staff and faculty, programs and perks. Much like any energetic government agency with a blank check, the school added as many positions as it could in the expectation that the budget would follow. International conferences, student trips, research proposals, and supportive infrastructure were all encouraged. And construction of the $150 million permanent building for the school was well underway.

In its first years, the school had been somewhat sporadic in its hiring practices for faculty. On one side were some well-credentialed scholars, such as professors Amira Sonbol and Robert Wirsing, for whom Doha had special appeal. On the other side were those faculty, usually in fields far outside Middle Eastern studies, whom administrators could grab without completely eviscerating Georgetown's standards. (This group included me, burdened as I was by an itinerant nonacademic career.) This was despite the perks of the positions, including a 50 percent bump over stateside salaries along with tax benefits, housing and transportation allowances, and education stipends for children to attend private schools. Over time, the faculty subtly changed. It came to increasingly resemble its host region; fewer old white guys from the United States, with younger, darker colleagues from all over. Arguably, it made the faculty more compatible with the students, the environs, and the politics of both. But this evolution also posed challenges to the liberal education being advertised.

A number of pinpricks occurred, minor events that raised my concerns about the ideological bent of the faculty and the direction in which the school was headed:

- A junior professor gave an incendiary talk at a Martin Luther King Jr. Day celebration in early 2009 on the dominance of Jewish (or Zionist, he said later) financial influence over both MLK and Obama. His theme: the control of black leaders made any change in American Middle East policy unlikely. While not exactly in line with the celebration of Dr. King, nonviolent change, and the recent election of a black president, it did legitimize the prevailing local conspiracy theories concerning how American politics operated and put a Georgetown professor's brand on them. It furthered previous classroom discussions of his that proclaimed the Israeli lobby a "fourth branch of government."
- Some members of the faculty steering committee quietly attempted to derail invitations to speak in Doha for *New York Times* columnist Tom Friedman and distinguished Georgetown professor of international relations Robert Lieber. Perhaps coincidentally, both were Jewish and were considered supporters of Israel. Both invitations were in fact sent and both lectures given— neither, however, touching on the Middle East.
- In the fall of 2009, a group of teachers and students presented "a staged reading" of the play *Seven Jewish Children* by noted British playwright Caryl Churchill—described by Israeli critics

as pro-Palestinian—as well as a parallel short play. Together they offered the perspectives of seven Palestinian and seven Israeli children. It was described by one of the presenters as an attempt to show how a traumatized people can traumatize others and presented contrasting views on the conflict.

In the manner of liberal educators, it was staged with an audience discussion afterward. A newly arrived Egyptian/Palestinian professor commandeered the discussion, denouncing the production as presenting a false equivalence between oppressors and oppressed, describing the participants as unethical and proceeding to intimidate students who attended into silence. One faculty member involved in the reading said he had made her students feel "like worms." No one tried to repeat the performance.

- Shimon Peres, Deputy Prime Minister of Israel, had come to Doha to televise *The Doha Debates Special* (sponsored by Qatar Foundation) on January 30, 2007. He spoke at Georgetown and mixed with students afterward. While he was greeted cordially on campus, students reported that after they had posed for photos with Peres, the pictures were put on Facebook without their knowledge and they were subject to online threats.

Afterward, a poster appeared outside the library signed by "Students for Qaradawi," referring to the anti-Semitic cleric's advice to the emir: that after greeting the visiting Israeli deputy prime minister, Shimon Peres, he should wash his hands seven times, including once with sand, because of the Palestinian blood Peres had shed. As told by Qaradawi, the emir, in a Qatar version of a good ol' boy talkin' trash with a populist bigot, joked that he had washed his hands fourteen times because he had shaken Peres's hand twice.

Neither of these reactions to the Israeli visit could exactly be taken as encouraging a more relaxed, liberal attitude toward this most sensitive of Middle East issues. Or fostering any further contacts by the school.

- The eclectic, televised *Doha Debates* was taken off the air. A "unique venture in the Arab world, providing a battleground for conflicting opinions and arguments about the major political topics of the region," it was broadcast worldwide by BBC and Al Jazeera. The *Doha Debates* provided a freewheeling forum for discussions of a range of controversial issues including the role of women in Muslim societies, the role of the Israel lobby in US foreign policy, and the right of return for Palestinians. After the English host, Tim Sebastian, left the show (apparently under pressure) in October 2012, the debates were canceled without explanation. The rumors were that the program was a victim of the financial downturn in the Gulf and the Qatari regime's wish to lower its own progressive profile amidst the conflicts of the Arab Spring. More to the point, someone in power somewhere got pissed off.

- A prominent Israeli academic had sent a letter of inquiry about teaching philosophy at the school. Although there was some interest in pursuing his hiring, informal conversations with Qatar Foundation officials made clear he would not be granted a visa, even if he was offered a position. The matter was dropped.

- A senior Egyptian economist emailed fellow faculty members two rows of incendiary photographs. One row displayed historic pictures of Holocaust victims being led away by armed Nazi soldiers. The other row matched them with news photos of Israeli soldiers shooting and arresting Palestinians in recent invasions of Gaza. Each of the matching pictures was accompanied by anti-Israeli propaganda for those not getting the parallels. The professor asked that the photos be circulated to students. I found them offensive—but was it harassment? I complained to the dean and left it at that.

This last incident highlighted the dilemma I faced. In part, this was a matter of personality and style. I was not raised in an era of filing lawsuits to enforce politically correct codes of behavior. Nor did I particularly want to argue about the asymmetric violence that Israel inflicted on Palestinians; many of my colleagues probably agreed with the sentiment behind the photos, if mildly dissenting from the stretched historical parallels. Once again, I felt I would be focusing on tribal rivalries, not engaging in a debate on the adequacy of the analogy.

Usually, these slings and slights—often about the Palestinian-Israeli conflict—washed over me. The elderly Egyptian economist who posted the photos was in his last year of teaching and had gone out of his way to be personally gracious to Ann and me. The young historian who had denounced Jewish influence over the civil rights movement was someone I had gotten friendly with. I never felt any personal antagonism or heard the slightest bias from him (or from anyone else at the school, I might add). And believe me, I was sensitive to the possibility. He didn't consider himself anti-Semitic or biased toward Jews. Were these any more than normal political differences among a fractious faculty in a tense part of the world?

However personally comfortable I felt with my colleagues, when I looked around at the faculty I could see it changing. Several of the Americans who had been present at the creation of the campus had left. One went to Iraq to lead a university in the Kurdish region; another retired to part-time teaching; a third, the dean, returned to the main campus. I feared the faculty was "going native"—becoming more Middle East–oriented with expatriates focusing on the Arab world rising to prominence in all the disciplines. And it felt like a drift to the left politically. Being an Obama liberal now positioned me on the right-wing fringe of the faculty. There were no political conservatives, no Republicans, no one interested in American security policies, and no one sympathetic to Israel whom I knew on our faculty. Arguably, Georgetown was adapting to the brave new world it faced in the region.

I felt this all reflected a slowly changing balance in the education we were delivering. Qatar Foundation, which had contracted with Georgetown University to establish the School of Foreign Service, could have gone to Egypt to set up a branch of one of their universities if it had wanted a "Middle East" school. Instead, it seemed to want what Georgetown provided on its main campus in Washington. And this model provided the initial guidance: if we did it in Washington, we should be able to do it in Qatar—the same diversity, the same balance, the same open market of ideas should exist here. Qatar Foundation evidently agreed with this when the contract it signed stated its belief in promoting "active and creative world citizens." Although committing to Islamic values, the Foundation stressed that these values "nurture openness, tolerance, and cross-cultural dialogue." Not to mention that diversity, intellectual openness, and Georgetown's international character would guide the campus in Qatar. But the vehicle for delivering these goals was now being steered by an altered academic community. Later, when Qatar's own political leadership—whose vision had established Education City—disappeared and was replaced by a more conservative, less innovative group, these concerns would grow.

My own attempts at encouraging diversity in Doha met with decidedly limited success. The existing consensus, often bragged about in administrators' public addresses, was that the school was already tremendously diverse, with some twenty-nine different nations represented in the student body. When I pointed out that some American groups—evangelical Christians, African Americans, Jews, Mormons—were not well represented in this diversity, it was acknowledged and then ignored.

One administrator who did fret about diversifying the school was the university provost, James J. O'Donnell. He had raised the question during a visit to Doha in a talk to faculty in late 2010. In response to his call for suggestions for broadening a small, insular school, I had suggested admitting Israeli students, a comment that, as I recall, was treated like the utterance of a drunk uncle at a holiday dinner—affectionately unheard. I followed up in a letter to the provost suggesting that "encouraging Jewish students and faculty to come here, especially from the main campus, would not raise political objections and would add a needed diversity to our school." I noted that to fulfill this goal he might harness programs such as junior year abroad and short-term faculty appointments. "Distinguishing between Jews and Israelis would be a step forward for a student body that doesn't know either," I told him in December

2010. He was sympathetic about pushing diversity in a meeting we had a month later in his Washington office but nothing happened, perhaps because his tenure as provost ended the following year.

I still thought Georgetown was missing an opportunity at building a broader-based campus in Doha—one that could allow students to learn from others of diverging backgrounds and beliefs. Despite offering a course on the problem of God, which introduced a range of religious opinions regarding the deity, the students were limited to Doha campus enrollees. I discovered that on the main campus there was an interfaith class taught by the campus ministry's Catholic, Muslim, and Jewish chaplains. Through the use of our distance-learning facilities, it would be possible to have the three chaplains teach in DC with Washington students complementing a class based in Doha. Each of the chaplains might visit for a week or so during the semester to teach the course in Doha and talk with students there.

Meetings with the Washington campus ministers, Imam Yahya Hendi and Rabbi Rachel Gartner, several Jesuits, and administrators in Doha engendered sympathy but no changes. The mandatory curriculum was already considered packed and there was reluctance to add to students' academic burdens. But perhaps most importantly, no one in the Georgetown hierarchy saw much to be gained by this interfaith initiative. Surprising to me was how indifferent the leaders of the Jewish community on the Georgetown campus proved to be. They saw little benefit in using scarce resources for what they viewed as a futile outreach to Muslims.

Interfaith dialogue was an easily embraced concept but implementing it through a unique Catholic campus in an Arab land required a high-level decision that this too was part of Georgetown's mission. That never happened.

Visiting Israel and Palestine: Zone of Conflict, Zone of Peace

As early as 2006, the idea for a student trip to Israel and Palestine surfaced. Opinion varies on where the idea came from. In the Summary Report of the trip, the concept "grew naturally" from the school's emphasis on international relations and its wish to expose students to "experiential learning" inside and outside the region. Under the program called "Zones of Conflict, Zones of Peace," sponsored by the Office of Student Affairs and led by Dean Brendan Hill, similar trips had been taken to India, Kenya, and Jordan, and later ones to Rwanda, Lebanon, the United States (Detroit), South Africa, and Poland (Auschwitz).

As recalled by some of the administrators involved (including Brendan Hill and Jim Reardon-Anderson), the idea of a trip to Israel/Palestine was suggested by members of the Qatar royal family. Others were not quite as sure where the idea came from but were certain the trip had high-level Qatari approval. This was ironic, given that no Qatari students went on the trip.

Initially, the hope was to make the trip in spring 2007. A couple of Student Affairs staffers went to Israel and Palestine to plan the trip and reported back to a town hall meeting. They also contacted Ambassador Roi Rosenblit of the Israeli Trade Mission in Doha. (The Mission was closed in 2009 after the Israeli invasion of Gaza, as Qatar nudged its policies closer to those of its neighboring Arab states.) The Ambassador agreed to the trip and helped make arrangements with the Foreign Ministry in Tel Aviv. This involved bending some rules to allow students from countries that didn't recognize the Jewish state to visit. Georgetown, for its part, insisted it would not sponsor the trip if any of its students were denied an Israeli visa because of their national origin.

The staffers presented their findings at a town hall meeting of students, teachers, and staff. The meeting, in the words of the official report, "revealed a genuine divide" among those attending. This was a generous interpretation written by administrators who supported the trip. The dominant reaction was that the trip was a bad idea, haram ("forbidden" in Arabic). Dean Reardon-Anderson remembered the attendees having a mostly negative attitude toward the trip, with Qataris worried they would be "besmirched" in the Arab world. Some of the Arab faculty reminded the gathering that such a trip would violate BDS—the Boycott, Divestment, and Sanctions campaign endorsed by the Arab League.

Coming out of the town hall meeting, the dean agreed to set up a staff-faculty-student committee to consider how the trip should be organized. A consensus among those wanting the trip was that more time needed to be spent visiting Palestine and talking to the Palestinian Authority. One of the first decisions of the committee was to delay the trip until spring 2008 to arrange more visits to Palestinian sites as well as allowing tempers at the school to cool.

The students' reservations about visiting Israel included "the Facebook issue." This was the fear that photographs of Arab students in Israel would be circulated in their own countries, putting them in an awkward, if not dangerous, position. (In some countries, such as Lebanon, it was illegal to visit Israel.) This problem of "intimidation by photos" had been illustrated by a visit to the school by the head of the Israeli Trade Mission, who was photographed speaking with a student who was the daughter of a prominent Qatari businessman. As mentioned earlier, when President Shimon Peres visited Georgetown before a televised Doha Debate, students who posed for pictures with him found their photos on Facebook and received threatening emails.

This concern over public exposure was reinforced by Sheikha Mozah when Dean Reardon-Anderson talked with her as the Israel visit was under fire. She thought visiting occupied areas in Palestine was a great idea. She did have one note of warning for the students who would be going, the dean recalled: make sure they know that if they talk to the press, they could receive negative reactions from militant Arab opinion leaders, inside and outside Qatar.

Fierce opposition to the trip came from the faculty. The professors' stance reflected the region's customary emotional intensity regarding all things Israeli. One soon-to-be-hired colleague, in Doha for a job interview, was treated to dinner at a posh downtown restaurant where two faculty members, forgetting the dinner's purpose, engaged in an ugly shouting match over the Israeli trip. Several Arab teachers denounced the trip, saying it would violate the Arab boycott and position Georgetown as a pro-Zionist outpost. One senior professor warned Brendan Hill that if the Israel trip went ahead, bombs would be planted in the school's building. When Brendan responded that he should tell the dean, the professor replied, "Oh no, don't take it that high."

At a spring 2007 faculty meeting that followed the town hall, an Arab history professor declared, "No Qatari worth his name will go on this trip." Another teacher denounced Dean Hill as "the King of Zion" and yet another revealed to her class that he was gay. The Egyptians on the faculty took the lead in opposing the trip, perhaps not surprising given that Egypt had lost four wars to Israel along with its leadership of the Arab world. Gulf Arabs echoed the anti-Zionist rhetoric but generally didn't seem to be as emotionally antagonistic toward a country they had never actually fought.

Faculty defending the trip were harder to find. Arab members of the faculty said the time wasn't right for such a visit, given the continuing conflicts in the region. Josh Mitchell, who later led the trip, recalled that his father, a professor of Middle East Studies, had pointed out that in 1967 the same argument—that the time wasn't yet right for reconciliation with Israel—had been raised. What was meant was: it will never be the right time, Josh concluded. He was later subjected to charges of harassment filed by an Arab faculty member for his remarks at the meeting. (The charges were eventually dropped.) Dean Reardon-Anderson, while pushing for the trip, attended the meeting but remained silent during the faculty debate.

I too stayed out of the fray. No one doubted where the only Jewish member on the faculty stood and I had in fact made my opinion clear in conversations with colleagues. But I was hardly a public profile in courage. This was not a debate being resolved by intellectually convincing arguments and I doubted I had anything to add. I also felt vulnerable. This had started during my first year of teaching and I still seemed every bit an outsider in a clannish blood feud. I thought any remarks I made would be interpreted as knee-jerk loyalty; once again demonstrating the strength of tribalism I frequently denounced when exhibited by others. Not that I was about to turn against Israel just to demonstrate my freethinking ways. In general I kept my mouth shut.

Student discussions with one another about the trip were considerably more varied than their public posture. Their positions included sincere curiosity about visiting an unknown land to "decide for themselves" or, as one young Egyptian put it, to "learn more about the enemy." At least four Qataris applied to go on the trip but apparently didn't make the cut for reasons the trip organizers can no longer recall. The two Qatari students on the planning committee withdrew after hearing faculty denunciations of the trip. Dean Hill summed up Qatari reactions: "Some were eager and intimidated; some were either opposed or indifferent."

The vehemence of the Arab faculty reaction largely explained why, when the trip did take place, no Qataris went.

Although there was curiosity among the students, there was also fear that those from the region would encounter reprisals from their own governments. With the recent fighting in Gaza, many fell back on the cliché of moderate Arab opinion that this "wasn't the right time." But students remarked to me that the debate about the Israel trip never became uncivil among them. One of my best students, a Lebanese national, did not apply to go. She saw risks in going home after making what might be an illegal visit.

Ultimately, the trip went ahead a year after it was first scheduled, from May 8 to May 17, 2008, with eleven students and five chaperones. The students represented six nationalities: Polish, Bosnian, Indian, Egyptian, American, and Palestinian. Josh Mitchell took on the role of faculty representative for the trip. Although they spent considerably more time in Israel, the group did visit Ramallah, Bethlehem, and Jerusalem in the Palestinian territories. The Georgetown visitors met a mix of public authorities, private citizens, social activists, other students and professors, lawyers, politicians, pacifists, and musicians. They prayed in Jerusalem's Al-Aqsa mosque, visited Arafat's tomb, and spoke with Arab members of the Israeli parliament and courts. One Palestinian girl was moved to tears when she visited the Holocaust memorial at Yad Vashem.

Sometimes the encounters were misunderstood, on occasion humorously.

One girl remarked at an Israeli dinner that she thought "Hamas" was a gift from God. The stares she received for this unsolicited praise for the militant group governing Gaza induced her to more

145

clearly pronounce "hummus," the traditional Arab chickpea spread. Nervous laughter around the table greeted her correction.

The response to the trip, especially among the students who went, was positive. Dean Hill, unsurprisingly, described it as "eye-opening for everyone, students and leaders alike." Some of the polarization seemed to dissipate after the trip as returning students spread their favorable impressions of their visit. The possibility of students learning something from such an experience had to be given consideration even by staunch political opponents.

But another visit by Georgetown seemed doubtful. The faculty leader of the trip, Josh Mitchell, bluntly declared, "It will be repeated when hell freezes over." The process was too disruptive. Small campuses were rather delicate constructions. They worked better quietly, surrounded by an implicit consensus that allowed the individual academic entrepreneurs who composed them to get on with their solitary career outputs. A forceful dean could drive an unpopular action, such as this trip. But there was a price, and it was unlikely that our school's emerging leadership, which increasingly was acquiring the coloration of its surrounding region, was willing to pay the cost. Georgetown might have lost something by its reluctance to fight for the liberal values embodied in such a trip. But will anyone notice?

*

You teach who you are. And I could see now that part of my calling in coming to Doha was being Jewish. Whether who I was or what I taught made any difference to the school, students, or numerous people in between, I was not sure. I knew what I taught; I was never certain what my students learned. This gap between teaching and learning was even greater when the separation required bridging different nationalities, cultures, ages, and religions. But there were moments that might have justified the effort.

Hussein was a student in my Introduction to International Relations class. He wore the thobe of a young Qatari man. He had sharp Arab features and a wispy, crisp, black beard fringing his narrow face. He was a bright, attentive, hardworking student who spoke up frequently in class. But all too often, whatever the topic being discussed, his comments led the subject back to Zionism, Israel, or Jews. Issues of international law would merit a reference to the invasion of Gaza; the causes of World War I might induce a question about the Zionist movement; the boycott of Cuba somehow got tied to the pro-Israel lobby in Washington. You get the idea.

I was in my sixth year of teaching in Doha and when a student tried to steer the subject in directions that seemed off point, I generally let the class remind the maverick of the boundaries for discussions. After a while, they did. Hussein didn't completely give up his commentary parading as questions and at some point, I asked him to come to my office. Speaking one-on-one, I said I was willing to give him the benefit of the doubt but I thought his comments diverted the class and wondered whether his questions were aimed specifically at his teacher.

I am sure I communicated more annoyance than I had intended. He denied any but scholarly motives. And I concluded our meeting by suggesting that at some point he take a class that might answer more of his questions. At the time, I didn't consider our chat terribly productive.

Hussein did well in the class. As I said, he was a good student. But we didn't keep in touch and I didn't see him for about a year. It was mid-spring semester of my final year in Doha (2014) when he knocked on my office door and asked to come in. After exchanging pleasantries, he said he had spent the fall semester of his junior year at Georgetown's main campus. Smiling, he said he had enjoyed his time in Washington, liked the professors there, and had gotten into topics that he hadn't expected to be interested in. Here he seemed to pause, perhaps for effect. He had taken a class on the history of Jewish civilization. Another pause. He said he liked the class a lot, adding, "Y'know, I never would have taken that class if I hadn't been in your course." Now it was my turn to smile.

Go know.

CHAPTER 8

The Expat Bubble

I n fall 2010, Georgetown moved into its sparkling, not-quite-completed building at one end of the Education City campus. This marked the end of the start-up phase for the School of Foreign Service. It was an impressive building; the structure was a testament to Georgetown's strengthening ties to its new home and the money lavished on the school. But it also underlined the conditional nature of Georgetown's mission and its status as an expensive import: paid for, delivered, and walled-in.

The New School of Foreign Service Building

The new building, built and owned by Qatar Foundation, cost some $150 million, significantly more than was budgeted. Built by the prestigious Mexican architects Langoretta & Langoretta, who also oversaw the Texas A&M and Carnegie Mellon buildings on the Education City campus, it is considered—and was designed to be—an "architecturally significant" building—much like Oxford's and Cambridge's medieval towers.

Ground was broken for the large (360,000 square foot), multi-sided structure in 2008 and formally opened on February 13, 2011. Classes had actually begun earlier—in fall 2010—with workmen, wiring, and dust uneasily sharing space with students, teachers, staff, and administrators.

The school was involved in construction through a building committee with Qatar Foundation and Georgetown representatives. Under prodding by Dean Reardon-Anderson, the committee took an active interest in worker safety. They hired a third-party safety consultant who oversaw the construction and gave rewards for safe working practices. As a result, in the eight million man-hours required for construction, no serious injuries of workers were reported. This record was unique in Education City and a source of justifiable pride to university administrators.

Georgetown was considered an "intelligent tenant," which meant it had input, through a building committee, on the plans for the building. The limits of this input were reflected in the comments of a Qatar Foundation representative during a disagreement with a Georgetown member of the building committee: "It's not Georgetown's building; it's Qatar Foundation's building. Georgetown is a tenant." This implied that the building might have future uses other than education—which Georgetown staff were reminded of, again, when they unsuccessfully objected to some of the decorations on the walls.

Describing the structure itself was a formidable task. Its Mexican designers claimed it "represents the universal character of Qatar" as well as being "the symbol of Georgetown University at all levels and activities." Whatever this archi-speak meant, most of the structure was primarily stone and dark wood, somewhat echoing Georgetown's nineteenth-century Washington, DC, campus.

The building was designed as a series of overlapping boxes. The entrance, with a courtyard and the dean's offices, was one box; the faculty rooms off to the side were another; the atrium and library provided another; and the classrooms and Center for International and Regional Studies offices were still another. A lot of stone was used in the construction. Trellises and mesh-structures on the outer wall provided a covering that cut down on the light and heat from the desert sun. Nearly every office had windows.

The three-story-high atrium provided the fulcrum the school wrapped around. This central space, which served as a lounge and eating area, led to the library on one side and the auditorium on the other. While the multistory library was arguably too large, with room for sixty thousand volumes, the auditorium, seating 350 people, was too cramped for graduation ceremonies that usually had to be held elsewhere.

Light and color were displayed throughout the building, a distinctive hallmark of the Langoretta architects. Although apparently held back by the building committee from using too wide a range of colors, nonetheless the inside of the school had quite a variety. The library and atrium shared yellow ceilings; the auditorium boasted a gold stage backdrop with a red-walled lobby; each seminar room was painted a different color.

Expensive modern art around the building added to the feel of genteel exhibitionism. This included Plexiglas world maps made up of images—seeds, plants, faces, flowers, houses, etc.—hung on the painted walls of the seminar rooms. As far as I could tell, these were glanced at on the first day of class, never to be noticed again. Alabaster sconces were fixed along the walls. Column-like chandeliers filled the faculty lounge and the library with the latter one covered in a copper casing. The dean's offices opened to a lounge and, somewhat jarringly, a water pond that adjoined the seldom-used VIP entrance. The atrium, where faculty and students would gather for lunch, was filled with sunlight. In the evening, the space was dark enough so that those inside felt they were outside. Modern color photography, clay and gold leaf, Mexican figures, and prints throughout the halls culminated in lightning bolts in the atrium, all of which produced an over-the-top, palatial quality to the interior.

The $30 million worth of expensive, high-end furniture added to the inside luster but had a style that could not be described as Hoya-like. The lounges reflected a modern Italian leather flair rather than preparation for the hard use of careless undergraduates. This included a much-remarked-on white leather "snake couch" that twisted along dozens of feet in the center of the student lounge. The building itself, despite the architects' claims that it was "human and inviting," put off some visitors who were used to the seasoned wood and coziness of the aged gothic structures in Washington. A German architect leading a tour of buildings in Doha offered the opinion that the school building looked "more corporate than educational."

Faculty, true to their traditional resistance to change and authority, greeted the new building with muted griping. Their offices, though ample and featuring windows, were all the same size, leaving some senior faculty feeling slighted. They were also considerably smaller than the dean's complex of offices with its fountain and lounge attached. One dean complained that everybody was too separated from everyone else in the expansive structure, leading to a sense of alienation among the different departments.

The faculty wing, on two floors, was some distance from the cafeteria and library. The fourteen classrooms and lecture halls had the usual problems with technology and seating arrangements. Personally, I always hated being elevated on the lectern, standing over students as wisdom rained down on their upturned faces. When possible, I would switch my classes at the beginning of a semester to seminar rooms, where any class under twenty could rearrange tables into a square with students facing one another.

The building was understandably touted as a tremendous accomplishment; it just never looked like what it actually was. It lacked what it tried so hard to conceal: the casual feel of an American campus. There were no posters on the walls advertising campus events, no cigarette butts on bathroom window ledges, no half-erased graffiti slogans, no computer rooms smelling of one-too-many all-nighters, and no cluttered library tables. The dean's offices came off as an expansive celebration of centralized authority. The building was impressive—a little too intimidating, perhaps because it aimed higher than higher education.

The overall impression was that this was not Georgetown's building. It was Qatari, built with Qatari funds and serving the host's objectives. The new building separated Georgetown from Education City's other schools, which generally had little to do with one another. Behind closed gates, the building also underlined the separation of the school from the residents of the rest of the country it had come to serve. Whether a recent policy change allowing visitors onto the campus without permission—an attempt to show a more welcoming face to the surrounding population—symbolized an end to this detachment was questionable.

Driving Me Crazy

There was almost no socializing between Qataris and Western expats, most of whom didn't have Qatari friends or acquaintances. I included myself in this group. After his first four years as dean, Jim Reardon-Anderson said he had never had dinner in a Qatari's home. The simplest explanation for this separation might be the most relevant: both sides preferred it that way. Perhaps the expats didn't want to take the trouble to overcome the cultural and language barriers their hosts maintained.

One of the few places that Western expats and Qataris did interact outside of work was on the highways. It wasn't pretty.

My colleague Robert Wirsing presented an expat's dark view of driving in Qatar in his customary graphic manner: "It is the single worst feature of Qatar. Forget the heat; it's the total lack of civility and courtesy on the road." Amen, brother.

Robert was a tall, commanding presence. With a booming voice and frequent gestures, he was a force both in front of a class and to his colleagues, who elected him faculty chair several times. Now in his early eighties, he has retired to a family ranch in South Dakota, where I spoke to him at the kitchen table about his seven and a half years in Doha. As he warmed to the topic, he animated his conversation with his hands and by raising his voice:

"There's no concern for their own lives or others'. I dreaded driving. When I did, sure enough I'd encounter some bastard who comes up at high speed on my tail. . . . Getting onto the Tilt Roundabout on the access road from the school, you'd have to fight your way onto the highway; drivers rarely made space for you. Y'know, home in South Dakota, people wave to each other when they pass on the highway. In Doha, no one else merited drivers' concern."

I asked Robert, a veteran of Asian travel, whether the driving was any worse than elsewhere on the Indian subcontinent where he'd lived. "I loved driving in Pakistan. In Doha, I rarely went anywhere. Pakistan was rule-less, not reckless; people were more merciful. Here they were merciless."

Driving might seem like a peculiar way to understand expat life until one actually takes to the road. If Ancient Rome had cars and freeways, then Doha would resemble the last five minutes of its empire. Everyone rushed to where they were going yet everyone was always late. One Georgetown dean thought the greatest danger the school faced in Doha was young Qatari men driving in Education City. He thought there was no public ethic on the highways recognizing other human beings with rights.

The stage on which this drama unfolded featured well-maintained, multilane, modern highways broken up at major intersections by roundabouts designed for the less-hectic traffic flows of an earlier era—or the more repressed driving habits of the British. These traffic circles were, in turn, being torn up and replaced by traffic lights and four-cornered intersections. Highways were perpetually under construction; if they were not being expanded and improved, then something underneath them—be it pipelines or subway tracks—was being implanted. Bordering these veins of the city and separating them on medians were shining green grasses and bushes, watered and tended at daybreak by throngs of Asian workers. Beyond this narrow zone of unnatural lawns lay the desert—brown, dry, and often churning—reminding motorists speeding past where the city began and where its limits lay.

Somewhat surprisingly for a place where security seemed a paramount concern from the outside, police were seldom seen. Other than on visits to government offices, I don't recall seeing cops much at all. They were sometimes on the highways attempting to speed up stalled traffic, usually to no avail.

My one interaction with police came while sitting in a traffic jam. A policeman walked down the line of traffic that was barely inching along. He paused at each car, wrote a ticket, and handed it to the driver. He did the same when he got to me. The ticket said I was going below the required minimum speed, which I clearly was. The cop, who I don't think spoke English, didn't explain what my alternative was to being stalled in traffic. Later, friends advised me to pay the ticket without complaint, which I needed little encouragement to do.

To mix metaphors concerning the highway: a repressed Arab state became cowboy country—with all the restraint, good manners, surface politeness, and respect for guests and age going out the window on the driver's side. Georgetown administrator Maya Primorac described the drivers she encountered: "Drivers don't see you till you make eye contact; then they'll be polite." Joe Hernandez, the head of admissions, found local drivers not only aggressive but—as Maya noted—prone to avoiding eye contact. He thought that as a brown-skinned man, he would be ranked lower in the hierarchy of drivers. "But if you're in a bigger car, they'll yield."

The simple explanation for this was that prior to their seeing you behind the wheel, the other drivers merely viewed you as a rival car in competition with them on the highway. Game on.

The authorities had a rather ambivalent attitude toward this chaotic sport. One faculty member, an Arabic-speaking scholar, recalled her driver's test shortly after she arrived in Doha. After carefully performing the tasks required for gaining a driver's license, the inspector seated next to her in the car told her she had passed. A not unexpected result because she had driven for decades. Making casual conversation with this official, she asked him if he had any suggestions concerning safe driving. "Don't depend on your turn signal so much," he replied. Perhaps he was reminding her of the need to take other drivers by surprise.

It was widely believed among expats that police wouldn't file reports on any Qataris involved in accidents—or at least, prominent Qataris.

Our neighbor related that she was stopped at an intersection when she looked at a Toyota Land Cruiser across from her. She saw two small children jumping around in the front seat with a woman in an abaya driving—a common if risky practice on Doha's roads. She motioned to her own kids sitting in the back seat of her SUV and drew her hands across her chest, signaling to the woman that she needed to buckle her kids' seat belts. The Qatari woman didn't respond and our Dutch neighbor drove off.

That evening, she was visited at home by the police. The two cops at her front door were stern and frowning. After establishing that she had been involved in the "seat belt incident," she was warned never to tell a Qatari driver what to do. Don't ever let this happen again, she was told. They didn't mention the driver's violation of Qatar's seat belt laws, which require buckling up, or the danger to the children. The message had been delivered. Any expats hearing the story were reminded to keep their unwelcome, alien conclusions to themselves.

Just as bad, after a few years, most expats' driving habits came to resemble those of the locals.

By custom, bigger, more expensive vehicles—especially if driven by a male whose head was covered with a keffiyeh—always had the right of way. Seat belts were for sissies and certainly not for children. Merging two lanes of traffic was not an exercise in civility. In Western democracies, cars from alternate lanes merge seamlessly together: one from the left, the next from the right, in zipper fashion. In Doha, merging was yet another opportunity for personal advancement. I squeeze in and edge you out.

Traffic accidents were the fourth leading cause of death in Qatar in 2015. This meant some 14 percent of all deaths were caused by these accidents; worldwide, the rate was 2 percent. In spring 2015, *Doha News* announced the number of people killed in traffic accidents had reached a new high. Even worse, those dying or crippled were disproportionately young. Reports of high-speed vehicle deaths were a regular feature in the local newspapers. Yet the public's response seemed to be a fatalistic resignation when it came to safety.

Vehicles of Choice
As unthinking as this recklessness on the highways might appear to those of us confronting it every day, scholars have uncovered some logic to these patterns of road behavior. In their choice of vehicles

and their driving style, Qataris might be demonstrating something important about their lives.

Andrew Gardner was an American anthropologist who has written widely on migrant populations and modern culture in the Gulf. Working under a grant from the Qatar National Research Fund, he coauthored an article titled "Car Culture in Contemporary Qatar." In it, he discussed how automobiles, as "vehicles for our humanity," provided a window into modern Qatar and how highways served as a public theater where local identities—particularly masculine ones—were exhibited.

Central to Qatar's car culture was the Toyota Land Cruiser, usually white and suitable for Qatar's large families as well as the needs of off-road driving. Their early adoption by powerful members of the royal family created a trend imitated throughout Qatar. They incorporated so-called masculine qualities: rugged enough for desert driving; capable of high speeds, thus suitable for racing; and sufficiently expensive to flaunt wealth. The Land Cruiser and a few other "status vehicles" became a significant public marker of citizenship and in-group membership on streets crowded with oblivious foreigners.

So-called feminine cars were models lacking these qualities, inexpensive urban sedans and coupes. As one Qatari declared, "If a guy is driving a Camry, that means he doesn't have any money." Often, these déclassé cars were black, matching the color of abayas and thus associated with women. They contrasted with the white thobes and Cruisers with their masculine connotations. (During my years in Doha, we rented nondescript, always grayish Toyota Corollas and Mitsubishi Galants, like many of my colleagues. My functional, uninspired choices clearly marked me as foreign, professional, middle class, and clueless—characterizations that, alas, were not far off the mark.)

At the wheel, Qataris turned the roads and deserts of their country into performance spaces. Here they established a collective identity that set them apart from foreigners. Within the Qatari population, there was a sophisticated and intricate conversation going on among peoples from varied backgrounds—ranging from sophisticated urban elites to rougher, rural Bedouins. In a society where appearances were crucial, cars and driving had become a way to establish social identity.

Drinking

For a country in which alcohol was prohibited for its citizens, Qatar was not a difficult place to get a drink. Most but not all of the drinking went on in the expat communities behind the walls of the compounds. They were supplied by the one place to buy alcohol legally: the Qatar Distribution Center. This was a store open to members. Membership was easy to get if you weren't Muslim; and if you were, it was easy to have your Asian servant get one. It sold goods such as booze, cigars, and pork that were *haram* (forbidden) elsewhere. Inconveniently located on the outskirts of the city, the Center was the destination of monthly supply runs by expat families gathering a harvest of full-price beer, wine, and hard liquor. The result, at least for Ann and me, was that we ended up with more alcohol on hand than I ever had back home. Cases of beer, dozens of bottles of wine, and hard liquor: more than we were ever able to consume. But people liked to have them on hand for emergencies. This was even more true when Ramadan loomed and the Center would close for a month, requiring unbelievers to stock up before their access to forbidden pleasures was temporarily clamped off.

The existence of one retail outlet for alcohol was a concession to the presence of expat drinkers, balanced by the prohibitionist religious impulse within the Qatari community. Given the profits accumulating from this operation 'to the owners of Qatar Airways that managed it, the attraction of expanding it were obvious. However, there were roadblocks. The attempt to open another store ended badly and quickly. That store was planned for The Pearl, a multibillion-dollar, artificial island consisting of upscale residences, docks, shops, and restaurants, and aspiring to replicate the success of Palm Islands in rival Dubai. Alas, it was not to be. The new alcohol shop stayed open for four hours. Gossip suggested threats of violence had forced the authorities to close it down permanently. This paralleled the earlier banning, in late 2011, of alcohol at several upscale restaurants after complaints from locals about intoxicated expats at The Pearl. The result was several closures when business dried up.

Legal bars in Doha were found in upscale hotels and in some private clubs. This tended to make a night out at fashionable places—such as La Cigale's Sky View Bar, the W's Crystal Lounge, or the Four Seasons Beach Party—an expensive proposition. The Khaleejis (Gulf Arabs) who went to such places often discarded traditional robes for Western sports jackets if they were drinking in public. The city itself was considered a rather naïve newcomer compared to a Sodom-and-Gomorrah metropole such as neighboring Dubai. The daytime atmosphere of strict public morality didn't inhibit any number of nightly reveries, as in most cities of the world. With a ratio of three and a half men to one woman, drinking tended to be the evening sport of choice for unattached males.

Flush with disposable income and far from home, an element in the European community—usually single white males—reverted to adolescence in Doha. As one journalist put it, "People tend to find a way to get shitfaced in an undignified manner if that's what they're after." There was an oft-repeated warning that drunken driving got expats deported immediately. Nonetheless, drivers closely resembling drunks—not all of whom were Qataris—wove around the highways late at night. Though Americans and Britons made up only about 1.5 percent of the total population, they seemed to disproportionately populate the trendy bars and enjoy extensive mutual friendships.

Yeah, But What Do They Do?

Expats' talk about their occupations was usually private and subtle. Expats' assets lay in the Qataris' deficits. Because the locals couldn't do certain things or didn't wish to, skilled and unskilled labor was imported. The gossip among expats reinforced this dependency and their own value as imports. Stories abounded of Qataris filling government jobs with fancy titles in offices where they rarely showed up. There was the iconic tale of the Arab sheikh who airlifted his

Ferrari to Rome for an oil change. More reliable was a story told by a neighbor: a government minister, ignoring the plans of his expensive German consultants, crossed out the stops they had proposed for a new subway system and drew x's where he wanted the new stations to be located instead. He then returned the plan to the now-irrelevant but still well-paid advisors.

Much like colonists of an earlier century, the expats needed to see the locals as flawed or at least as not quite good enough to operate on their own. As the economy got more complicated and the citizenry got wealthier and ever more indolent, the case became easier to make. For their part, the Qataris seemed to expect the foreign professionals to eventually be replaced by locals. As each month brought more expats to manage the still-growing, increasingly convoluted economy, the case for their disappearance became less and less convincing.

Expats were immigrants yet not immigrants; invited if not quite welcomed. They were politely viewed as a temporary necessity: "bubble immigrants." Most of them were segregated into well-appointed, walled compounds, given limited visas, and not expected to mix too much with the natives. Expats self-isolated themselves by retaining differences in language and culture, by drinking alcohol, and by socializing with the opposite sex. Most expats willingly accepted being fenced off, although there was the occasional, "Why don't we know more Qataris?"

The expats' bottom line remained the bottom line. For those who had overcome the paperwork required to get in, the imperialist imperatives of "Gold, God, and Glory" had been reduced by two-thirds. The yellow metal was retained. The money was better—much better—than expats could get at home. Most enjoyed an affluent lifestyle that would be out of reach in their own country: servants, expensive cars, free private education, and no pesky income taxes. (The IRS insisted that American expats be taxed but a Qatar-paid tax reimbursement largely fixed this.)

For example, when Georgetown was hiring teachers, it might consider an applicant who was a full professor at an English

159

university—say Kings College or the London School of Economics. The applicant might be making $50,000 a year in England. Not only could our school offer almost two and a half times as much but it could also throw in free housing and free cars, free private schools for children, two round-trip airfares back home per year, and ample research money. The new hire would add at least a third to whatever earnings they were getting in the UK because they no longer owed any British tax on their income. Uniquely affluent Qatar was a swell enough host not to require an income tax on anyone, even tax-obedient English academics.

Most expats, professors included, ended up staying longer than they intended when they first arrived (as did I and my wife). Although these so-called "golden handcuffs" were disparaged, they didn't chafe at the expats' pale wrists terribly much. And despite some complaints heard, the price to be paid wasn't terribly stiff: it included staying out of local politics, remaining isolated from the native population, abstaining from drinking and driving, and following social customs—especially ensuring women didn't expose arms, legs, or various other body parts. Spouses frequently voiced unhappiness, with the recurring complaint of having "nothing to do."

Most expats eventually left. Whatever the financial incentives, Doha tended to be a side street off the main avenue of most foreigners' lives. Although it might make sense to stay for a while, it didn't make sense to stay for a *long* while. The journalist Dane Wisher put it well shortly after he finished three years in Doha: "Bureaucratic hassles, professional roadblocks, homesickness, geographic fear of missing out, and boredom erode the wall of comfort people build up around themselves in Doha. Financially, it's almost always stupid to leave, but there is a powerful sense that the world is moving on without you and that Doha isn't part of the real world."

Although Qataris might express mixed feelings toward the large expat community in their midst, one thing that didn't come up was jealousy toward the expats' privileges. Unlike a traditional colony, the colonized were living a step (or two or three) up from the invited invaders. The status clashes that existed among Qataris were mostly directed toward one another in a competition to flaunt the wealth. One Qatari student told me how her mother wore a new Rolex watch—a real bargain at $200,000—to a family gathering. One of her relatives, after admiring her watch, asked the woman why her daughters didn't have their own Rolexes. Sure enough, by the next gathering, each of the daughters was compelled to show off her newly purchased, diamond-encrusted Rolex. The boys in the family were not forgotten: they got Porsches.

The trick Qataris aimed to perpetrate on expats was to extract their expertise without integrating them into Qatari society or adapting Qatari society to them. One Qatari student acknowledged a sense of suspicion by locals toward professional expats: "People suspect that they are here to exploit us without really giving us their knowledge." Although the official narrative was that the expats were here temporarily, she recognized these jobs would not be "Qatarized" anytime soon. Another Qatari woman voiced a local view: "They're supposed to teach me and then I take over. But I don't think that will happen. This guy got his wife hired, instead of me getting his job."

The most corrosive part of the expat presence for Qataris was the sense of "domestic encirclement." Nationals found themselves a minority in their own country—and at an estimated 9 percent of Qatar residents, they were indeed a small minority. In cyberspace and in home Majlis (the all-male family councils held regularly by Arab households), this topic raised the temperature of Qataris young and old. The resentment surfaced in arguments about why society should "respect our values" by banning pork and liquor, enforcing female dress codes, and increasing the use of Arabic. The issue of language was a sore point for locals because the mother tongue—Arabic—had been reduced to a second language. This sentiment lay behind the push, in 2013, to replace English with Arabic as the major language of instruction at Qatar University with a resulting upheaval in the English-speaking faculty. At the same time, English was the admission ticket to the globalized world as well as the universities of Education City. This reality was not changing. And so, the language dilemma remained.

For Qataris, isolating expats seemed a small price to pay for retaining their customs, religion, and family-centered social lives. But pursuing this bifurcation in the workplace came at a cost. With only 2 percent of Qataris employed in the private sector, there appeared to be relatively little opportunity to learn about management of modern organizations from professionals on the inside. Under the direction of a few Qatari leaders, expat administrators seemed to operate well—if expensively—as they rapidly grew the nation's infrastructure. But as a dynamic model of development—one designed to stimulate the local population to change its behavior and adapt to the demands of a newly emerging global economy—the impression was that it didn't work. The Qataris were on the sidelines of their own economy: beneficiaries but bystanders. The Qataris weren't players; they were the paying audience.

In the little English he spoke, the Tibetan masseur at a downtown Chinese health clinic voiced a conclusion reached as well by more articulate Western expats: "No gas, no Qatar."

Compounding Social Life

Living in an expat compound was like cruising in a well-appointed lifeboat. Serving overseas meant leaving the mother ship behind, shoving off from the familiar friends and family in your life. From the time that we plunked ourselves down in new and comfortable (if confined) quarters, we were sharing our backgrounds with others from around the world for an uncertain and temporary journey.

Whatever the personal disruptions involved in getting to Doha, expats ended up thrown together pursuing similar missions, consuming the same goods and services, and exchanging broadly similar outlooks. Toss in the awareness of an alien environment outside the compound walls—with just a hint of threat—and it was not surprising how easy solidarity formed.

My wife and I mixed mostly with four couples in the compound. Helmut and Helga were from Germany via a university in Minneapolis. He was an academic dean at Georgetown, a nuclear energy specialist, and an avid photographer. She was an environmental, green roof specialist and president of the nonprofit Sustainable Qatar. A great cook, she filled her frequent dinners with authentic German dishes and memories of a harsh childhood growing up in East Germany. Each year culminated in a rousing Oktoberfest evening with all assembled dressed in German outfits, dancing and laughing.

Sky was a straight-arrow American Midwesterner from small-town Missouri, in Doha working for an oil company. He was married to a Lebanese Palestinian woman, Naila, a senior staffer who ran an office at Georgetown. Their memories often turned to their early married years, before their two boys came, when they lived in a Queens, New York, walk-up mixing with Orthodox Jewish tailors, Italian butchers, Indian deli owners, and Dominican barbers. It brought Sky to the world outside Missouri and perhaps enticed him into seeing the rest of it.

Jonathan and Sue were born in Britain and migrated separately to Australia, where they met and became ardent fans of all things Aussie, starting with rugby and beer. Jonathan had worked his way up in Georgetown's administration and combined restless energy and Australian informality, both of which led to frequent invites to hoist a pint. Sue took her efficient competency to work in the Georgetown library and in organizing social gatherings. She also spent much of her time managing their son, Jack, who started in Doha as a newborn and grew into an energetic sports fanatic.

Ang-Ling was a lovely Chinese Malaysian woman, married to Patrick, a French philosophy teacher and Ping-Pong devotee. They shared their stories: she of growing up as a privileged yet not-quite-accepted minority in Malaysia; he as a French migrant teaching college in rural Oklahoma. A spiritual couple, they were frequent visitors to India.

My wife summed up our relations with our neighbors: "You could borrow anything. And anyone would help you." At the beginning of our stay, Ann had fallen and injured her head. Three neighbors, not well known to us yet, came to the house to stay with her until I came home that night.

Because the town houses were grouped close to each other in three concentric rectangles, we were a short walk from everyone else in the Barzan compound. Venturing outside the compound on foot was a rare occurrence because the immediate surroundings consisted of little more than a couple of Indian dukas (small supermarkets), a bakery, and cleaners. Surrounding them was uninviting, unkempt, rocky scrubland, spotted with desert bushes and scattered piles of trash tended by groups of feral cats. The emir's land—parks, highway strips, and other plots—was easy to identify: it was covered in manicured, green sod. The rest of Doha was unremarkable, rocky unappealing desert: a blank slate to the untrained eye, requiring and receiving little maintenance. Civic duty in Doha toward public space didn't extend beyond the clear limits of one's own domain.

The outer ring of houses backed up to Barzan's surrounding walls. They fronted an encircling car road that also functioned as a walking and jogging track for residents. Pairs of chatting women, married couples, mothers pushing their baby strollers, dog walkers, and occasional runners would take advantage of the cooler evenings to circumnavigate. This asphalt road provided an outlet to exercise and to meet and chat with neighbors. Our cat, Ginger, named for her orange coat streaked with white bands, generally followed us on our evening rambles, disappearing only when we crossed some other cat's turf and then reappearing a few houses later. (Ginger had adopted me when, as the most assertive member of a large contingent of street kittens, she had come to the back door during my sixth spring in Doha; with little forethought, I fed her. We were friends for the duration of my contract; we left her with our town house's new tenants when we left Qatar.)

Just inside the gate, a stucco clubhouse was centered behind its own semicircular driveway. Its sandstone exterior wouldn't have looked out of place in a Florida retirement community. The clubhouse contained a workout room with a half-dozen exercise machines and two occasionally operating small TVs perched high on the wall at one end. A central room opened onto an outdoor pool with a fenced-in tennis court on the far side. Adjoining the workout gym was a meeting room that had comfortable sofas and upholstered chairs as well as room for a Ping-Pong table that I and a neighbor set up every Saturday for our weekly games. At the other end of the clubhouse were separate men's and women's locker rooms with steam and saunas. Since these were for Barzan residents whose houses were located nearby, they were seldom used. Once, when the hot water went out in the women's room, the Indian workers at our compound at first refused to enter the empty locker room—fearful of being accused of crossing the line separating the genders. On their behalf, I stood in the open doorway to steer away any female residents as they worked.

Barzan was a world of its own or at least a village. The compound contained families from three overseas employers: Georgetown, Carnegie Mellon, and Maersk, the Danish shipping and energy company. The company's families tended to stay for shorter periods, say two to three years, while those in the universities stayed at least twice as long. Barzan was where we did most of our socializing and where we made most of our friends, all conveniently close by. No need to fight the traffic to go to a party. No worries about being caught drinking and driving; you could stroll to and stagger from the frequent social gatherings. No concerns for how you dressed—an important consideration for Western women in a hot, steamy city where many others of their gender were pressured to cover up hair or faces or entire bodies. And no anxiety about safety. The compound walls had TV cameras on each corner, complemented by sixty-four cameras covering every conceivable angle of the compound's streets. The front gate incorporated a truck barrier that was raised and lowered to provide further protection. No one seemed to mind that the contingent of a dozen unarmed, uniformed Nepalese guards were slight and small—and would never risk their hard-earned visas by preventing any insistent expat or Qatari driver from entering.

Our own town house, number 52, was on the corner of an inner row of residences just to the left as you entered the gate. It was not easily distinguished from its identically sand-colored neighbors, though the corner location gave us windows on three sides. The four ample-sized bedrooms upstairs had attached bathrooms. Each of these had a bidet, much prized by the resident American women as an exotic luxury. The presence of two downstairs bathrooms—one in the maid's room—meant the house had two more bathrooms than bedrooms. The high ceilings, light tiled floor, beige concrete walls, and large windows gave the place an airy, earthy feel. The small dimensions of the kitchen, with the even smaller maid's room adjoining it, led my wife to conclude that neither had been designed by a woman who would actually have to use them.

During our eight years in Barzan, our walls and floor became crowded with foreign objects we'd bought on our trips to Asia, Africa, and the Middle East. Thanks to a week off in the middle of each semester, a month between semesters, and three months of summer vacation, there was ample time for travel. Qatar enjoyed great airline connections courtesy of Qatar Airways. Trips to places as far away as Burma and as close as Oman—as well as India, Nepal, and Turkey—had supplied pictures, rugs, and furniture to spread around our house. A dozen small photographs of leathery Uyghur faces that my wife took on a visit to Xinjiang Province in China filled a wall near the back door; a green and yellow, intricately woven, beaded embroidery from India hung on the wall next to the door, while a yellow African textile print filled the space at right angles.

Our narrow backyard had enough room for a small, round, weather-beaten teak table with chairs. Ann and I sat there to drink our morning coffee. Beyond the small patio jutting out beyond the kitchen door, a garden ran along the back wall for the length of the house. Tended with motherly care by my wife, it was dominated on one end by a fast-growing, pear-shaped tree surrounded by a variety of flowers: purple desert lilacs, orange and yellow hibiscus, multi-colored lantanas, and white jasmine. Dark pink bougainvilleas ran along the wall to the far corner, where a squared, sandy plot was devoted to desert cacti, rocks, and a camel skull, in our bow to the native habitat.

The tree, labeled a conocarpus by our eco-knowledgeable German neighbor Helga, provided a shady centerpiece to the sitting area. Or rather, it did—until one spring day when our water pressure disappeared and we were suddenly confronted by a few slow drops coming out of the kitchen tap. Barzan's three Indian workers—Sandosh, Jitendra, and Mohammed—were there in an instant as usual, quickly dismantling the outside pipe going up the back-yard wall outside the kitchen. They seemed to identify the problem immediately.

Spiraling up the pipe's insides—as thick as a man's forearm—was a tightly coiled knot of roots. Our arboreal burglar had broken into the water supply. Ascending some ten feet up the wall in an aggressive search for moisture, it had finally strangled off any chance the human residents might have for enjoying water flowing through the faucet. The roots were cleaned out that afternoon and the pipe repaired. Although I was reluctant to surrender our only source of natural shade, we asserted our rights on the desert food chain and the tree was gone the next day.

The tree was doomed by its very success in the fight for survival. Helga noted that the conocarpus had also poisoned the surrounding soil to keep other plants from taking its nutrients. Under the strict supervision of our gardener, we replaced it with an Indian neem, a smaller canopy tree that was welcomed for its limited consumption of water and its medicinal qualities. Its tiny, white clusters of flowers smelled like orange blossoms. Harmony was restored to the garden.

Blue and Gray and Gay

Expats brought some nonconforming lifestyles that, while forbidden, were shared by surprising numbers of the local populace; homosexuality was among them.

Brendan Hill remembered when he first came out as gay in Doha. He had never tried to hide it, but it had become public knowledge when a faculty member opposing his leadership of the trip to Israel announced in her class that the dean of students was gay. He had already received a friendly warning by a Qatar Foundation representative to be discreet. When he was hired, Dean Reardon-Anderson had asked him if he was going to be comfortable living in Doha. The dean had gone so far as to say he would recommend pulling the whole school out of Doha if Brendan were subject to any discrimination. He added that he expected Brendan to comply with the Sharia law that governed Qatar, which meant "being" gay but not "doing" gay—a somewhat nuanced distinction for any employer to enforce.

Brendan said there were lots of gays in Qatar. Given the enforced separation between genders, arranged marriages, and strict barriers limiting any public expressions of affection, a "prison sexuality" dominated. Homosexuality was practiced privately and denied publicly. As long as the activities were kept quiet, didn't embarrass the family, and didn't undermine marriages, they were tolerated or at least ignored. Sexuality was viewed as more fluid in this society, with homosexuality less likely to be compartmentalized; hence there was less reason to "come out." When mentoring students, Brendan generally advised those who were gay to keep their orientation under wraps. "If you say it, then they have to do something about it." If "don't ask, don't tell" was good enough for the US military in the 1990s, it was a good enough guideline in the present-day Arab Gulf.

For expats with enough status, even greater flexibility was allowed. One story, told by a gay expat, concerned the hiring of a high-level administrator—not at Georgetown—who refused to accept the job unless he could bring his lover so they could continue living together. The difficulty arose in getting visas, which were limited to employees and their dependents. The issue was finally resolved by classifying the administrator's partner under the category of "long-time domestic servant." The couple stayed together in Doha for the administrator's three-year contract with no further problems.

Gay students faced more obstacles. Most kept their orientation to themselves, although they would confide in friends. When I asked whether there was much discrimination among students, only one person—a Qatari woman—came up with an example. In the early years of the school, there was a slender male Qatari student who wore a thobe and was suspected of being gay. Apparently, a Pakistani classmate made fun of him in front of others, telling him that he was acting contrary to the Koran and would end up in hell. According to my informant, the Pakistani boy's behavior was unusual and looked down on by other students.

Not that life for gay Arabs was easy. One son of a prominent Gulf family had stayed out of his country for years since he graduated from Georgetown. He began to live openly with a partner in a cosmopolitan city outside the Arab world. He was religious and accepted that what he was doing was a sin against Islam. But as he said to a woman friend in Doha, "This is not a choice. When people speak about homosexuality as a choice they don't know what they're talking about. Why would I have chosen this, putting at risk my family and religion?"

Gays did have some advantages living in Qatar. One expat staffer remarked that social life changed for him when "hookup" apps came to Doha. It was easy to meet and make friends. GPS coordinates were widely shared; you'd plug them into your smartphone, drive out into the desert, and arrive at a large, well-lit tent where a loud party was underway. There was also a refreshing lack of identity politics connected to being gay in the Gulf, said this staffer. The prevailing view among gay Qataris was that sex was up to each individual; you could do what you liked.

A straight Qatari modified this conclusion a bit. Now studying in New York, she said, "You can be gay in Doha as long as you don't practice it." She had not seen much discrimination either at our school or in Qatar generally. Many of the gay men she knew went along with their families' preference and entered into marriages, some sham, some not. She had gay women friends and thought they, too, found implicit acceptance. As she said, when compared to girls having extramarital relations with men, sex among women was "the lesser evil."

Strict gender divisions in Gulf society, which have made all-male and all-female social gatherings the norm, provided ample opportunity for same-sex relations to flourish among those so inclined. One gay Qatari, Saeed, thought social segregation had given him the space and time growing up to understand his attraction to other men. "I recognized the chemistry between men," he said, "and it became a natural way of fulfilling my physical needs." He felt that gender separation had encouraged robust lesbian and gay communities in Doha.

As long as same-sex relations were kept private and the family unit maintained, there was an acceptance that seemed surprising to those expecting strict obedience to the restrictions of the Koran. Saeed, a stout young man who I only barely remembered sitting quietly in an introductory international relations class, told me, "Anything sexual is taboo to talk about within the family. But I think my father knows already. He was educated in all-boy schools and understands what goes on. He sees me with my friends and knows they are gay. I would go with my friend to our family Majlis (gatherings) together and he would stay over afterward in my room. My mother just doesn't have the experience. If I ever tell them, I think my father would be more accepting than she would."

After finishing his graduate studies in Washington, Saeed expected to go home, get married, and have children. He had no plans to announce his sexual orientation. As the only son in a large family, he felt pressured to get married and carry on the family name. Sounding resigned, he concluded, "I can be comfortable enough living a parallel life. I'll have to give up the nightclubs I go to here. I pray five times a day and think of myself becoming a husband and a father. For the time being, there's no need to come out. That would just be creating conflict. Doha is much more tolerant than it used to be."

Georgetown, too, might have played a peripheral role in acquainting Qatar with evolving twenty-first-century attitudes toward sexuality. In February 2009, a few faculty members were asked to write articles for the *Chronicle of Higher Education* on our experience teaching in the Arab Gulf. I wrote a somewhat upbeat piece that concluded: "For a faculty that includes priests, Jews, and other nonconformists, the response has been welcoming and, assuming a degree of discretion, accepting."

In an earlier draft, I had included "homosexuals" as one of these tolerated groups. I showed the draft to a colleague with more grounding in the region than I had and he suggested I delete any mention of gays. I was in my "go along, get along" phase in Doha and didn't want to unnecessarily offend our hosts' sensibilities—so I substituted "nonconformists" for "homosexuals."

What I didn't know at the time was that Matt Tinkcom, then teaching communication and culture and later to become Assistant Dean for Academic Affairs in Doha, was being interviewed by a correspondent for the *Chronicle* for an accompanying article in the same issue. In that piece, he was described as a visiting teacher "who specializes in film studies and queer theory." Matt, having just completed a semester of teaching in the Gulf, denounced outsiders' "dumbest stereotypes" of the allegedly stifling intellectual atmosphere in Doha. In his one semester of teaching, Matt had found just the opposite: "a culture of critical thought, engagement, and dialogue." To prove his point, he declared that in his course he had included "queer theory" in discussing same-sex sexuality, "and my students here have been receptive to it."

Well, good for Matt, I thought, when I read his interview. Perhaps I had been living in a parallel universe from his in my years teaching in Doha.

Both articles appeared in the *Chronicle* on February 9, 2009. That very afternoon, I received a panicky phone call from a friend who was a consultant for a senior member of the Qatari regime with a particular interest in higher education. His boss, a dignified, conservative sheikh, had asked my friend, a British expatriate, to explain this "queer theory" that Georgetown's Foreign Service School was now teaching to apparently eager young Arab students and that—though he was too polite to mention it—his Sharia-based government was paying for.

So my buddy passed on to me the sheikh's question: Did I know what, exactly, "queer theory" was? Well, no I didn't, but I did know that this was way above my pay grade. I told him, "Sorry chap, you're on your own."

By way of postscript, I spoke to my English friend a few days later. He said he had briefed his employer, informing him—courtesy of Google—that queer theory was the study of film and literature that emphasized sexual orientation. The elderly sheik didn't ask any further questions.

CHAPTER 9

Freedom as a Teachable Moment

This is American education. And for many of our students, that's a very big change. Almost all of them went to single-sex secondary schools. As recently as six years ago, the elementary reader in Qatar was the Koran, so students learned beautiful classical Arabic, but they had no experience with questions like 'What do you think the author meant by that?' or 'Do you agree or disagree?'
—Charles E. Thorpe, former dean of Carnegie Mellon in Qatar,
The New York Times, February 12, 2008

The Classroom Bubble

Most faculty believed that our classes, with all their limits, served as a buffer to the immediate outside world. They viewed American universities as a bubble of safety and tolerance within which students could speak freely, at least about the topics of classroom discussions. Heated debates arose that would have been taboo elsewhere—on everything from feminism to punishing dissent to treatment of migrant workers. Women students, however they might have restrained themselves outside of school, were assertive, knowledgeable, and confident in class arguments. I and most of my colleagues would encourage conversations on what we had presented. These discussions stood as implicit reminders to students that their professor's lecture was not the final word on the subject.

I thought faculty in all the Education City schools were proud to deliver something distinctive to their students: an American education. Both teachers and students understood this to be a novel experience in this part of the world.

Teachers certainly took pride in the freedoms they fostered in their classes. Robert Wirsing, after fifty years of college teaching, declared his years in Doha "the best work environment I ever had," adding, "there was no subject that can't be discussed in class." Other faculty members would agree. Whatever the political temperature was outside of school, students would know that what they wanted to say was welcomed on our turf.

Or at least that's what we had convinced ourselves. It was a bit surprising to find students who didn't agree with these conclusions—even students in my class.

Sitting in a Chinese restaurant near Harvard Square a couple years after she graduated, Aatikah delivered the bad news to me:

"I felt like you had to be politically correct in your classroom. Discussions about 9/11 were very sensitive. You didn't exactly welcome outsiders with conspiracy theories talking about what happened back then."

Fair enough. And true. I was about to engage her, a bit defensively, in a discussion about academic standards but, seeing my dismay, Aatikah moved on to the point she wanted to get to.

"Georgetown classes generally resisted talking about the Qatari government, both faculty and students." She then added another reason for this inhibition on free speech that frankly had never dawned on me: other students.

"People didn't want to talk about sensitive issues with a member of the royal family in the classroom. I can remember one of my friends coming up to me after a class talking about what another girl had said. 'Can you believe this? She said that with Abdullah Al-Thani [the younger brother of the emir] in the room.' You can say whatever you want about the Middle East but not about Qatar. Students were more outspoken in the classes I took in the US."

She saw this faculty reluctance to discuss Qatar most clearly in her classes that covered Middle Eastern subjects: "The longer teachers stayed in Doha, the more likely they were to be silent."

An Egyptian graduate added his memories to this chronicle of faculty restraint. During freshman orientation, the late Foreign Service School dean, Carol Lancaster, was asked a question by a Lebanese student who referred to "a democracy like Qatar." Carol interrupted to point out that you couldn't call Qatar a democracy because it was governed by an unelected emir. All well and good. But what the Egyptian student remembered was that several weeks later, in a political theory class, there was a discussion of Plato's *Republic*. One student, a member of the Al Thani royal family, declared that the best-governed countries were constitutional monarchies, like Qatar. What the Egyptian recalled was that this description of Qatar went unchallenged by the professor, a notable contrast to the dean's response.

Another perspective came from an Indian student from Doha reflecting on the dynamic within the classroom. This student wrote me about how careful non-Qataris who grew up in Doha had to be when they were around nationals and why so few of them actually knew any. As children, they had been warned to steer clear of Qataris because they had the power to deport anyone who rubbed them the wrong way. This social hierarchy, though put to the side at the school, had to have an impact on what went on in the classroom.

One European colleague in the social sciences acknowledged the faculty's self-restraint and called it a form of soft censorship. "We were changing or withholding what we would otherwise express in response to perceived threats," he declared. Perhaps it was caution bred by faculty members at the beginning or end of their careers, he speculated. Further, many students lived as noncitizens with families in Qatar and virtually all depended on government funds for their education; as one student observed, this might have made them "insecure and cautious," fearful of getting out of line. They didn't appear that way to me—but as I frequently asked in class, "What do *I* know?"

Soft Self-Censorship

Scholars who have written about Qatar and taught there add insight to these observations. Allen Fromherz, a historian who taught at Qatar University and authored *Qatar: A Modern History*, which happens to be banned in Qatar itself, described teaching there as walking "a very delicate tightrope. . . . At times, it feels like you're in a traditional American setting, where everything can be debated. But there are certain lines that really can't be crossed and they are invisible to you until you cross them."

Such lines would include criticizing the royal family, questioning religious orthodoxy, or "dishonoring" Qataris. Even on foreign branch campuses, Fromherz pointed out, "you don't know when you're going to have royal protection or not." Fromherz declared that higher education had been brought into Qatar to create marketable, international skills that could connect the country with the outside world, not to reform governance and society within Qatar itself. The country remained, he concluded, a tightly controlled tribal political system.

Other academics were skeptical about the viability of the relationship: could academic freedom ever exist without free speech in the society surrounding the university? Lina Khatib, who headed the Program on Arab Reform and Democracy at Stanford University, told the *Chronicle of Higher Education*: "It goes against the very principles that form the core of academic life in the US to go and install a campus in countries that have spoken and unspoken red lines on what can be debated. No financial incentive is . . . good enough. . . ." In a statement directed at New York University's campus in the United Arab Emirates, the American Association of University Professors worried whether academic freedom could survive: "In a host environment where free speech is constrained, if not proscribed, faculty will censor themselves, and the cause of authentic liberal education, to the extent it can exist in such situations, will suffer."

Other Education City schools have had their problems with academic standards. In a bow to local cultural norms, Virginia Commonwealth University didn't use nude models to teach art. More

175

serious was the criticism leveled at Northwestern University for the way it educated students for careers in journalism and communications. A former president of Northwestern's faculty senate, Stephen F. Eisenman, visited Doha and afterward criticized the authoritarian atmosphere that "inhibits free expression" in which their journalist students were being prepared. "Teaching journalism as an enterprise in which you must first learn what *not* to ask," he added, "is no kind of journalism instruction at all." And he pointed to the most interesting questions about Doha that faculty and students were definitely not interested in asking. These included inquiries about "all those tall, half-empty office buildings" in downtown Doha; Qatar's role in funding Sunni extremists; and the living and working conditions of the vast majority of residents who were migrant workers. Eisenman concluded that Northwestern should withdraw from Doha because ". . . in its current form, the program is not legitimate or defensible."

A faculty member who taught in Georgetown's Arab and Regional Studies program, and who preferred not to be identified, thought there were implicit boundaries on what was discussed in classes about the history, culture, and politics of the region. He found major political issues curiously absent. The Sunni-Shia division, a central topic in numerous Western explanations of Arab conflicts, was a source of considerable embarrassment in the region and seldom publicly debated. This professor charged that tribal identities and their importance in domestic politics in Gulf states as well as other Arab countries seldom surfaced in debates in class or forums outside of class. In Qatar's case, this would entail discussing the Al Thani dominance of palace politics and the domestic economy. The US Army and Air Force bases in Qatar did not provoke much academic debate. Regarding religion, my colleague said, "It is unlikely that anyone too critical of Islam would be hired at Georgetown." Critiques of Islam or local Arab regimes in state-supported universities were definitely not welcomed, this instructor concluded.

Current professors at least partially agreed with these conclusions. One professor of government somewhat flippantly concluded it would be "impolite to criticize the emir and insane to insult Islam."

Another faculty member felt concerned enough about the issue of sectarianism to publish an article in an international journal on Shiites and Sunnis under a pseudonym.

Students also considered the sectarian conflict in Islam a "no-go area." One Shia student from Lebanon noted that this religious division never came up when she was at school. Some Arab students took a darker, more conspiratorial view, attributing the Western focus on this division to a desire to factionalize the Muslim world. As another Arab colleague put it, denial was not just a river in Egypt.

Most Georgetown faculty argued that the limits of what could be taught were a bit murkier than their colleagues' view allowed. Mehran Kamrava recalled being a young professor from Iran teaching Middle East politics in a state university outside of Los Angeles and feeling implicit pressure on what he could say. He thought there were limits on how much criticism of Israel would be acceptable to the Jewish community there and it affected what he felt could be taught. One graduate of Georgetown's first class in Doha pointed to the number of Arab faculty members who had previously taught in national universities and learned the constraints on expression under which these schools operated. Many had outgrown their country of birth. They were familiar with the dangers of criticizing their own regimes; certainly, denouncing Israel or America in class was a safer route to firming up progressive nationalist credentials.

Any faculty, including Georgetown's in Doha, shaped the messages that were being delivered in the classroom by whom they hired or didn't hire. The dearth of political conservatives teaching at our school and their perspective on American national security or free market economics, underlined the point. Consider once more the Israeli academic (mentioned in chapter 7) whose inquiry about teaching at Georgetown was deferred by administrators who were convinced he would never be granted a residence permit by the local authorities.

This was not to say that many faculty were not willing to engage in a vigorous discussion of sensitive issues. Professor Kamrava disputed that there were constraints on his work, despite the warnings he received from American colleagues before arriving. "I had no limitations on what I could teach, and what I could write and do research on," he said. Kamrava's book, *Qatar: Small State, Big Politics*, was unavailable anywhere in Qatar except Georgetown's bookstore. Former dean Gerd Nonneman pointed to Kamrava's writings as an example of the tolerance for informed critics among Qatar's leadership. The dean noted the Iranian-born scholar's critique of the regime's centralized, often personalized decision making, and the lack of democracy, accountability, and transparency. (He might also have added Kamrava's publications on the uncomfortable topic of migrant labor in Qatar as well as sectarianism in the Gulf.) Nonneman concluded, "There is an appreciation at the highest level that 'critical thinking' is a crucially important skill for the development of the country."

Women scholars such as Amira Sonbol and Rogaia Abusharaf taught courses that incorporated their own and others' progressive scholarship on women's roles in Islamic history and law. They also served as models for women students who flocked to their popular courses. Amy Nestor led theater groups and taught English literature emphasizing feminist and lesbian perspectives in American culture. Birol Baskan—before a painful confrontation with Qatari security interests that I describe later—vigorously attacked numerous popular conspiracy theories in his comparative politics course. Patrick Laude used his position as a professor of theology to explore Sufi mysticism in religion classes and started a well-regarded interfaith journal in Doha.

Perhaps the course that most surprised academic visitors and journalists to the campus was a required class called The Problem of God. Taught in the theology department by a variety of faculty, from a Jesuit priest to a Protestant minister to a Sufi Moslem, the course aimed to present students with a variety of religious perspectives on the Deity. *Washington Post* education reporter Nick Anderson, who visited a class in late November 2015, found Professor Akintunde Akinade, an Anglican theologian from Nigeria, leading a discussion of Judaism focusing on Psalm 91 ("the Lord is my refuge") and Elie Wiesel's Holocaust memoir, *Night*. Akinade was quoted in the article: "We're not here to preach to you. We're here to engage you, to make you think as a scholar."

Many students to whom I spoke after they graduated named The Problem of God as the most challenging class they had taken at Georgetown. Some had found it deepened their faith; others that it had accelerated their drift away from organized religion. One Egyptian graduate recalled starting college with a sympathetic view of religion: it had a decent humanitarian core, too often covered over by ideology. He later grew disgusted with organized faith and just "dropped all of it." A young Qatari, now in an American graduate school, fondly remembered the controversies discussed in class: "I enjoyed how much space we were given to say what we wanted. Sometimes I wish I could go back to the Problem of God class; I would say more."

Not-So-Soft Censorship

Why, why do these regimes
Import everything from the West,
Everything but the rule of law, that is
And everything but freedom?
—Rashid al-Ajami, Qatari poet; served four years in prison for writings such as this poem seen as critical of the emir. He was pardoned in March 2016.

Can an "obscene" book be used in a college class in Qatar?

Opening a liberal arts American college in a nondemocratic Islamic country was one thing. Operating it—in a place where controversy arose from the practical realities—was something else. One sticking point was the need to import books for the library, classes, or research. Some of these books might cover subjects that would ordinarily be kept away from Qataris, including dissenting religious views, sexual topics including homosexuality, and views critical of the ruling regime. In principle, Georgetown was to be treated as a part of Qatar Foundation, which meant it was exempt from custom fees and the inspection procedures of the Qatar agencies that regulated what was allowed into the country. This had been granted to the university in May 2005 and reasserted in August 2006. However, this arrangement unexpectedly began to fall apart in the summer of 2010.

Kara Walker was a modern African American artist unlikely to know her impact on academic freedom in the Arab Gulf. Provocative and complex, Walker worked frequently with black-paper silhouettes echoing eighteenth-century art that she organized into stories. She gained international recognition for her presentations reflecting the sexuality and violence of slavery in the American South before the Civil War. Her shocking pictures played on racial and gender stereotypes both of the past and present that critics have hailed as original and illuminating. Her book, *Kara Walker: My Complement, My Enemy, My Oppressor, My Love*, collected some of her artwork, including a number of graphic portrayals of sadism and rape, as well as satires on sex and slavery.

In fall 2010, an assistant professor of English, Amy Nestor, wanted to use the book for her course, The Poetics of Catastrophe. You wouldn't call Amy a typical foreign service schoolteacher or her class a mainstream social science offering for aspiring diplomats. Hailing from Alameda, an island in San Francisco Bay, Amy was wafer-thin, frequently ill, and prone to migraines. She made up in energy what she lacked in health. A knowledgeable follower of HBO's *Game of Thrones* (she used to explain the previous evening's episode on Monday mornings to this befuddled fan) and an instigator of the School's modern theater group, Amy had carved out a following among students for her edgy feminist leanings. In this particular class, she aimed to address how literature and art represented trauma as reflected in historical genocides including the Holocaust, Stalin's purges, and American slavery. By necessity—according to Amy—she presented avant-garde art trying to grapple with these atrocities. Perhaps because it consisted in large part of striking visuals—including the horror of the rape of children—that were easily understood across language barriers, the Walker book was held up at customs and forwarded to the Ministry of Culture for review in September 2010.

Notice of the book banning—or at least its sidetracking—was first communicated to Amy by the faculty chair, Judith Tucker, a noted Middle East historian. Judith asked Amy not to fight it and suggested using other historical texts. Amy objected because she wanted to demonstrate contemporary artistic representations of these traumas as well as their sexual aspect. She felt she was being told the Walker book was obscene and inappropriate. Professor Tucker advised her to hide the books she had and tell no one she possessed such apparently volatile volumes.

Distressed by the lack of support she had received, Amy raised the issue with the academic dean at the time, Matt Tinkcom, who encouraged her to fight the censorship. The issue eventually made its way to a meeting of the deans of the schools of Education City. That meeting supported the use of the Walker book in class. None of this was publicly revealed at the time and most of the faculty remained in the dark concerning the controversy.

The deans' approval, however, didn't mean the book was actually available for use in that fall class. The Qataris had not released the volumes. Like most oversized art books, it was not available online as an ebook.

At this point, undergraduate creativity came into play. One student had a sibling who traveled on a diplomatic passport so was not subject to search at the airport. Three copies were ordered from Amazon, delivered to a New York City hotel room, and subsequently smuggled into Doha two weeks later. The three-hundred-page book was photocopied with the originals passed around the class for images that were not easily visible on the copies. The result? In Professor Nestor's words: "Discussing her work was difficult, discomforting—but it is supposed to be, and the class was fully engaged in it."

Subsequently, Georgetown's administrators had to face further actions from the government bureaucracy, which—in the months that followed—proceeded to block other books coming to Georgetown. Despite letters exempting university-ordered books from inspection, many were held up at customs and forwarded to the Ministry of Culture. This went on for the next four years. According to the director of the Library, Frieda Wiebe, the total number of books censored, lost, or for some reason never returned to the library from the Ministry, totaled four hundred volumes.

Befitting an inept bureaucracy under pressure from religious conservatives within and a liberalizing leadership on top, the books in question were treated in a variety of ways. Packages of books that had been forwarded to the Ministry of Culture were returned to Georgetown missing one or more specific titles. Some of these books would later be released; some would be misplaced or lost; others would never reach the library. Many of them were censored, not to be heard of again. Several missing titles the Ministry claimed not to have seen. In one instance, the Georgetown librarian visited the Ministry of Culture and "was able to retrieve some of the books that were scattered about in their offices and storage room."

Despite a good deal of incoherence regarding the censorship, there was a pattern to it, as the director of the library noted: "So you can see, the titles that are held for review are typically on topics of politics (Qatar in particular), religion, and anything that would seem from the title to be about sexuality. All of the books on Islam and homosexuality were held and never returned."

Included in this tally were forty-six Arabic language volumes that were ordered for a researcher working on temporary marriage customs in Shia Islam. Other "missing" volumes included titles such as *Women and Islam*; *Hatred, Lies and Violence in the World of Islam*; *Islam's Jesus*; *Study of Shi'i Islam*; *Buddha, Jesus and Muhammad: A Comparative Study*; *Qatar: Politics and the Challenges of Development*; *Mohammedanism: An Historical Survey*; *The Islamic Context of the Thousand and One Nights*; and *The Life and Times of Muhammad*.

Two of the "missing" titles were later explicitly banned: *Prophet Muhammad: The First Sufi of Islam* and *The Qur'an and Woman: Rereading the Sacred Text from a Woman's Perspective*. Recent scholarly treatments of Qatari politics were also censored: Georgetown professor Kamrava's *Qatar: Small State, Big Politics* and Alan Fromherz's *Qatar: A Modern History*. Theology professor Patrick Laude had four books banned from use in his classroom: *The Spiritual Teachings of the Prophet* by T. Chouiref; *Mirror of His Beauty: Feminine Images of God from the Bible to the Early Kabbalah* by Peter Schafer; *The Bhagavad Gita* (banned after it had been used five times in previous years); and, ironically, *Pray Without Ceasing: The Way of the Invocation in World Religions* by Laude himself.

The logic—if there was any—behind censoring these books remained perplexing. For example, they included an obscure academic publication on the painters of miniatures during the Timurid period in fifteenth-century Persia. Even artists of very small works apparently needed to be scrutinized for their political implications.

Many of the censorship obstacles were overcome by a persistent library staff that requested books in electronic format or simply ordered another batch. Some complaints were taken to the leaders of Qatar Foundation, who reaffirmed their support for unhindered access by Georgetown to texts and books. The dean and other administrators had a "very cordial" meeting with the Minister of Culture in April 2015. At Georgetown faculty meetings, book censorship was blamed on conservative religious elements within the government who were resisting the reform measures supported by the leadership. There was a reluctance by the dean and many faculty to take the issue of censorship to the press or into the public arena. Hearteningly, the librarian declared in the summer of 2015 that "no library books have been confiscated since September 2014." This reflected the fact that Qatari parents were less likely to scrutinize library books than the texts their children were assigned. During a visit to the library in spring 2017, school officials declared that books ordered by the library were no longer subject to censorship.

Texts ordered by teachers for classrooms were treated differently. In 2015, a new agreement on reviewing books for use in class was put in place by the Ministry of Culture. Unlike the previous procedure—where books first went to the Ministry for approval—now they went to Georgetown directly. Then the bookstore made a list of the titles and sent the Ministry one copy of each book for review. The Ministry would then send the names of the books they wouldn't allow and Georgetown's bookstore would forward all the copies back to the Ministry for disposal.

The books rejected were usually on religious subjects or involved Qatari politics, though no reasons were given and the process often was inconsistent. One hint at the Ministry's motivations came when officials mentioned parents' calling into morning radio shows to object to books their children were reading for class. Sacred texts from outside of Islam or with dissenting views from within were not approved. Christian Bibles, including the *New Jerusalem Bible* and the *New American Bible*, were rejected. The *Bhagavad Gita* was nixed. Naguib Mahfouz—the Egyptian novelist and Nobel prize winner—had his *Children of Gebelawi*, a fictional representation of religious figures, banned. A book on Sufism, a mystical movement in Islam diverging from state-endorsed Wahhabism, was forbidden.

Few books were affected by the Ministry's restrictions: none during the 2015–2016 school year; four banned in fall 2016; two more in spring 2017. But halfway through the spring 2017 semester, fourteen were still under review and there was some concern the authorities were tightening up.

Although Georgetown conformed to the Ministry's wishes in all cases where printed books were banned, they were retrieved via other methods. Websites such as JSTOR provided access to some volumes; chapters were transmitted in PDFs; Amazon's Kindle allowed the purchase of other material. Because the school was on the Washington campus's virtual private network (VPN), content could not be tampered with by the authorities. When necessary, publishers were contacted for permission to photocopy material. The other schools in Education City who were under similar restrictions all handled the censorship restraints in their own ways.

Although pushback from the authorities remained a concern, the university was not lacking in techniques for dealing with government intrusion. When a Jesuit priest wanted his students to study the Bible for his fall 2015 class, he was advised to supply it in ebook format. Amy Nestor continued to teach themes of sex and violence, including a play, *Blasted*, by British playwright Sarah Kane. After she had taught the play for three years, someone in the Ministry decided to read it. Finding an account of oral sex in it, the bureaucrats tried to censor it. Amy argued that they had already approved it three times and couldn't censor it now. They sent her a photocopy of the play to use in class.

As for the Kara Walker book, Professor Nestor gave a copy to the student whose family member had smuggled it in. She kept the other copies in her office. The copy the Georgetown library ordered got through the censors without difficulty. It can be found on the shelves of the library today.

A Turkish Intrusion?

In early May 2015, Birol Baskan, an assistant professor of government at Georgetown in Doha, suffered a jolt to his plans for the coming year: his residency permit was not being renewed. What was usually an uneventful matter of filling out forms every two years was about to turn into something else entirely.

Since coming to Doha in 2007, Birol had been issued a residency permit every two or three years. As usual, he dealt with Omar Al Swadi, who was Georgetown's point man for dealing with the Arab bureaucracy. Omar, a take-charge ex-cop from Yemen, had not gotten back to Birol for two weeks—longer than usual but not terribly worrying. When Omar finally did return Birol's passport, he brought upsetting news: when his current permit ran out in September, Birol couldn't stay or teach in Doha. An agency of the Qatar government was removing a Georgetown professor with no reason given.

A Turkish citizen with a PhD from Northwestern University, Birol had previously taught at Qatar University before being hired by Georgetown in 2010. He taught courses in comparative politics, religion and politics, and methodology. A somewhat laid-back instructor, often casually dressed and unshaven, Birol was more interested in publishing than in organizing his lectures. Among a faculty in which grade inflation was widely acknowledged, Birol was unusual in his willingness to flunk unproductive students in his classes. In the classroom, Birol had a reputation for eviscerating the conspiracy theories popular in the region.

A couple of days after getting his bad news, Birol went to see the dean, who had been briefed by Omar. In the fourth year of his five-year term as dean at Georgetown in Doha, Gerd Nonneman had just finished overseeing the renewal of the ten-year contract between Qatar Foundation and Georgetown. Although the negotiations were successful, budget cuts insisted on by the Qataris had led to layoffs in staff and, as a consequence, morale was not at its highest. A Flemish Belgian, Gerd had come from an English university, Essex, and as an outsider to both Georgetown and American education, he was a surprise appointment. But he was a Middle East expert, and his cultural sensitivities and engaging personality held him in good stead in relations on the ground in Doha. As an outsider to Georgetown's insular culture, however, his ties with the main campus were often more strained.

Gerd was reassuring if noncommittal in his conversation with Birol. Gerd said he would look into the case. Birol felt pretty much left in the dark about what was going on. Familiar with the uncertainties of the region's politics, he understood that a public fuss would not be helpful to his cause. He kept quiet about the situation to his faculty colleagues and the media. Meanwhile, Georgetown's administrators, who estimated the odds of reversing the permit decision as fifty-fifty, were doing quite a bit.

The dean had followed up with the president of Qatar Foundation, Saad Al-Muhannadi, who promised to contact the Ministry of Immigration. Saad expressed his sympathy and offered his support for measures that would allow Birol to continue teaching. Unfortunately, the initial communications between President Saad and the Ministry did not produce immediate results or result in any information on why the visa had not been extended.

At the same time, Georgetown's Washington leadership had been brought into the issue. This included President DeGioia as well as the provost, Bob Grove, and the new Foreign Service dean, Joel Hellman. There was general agreement that this was a serious issue and, in

one administrator's words, "a matter of principle and public per-
ception (inside and outside) were at stake." President DeGioia asked
Grove and Hellman to go to Doha for meetings on the issue. They,
along with Dean Nonneman, held two high-level meetings early in
July 2015 with Qataris about Birol's case. One was with Saad; the
other was with Qatari members of the Joint Advisory Board, which
functioned as a quasi-Board of Trustees for the school in Qatar, and
included influential members of the royal family.

The administrators used these meetings to send a clear message that Georgetown, from the president down, treated this matter extremely seriously. While the administrators got a sympathetic
hearing, the Qataris' empathy came with a warning: if the decision
to pull the visa was made by state security, it was unlikely they would
uncover the reasons or be able to reverse it. In short, although senior
members of the royal family were responsive, they were not prepared
to overturn the decision.

Among Georgetown's deans, there was an attempt to understand
the Qatari position. One administrator, who asked not to be identified, pointed to parallel cases in the United States where visas were
refused for foreign academics where national security was involved.
A few years earlier, the noted Islamic scholar Tariq Ramadan
had been turned down for a visa allowing him to leave Oxford
University to teach at Notre Dame for a year. George W. Bush's State
Department—not a great fan of progressive Muslim theologians—
cited a charitable contribution Ramadan had made to a Palestinian
group to imply he was a supporter of terrorism, hence disqualified
from teaching in the United States. After six years of controversy and
court cases, Ramadan finally obtained a visa in 2010.

There were straws in the wind on the causes of Birol's removal.
He wrote frequently, and critically, about Turkey's leaders. In a 2011
piece in the *Turkish Yearbook of International Relations*, titled "Ankara
Torn Apart," Baskan complained that the "overambitious, overconfi-
dent, and highly personalized management of Turkish foreign policy
in two hands, and two hands only"—of the prime minister and his
foreign minister "is simply turning the Arab spring into Turkey's

autumn." Others pointed to Birol's appearances on Al Jazeera TV where he criticized the Turkish government. Apparently, complaints had come from within Turkish security agencies to allies in Qatar security forces.

But was academic freedom at stake? It should be noted that during the following academic year, Birol planned to teach a course titled Turkey and the Middle East. Any attempt to shut him down based on his outspoken views on Turkey, therefore, clearly impacted his academic interests and freedom.

With Baskan's existing visa due to expire, Georgetown needed to act. The deans were confronted by several competing interests. They wanted to support their employee and keep his career from being damaged. They didn't wish to concede the arbitrary withdrawal of his residency permit. And having previously defended their move to Qatar as no threat either to the Georgetown brand or its academic standards, they wanted to avoid any embarrassing public reaction from the Washington campus or the community of liberal American scholars sensitively tuned to blemishes on the record of Catholic universities. At the very least, this did not reflect well on their emirate host's stated dedication to freedom of expression.

The interim solution was to offer Birol a two-year arrangement, matching the years left on his contract, to teach on the main Washington campus. This would include teaching his Doha students through a closed-circuit TV global classroom. Qatar Foundation agreed to continue his funding in Washington.

By late August 2015, Birol and his young wife, Feyza, were on a flight to Washington—their American visas and accommodations having been supplied by what he described as a "very kind and helpful" Georgetown administration. The university was under no formal contractual obligation to offer him a teaching position in Washington. Later, as a result of this incident, permanent faculty in Doha were given explicit protection in their contracts by the university if there were ever a repeat of this case. Birol would stay in Washington for the 2015–2016 school year, teach the classes previously scheduled for Doha, and remain in the dark about whether his residency problem in Doha was being resolved. Or even what the problem was.

In May 2016, Birol returned to Doha for a brief visit on his way to Turkey. He dropped off a new application for his residency permit with Omar and left the country. At this point, none of the administrators in Washington or Doha could tell Birol whether his residency problem had been resolved. Ten days after he applied, Omar contacted him in Turkey to tell him that he had been granted a permit. In fall 2016, he began teaching again in Doha. Not surprisingly, the Georgetown administrators thought their efforts deserved credit. But consistent with the protocols of palace politics, no explanation was ever offered as to why his residency had been denied in the first place or why it was approved a year later.

Had Georgetown's relocation of Birol to Washington meant it accepted the removal of a professor for his public commentary—an act of retribution on behalf of a powerful allied state? Or was this, as a faculty colleague concluded, an example of Georgetown's leadership effectively engaging in quiet diplomacy and without damaging the larger relationship with the Qataris in the process? The administrators viewed their efforts as bearing fruit with Birol's eventual reinstatement, all while standing up for principle. As with most accounts of politics as practiced in the region, the calculations got murky.

But there might have been a cost to be paid in the lack of a public response to what was a clear infringement of the university's contractual right to hire and retain faculty without interference from the Qatari government. Georgetown's achievement had come in reversing an action that should never have occurred.

Unfortunately, the university's weakness was underlined suddenly in 2017. On returning from his winter holiday between semesters, Professor Baskan was denied reentry into Qatar. Following the failed Turkish coup in July 2016, the Erdogan government had increased its pressure on allied states to take action against overseas Turks accused of supporting the group behind the coup. The expulsion of other Turks in Doha, including a dozen from the faculty of Qatar University, further clouded the picture. In a replay, Georgetown invited Baskan back to Washington to teach for the remainder of the 2016–2017 school year and kept quiet about the incident. But the potentially explosive issues of hiring and removing faculty, which the university administration had thought resolved, were not. Nor did they seem likely to be.

Learning What to Teach
Why do we fear words?
Some words are secret bells, the echoes
of their tone announce the start of a magic
And abundant time
Steeped in feeling and life,
So why should we fear words?
—Nazik al-Mala'ika, Quote inscribed on Meditation Walk of Georgetown Building in Qatar

"We are not setting up a school in Belgium," is how the first dean, Jim Reardon-Anderson, aptly summed up the dilemmas facing Georgetown in Qatar. He was speaking of Qatar's system for managing migrant labor and the difficulty in trying to humanize the treatment of the low-income workers at Georgetown. We were sitting in his office in July 2015 at the Foreign Service School on the Washington campus, where he was serving as interim dean.

The dean's point could be applied equally to the issue of intellectual freedom. Perhaps he meant that Georgetown had the task of finding a place in a harsh desert environment for a liberal education more adapted to temperate climes and societies; of the need to be flexible to adapt to the local culture at times, but not break.

The alternative is pulling out, he went on to say.

And he said it like someone who had toyed with the thought before.

But if we stay, he went on, then we have the choice either of not engaging, or of trying to move a system with little respect for human rights, women's rights, worker rights, or dissent in the direction of protecting liberal education.

Unspoken but understood was that the school had skin in the game. Neither the dean nor the rest of the university were neutral bystanders. Any visible breaching of the walls of academia that infringed on the autonomy of the classroom or freedom of speech, or the independence of the university administration, threatened the Georgetown brand and this hard-earned experiment.

From Georgetown leaders' perspective, they had dealt effectively with the book bannings and the withdrawal of a professor's residence permit. Through a combination of administrative persistence and private diplomacy, decisions by agencies of the Qatar government were quietly circumvented. Books imported for library or classroom use were no longer stopped to the degree they once were or effectively restricted from use by the university. Professor Baskan, after a year's standoff, returned to teaching although he was later removed again. Whether the host's challenge to academic freedom had been sufficiently confronted remained an important question.

"All hat, no cattle" was a classic Texas put-down of an Eastern tenderfoot coming to a rough land to ranch with lots of ideas and swagger but little experience. Detached American scholars' declarations of support for academic freedom in the Middle East echoed this. Although endorsing the importance of academic freedom, they implored Georgetown to withdraw from Doha if this freedom was not ensured. This hardly reinforced the principle or those who required it. Elevating the concept of academic freedom did not mean removing the support it needed to endure, both inside and outside academia's walls. And beyond the modernizing elements within Qatar's Arab leadership, higher education's autonomy and importance in the country were neither long-standing nor widely accepted.

The point is that academic freedom was not an imported sacred altar on which liberal educators could stand unchallenged and hold forth as they thought best. It was, in fact, a vital tool for teaching students and fulfilling the tasks of thought and research that were the goals of a modern university faculty. And these freedoms needed to be taught along with the substantive education they guarded. They should not be hidden away. They were not something to be ashamed of. Violations needed to be loudly protested. These freedoms were integral to the learning process that Georgetown and others had brought with them.

The free exchange of ideas required a diversity of minds operating in an environment that encouraged thought and discussion and challenging critiques. Despite all its formal requirements for students, the university acted as a forum where younger generations were educated amid the widest possible expression of ideas. The assumption was that this approach served society's purposes, even if not every idea proved worthy of defending. Academic freedom was the method via which an educational institution preserved its members' independence while getting on with its broader service to society. In fairness, most countries—including the United States—did not yet fully embrace the protection of all these freedoms. But limits—whether scholarly or practical—should be minimized.

Censorship was especially onerous. Restricting the expression or teaching of ideas challenged the very nature of liberal education. Self-censorship had particularly harsh consequences. Implicit boundaries on what could be written, with equally vague punishments for crossing these lines, left individuals alone with their anxiety in deciding what they could say or write. The result would be even greater suppression of thought than more explicit limits might impose.

I can sympathize with the anonymous Qatari bureaucrat examining the daring artistic volume that Amy Nestor wanted to teach in her class. Arguably, its strong sexual and violent content would render it obscene in most societies at most times. (Not as obscene, however, as the actual atrocities afflicting the region that this art reflected.) The expression of these ideas was inconsistent with the traditions within which this bureaucrat was raised. Nor could their expression have been anticipated by his countrymen when they invited Georgetown to establish a School of Foreign Service.

Yet Georgetown was not brought to the Arab Gulf by timid clerks hiding in a faceless bureaucracy. The university was embraced by men and women with a bold vision of their country's future. They were leaders who understood their people could not retreat to the past or passively waste nature's bounty in present consumption. Instead, they needed to embrace the best in global education to prepare their youth and region for an onrushing future. But this liberal education required more from them than a beautiful building in which this "art on the wall" could be hung. It called for a supportive relationship with equally confident university leaders; ties that would inevitably test both sides' comfort zones.

On the green, manicured, unnaturally layered lawns that conceal the desert and encircle the campus buildings in Education City, there stood bright yellow word-sculptures that called on students to "Imagine," "Achieve," and "Create." At least in its signage, Qatar had taken the side of change. Using its plentiful resources, it had pursued the goal of becoming an innovative "knowledge society" that wanted the best a globalized world had to offer in educating its youth. And Georgetown had not come to Doha to escape its own values. Whatever the compromises involved in operating in the Arab Gulf, the university had a set of beliefs supporting its faculty, staff, and administrators. These guidelines preserved the four hundred-year-old Jesuit tradition that committed the university to the care of the whole person, to the importance of "the life of the mind as a means for uncovering truth and discovering meaning."

Values such as academic freedom needed to be articulated, promoted, and protected in public. Its defense must be clearly communicated within the academic walls and to the outside community. If there was anything a university possessed in abundance, it was talkers—and some of them ought to be speaking out on academic freedom. Georgetown should not be shy about publicly embracing the principles that it brought—and that brought it—to Doha.

Freedom can be a teachable moment.

CHAPTER 10

Qatar's Migrant Majority

G wakes up at around 4:30 a.m., usually with the other five workers in his dormitory-style room provided by his employer. There's a mix of Nepalese, like G, and Indians in their sparse, crowded living quarters in the Industrial Area district of Doha. His bus picks him up at 5:30 a.m. for what is an hour-and-a-half drive. Because of many stops for other workers, he gets to his job at 7:00 a.m. as a gardener at The Pearl. He has a breakfast of tea, rice, and cooked vegetables, and packs his lunch of rice and vegetables in his cooking pot, which he takes with him to work. (His dinner will also be vegetables, mainly cauliflower and rice.)

He coughs almost constantly, probably from the pervasive dust. He has no medical insurance and hesitates to go to a doctor for fear of losing his job. At thirty-nine years old, his health is generally pretty good, though he's put on an extra thirty pounds since coming to Doha eleven years ago—too much food with lots of calories but less nutrition. He seldom eats meat because it's too expensive. He misses the oranges and bananas he used to eat in Nepal.

G is painfully shy with anyone he feels is his superior. He seldom complains and feels fortunate to have a job when there are none back home. His day consists of going to and from work, and then food shopping.

Home is a small village in southwestern Nepal near the Indian border. G's father died when he was still quite young. G didn't finish his schooling but he reads Hindi. Although he worked in India for a year, he lacks basic knowledge of the larger world, its geography, culture, and food. Despite being from Nepal, he has never actually touched snow.

G found out about Qatar through a cousin who had worked in Doha. The cousin brought him to an agent who arranged his employment in Doha and his visa; it cost him QR1200 ($330), which he borrowed from an uncle and paid back out of his first months' wages. He has several cousins who work in Doha whom he tries to see on Friday, his one day off. They used to stroll on the Corniche, the walk along the waterfront, before Qatari families objected and single Asian male migrants were excluded.

His workday runs from 7:00 a.m. till the bus leaves at about 4:30 p.m., six days a week. He is paid QR800 ($220) per month, a recent increase over his previous QR600 ($165) salary. G has worked in Doha since 2006. He is quite happy about the raise because he is the sole support for his wife, mother, and two school-age children back in Nepal. The school fees for his children are five thousand rupees a month ($46) and since he sends about half his paycheck home each month, he has little left to live on.

The company he works for, Al Mazor, is the contractor for the building's owners. The company is supposed to pay for a ticket home every two years but G has only been back home three times. He sees his family every three or four years. When he goes back to Nepal, it is for three months. His next scheduled visit home is coming up but he does not yet know if and when he will leave. Trips have been delayed before. His employer holds his passport.

G hopes that with an education, his children will not have to follow his path. He has hopes that someday his family could open a small food shop in his home. But he has no plans to return to Nepal permanently anytime soon. A sympathetic American couple gave him $10,000 to build a house near his children's school. One-third of that money went to pay bribes to get the construction materials to his village. He does not seem to have any savings either in Doha or back home.

Migrants: From Where We Sat

Neither Ann nor I grew up with servants. Working-class American families didn't have them. Every other Thursday, my family had a "colored lady," whose name was Mary, come to the house to clean. In preparation, Mom would do the dishes, take the sheets off the bed, and "straighten up." Not wanting to show a dirty house to a cleaning lady was part of her attitude toward her home as well as to "the help." There was always a separation between Them and Us but it wasn't much.

Ann was similar. When our youngest, Laura, was a couple of months old, Ann needed to go back to teaching at Sidwell Friends School, where she taught ninth grade biology. She hired Marisol as a combination nanny and housekeeper. Marisol was, as the phrase goes, fresh off the boat. She had just arrived from Peru, with questionable legal status, no driver's license, and no English. Ann, fluent in Spanish thanks to a youthful venture teaching in Mexico, chatted with Marisol and formed a bond. She stayed with our family for the next twenty years and became part of it. We sponsored her for citizenship and helped bring over other family members; our son Daniel stayed with her family in Peru during a year off between high school and college. During the Christmas holidays, we went with her to visit them. Marisol became an American success story with a house in the suburbs and with relatives she brought in owning their own business. She came to both of our kids' weddings, still gossips with Ann in Spanish, and cried with us when our Jack Russell terrier died.

Doha was very different. We professionals lived among a sea of working Asian men in a relaxed state of security. Many of these migrants seemed to be there to take care of supplying all the creature comforts that made our lives pleasant.

As a result, I went eight years without changing a lightbulb—you can ask my wife. We didn't have a full-time housekeeper but many did, with a tiny maid's room provided in each house. Live-in child care was available and, at no more than a few hundred dollars a month, dirt cheap. Why wash your car when there were so many smiling men offering to do it—and at around five dollars, why not let them have the money? Expats adapted. For most of us, migrants became another limb of the body to be used unthinkingly.

None of us ever got to the point of the Qatari teenagers who would pick up their robes at the cleaners by parking in front and honking their horn. An Indian boy about their age would come out, usually under a blazing sun, pick up their receipt and money, go back to the store, and then return with their clothes and change as they sat chatting in their air-conditioned SUVs. The Americans I knew could never quite master that boyish insouciance. It helped to start young if you wanted to get the most out of foreign servants.

In fact, many expats had somewhat guilty consciences about using the cheap labor available. Although the longer you stayed, the less you tended to talk about it. The professionals who had grown up with servants—expats from the Middle East and Asia—tended to be less bothered and arguably a bit sterner in their dealings. The rest of us made peace with residual troubled consciences, one way or another. Ann taught English classes for the guards and staff at the compound, and frequently gave them money for their children's school fees. A neighbor smuggled gold into Nepal for a worker who wanted to get his savings back home. For the rest, dinners at Christmas, American-size tips for services, free trips home for those with live-ins, and extra leftover food would have to do.

What low-income migrants thought of their situation remained a bit of a mystery. It was generally considered impolite to pry, given the realistic apprehension that any honest account might get the workers in trouble. There were iconic stories of workers' success. One Arab professor told of her Indian driver who had built a large terra-cotta house for his family in Kerala. After a dozen years in Doha, he had returned to start his own business and relax with the family he had worked to educate and elevate. In our travels in Nepal and India, after identifying ourselves as residents of Doha, we heard tales about locals who were also in the Gulf and whose families now lived with newly purchased TVs, stoves, and refrigerators.

Two recent academic surveys of low-income workers reported fairly high job satisfaction levels. In the first, conducted by Andrew

Gardner, 78 percent of workers said they were "satisfied" or "somewhat satisfied." In the second survey, conducted by Georgetown economics professor Ganesh Seshan, almost 70 percent reported being either satisfied or very satisfied with work and more than two-thirds said they were in good or very good health.

This was not how it looked to us. Admittedly, the Western expats and the Asian workers had different points of reference. We unfavorably compared their situation to our own nations' familiar comforts, which produced, as Mark Twain put it, "the ethics of a Christian holding four aces." These migrants had been dealt a different hand, which they thought they played well. Emerging from the grinding poverty of the teeming Asian subcontinent, their starting points differed from ours. Their beginnings lay in the strength of families for which they sacrificed years of separation. Their trajectory was rooted in the weakness of their own nations that offered them neither jobs nor security. The rest of us were observers, left to imagine the conditions that would compel individuals to leave their homes and culture, and journey thousands of miles to work for poverty-level wages in strenuous, unhealthy conditions.

Qataris, who didn't take criticism of their treatment of migrant workers well, pointed out that these workers were better off than in their own countries, which was why so many were eager to come. Fair enough. Of course, saying that the wealthiest country in the world treated people from the poorest countries in the world better than their homelands left a lot of room for mistreatment. For these were workers without any rights as citizens; forbidden from forming trade unions; subjected to the whims of their bosses; cut off from women, families, language, and culture; and rendered powerless by a citizenry indifferent to their welfare and frightened by their numbers. Theirs was a story that preceded Georgetown's arrival and on which the university hadn't had much impact.

The Workers in Time and Space

Though Qatar was an Arab state, the majority of its residents were from South Asia. With only 9 percent of the population

Qatar-born, the country had the highest proportion of immigrants in the world.

As recently as 1970, Qatar's total population stood at around 111,000. When we arrived in Doha in 2006, the number was around 800,000; eight years later, when we left, it had grown by an additional million. By the end of 2016, with the increased construction for the 2022 FIFA World Cup increasing the demand for laborers, 2.6 million people were living in Qatar; some 1.75 million were migrant workers.

In the 1960s and '70s, most foreign workers came from neighboring, non-oil-rich, Arab states. Then oil and gas exports took off, which encouraged the launching of an ambitious building program. Over the next thirty years, Asian workers replaced Arab foreign workers and migrant numbers rose dramatically. Asians were considered more tolerant of arduous working conditions. (One student pointed out that fellow Arab Muslims had more of a claim for equitable treatment than nonbelievers—curiously making them less-desirable employees.) Most migrants came from South Asia: India, Nepal, Pakistan, Sri Lanka, and Bangladesh. The Philippines seemed to be second to India in total numbers. One recent survey found that Nepalese were the most numerous of the low-income labor force.

The duration of a typical low-income migrant's stay was five and a half years, though some remained much longer. Although migrants became a permanent part of Qatar, almost all of them were temporary, looking forward to returning home. This was a good thing since naturalization was rare and had stringent requirements, including twenty-five years of continual residency and fluency in Arabic. (Unless you happened to be a professional soccer player or Olympic-class athlete, for whom easier standards applied.)

At the end of their contract, migrants were expected to return home. Only workers earning more than a certain minimum—around $23,000 annually—were permitted to bring their families with them. This effectively meant those with low incomes were single men, visiting wives and family every two or three years if allowed and paid for by their employer. Further, according to a 2010 law, these single male workers were not allowed to live in neighborhoods that had families in them.

A Georgetown economist drew a profile of a "median migrant male":

He is thirty-one, single, high school educated, and has been in Qatar for 1.4 years. He works ten hours a day, six days a week, earns $3,945 a year of which he sends more than half back home to parents or family. To get to Qatar, he had to pay a placement fee to an agent equal to 1.25 months of his salary. He is generally satisfied with his work, the amount of sleep he gets, and with his life some of the time, but "also felt a little nervous."

Domestic workers were probably the most challenging group to learn about. In public spaces, they were usually on the job; in private, they were inside a family's home. Earning an average of $430 a month, they were not protected by Qatar's labor laws. Hence there were few standards their contracts had to meet, including any requirement for a day off, set working hours, timely wage payments, annual leave, or medical treatment. And if there was a breach in the contract, which the maid or cook or driver or gardener probably couldn't read, the worker had few places to turn, as this letter from a maid (in broken English) shows:

I am a house maid here in Qatar with Palestinian family I work 6:00 a.m. until 10:00 p.m., I eat my meals for ten minutes [after] every meals. I don't have day off, and even I don't have privacy for my self because I sleep with the children's room . . .

When I was two-three months, I told them to [take me] back to my agency because I can't take all the pressure at work, especially when they shouted me. But they said they will put me unto jail, and also my agency that's what they said, they are the ones who put me to jail if I leave. I needs all your advice. Thank you very much.

Do I have a right to report them?

The Kafala System

Throughout the Arab Gulf, migrants were under the supervision of sponsors, a system called the kafala in Arabic. This mixture of law and custom put effective control over the foreign worker in the hands of a private citizen, a kafeel. It locked the worker into a particular job and made the sponsor responsible to the government for the migrant. Workers could not change jobs or even leave the country without the sponsor's permission. Labor unions were forbidden.

Actually, getting into the system wasn't easy for migrants. The employer, say a multinational construction company, would go to a recruitment agency, which turned to a subcontractor in Nepal or India. Although the employer paid the recruiter, the recruiter often charged the low-income worker for the costs of the visa, or plane tickets, or their own fees. So a visa for an Indian worker that cost the agency one hundred dollars would cost the worker five hundred dollars. Attempts to regulate this exploitation of workers have proven difficult, especially in the worker's country of origin. Although labor standards adopted by many large companies and government agencies proclaimed ethical recruitment and declared laborers shouldn't pay any of these costs, in practice the workers paid what they were told.

Most ended up owing around two months' wages for the right to work in Qatar for two years, the usual length of a labor contract. Some paid half or more of their annual salary. One scholar's survey put the average at $1,031 paid to labor brokers in their home country. Other migrants found employment by using an informal network of family and friends already working in Qatar. In any case, getting to Qatar required cash from loans or family savings, putting most migrants in substantial debt when they arrived.

Almost all low-income migrants wired money home regularly. Typically, the first monies sent back were used to pay off the debts caused by getting to the Gulf in the first place. Professor Ganesh Seshan estimated yearly remittances of about $2,400, which was at least 50 percent of a migrant's income. Most of these funds went to parents, with spouses being the second-most-likely recipients.

This money was used for educating children or for family savings. Whether any of this money remained when the worker eventually returned home was the subject of ongoing scholarly debate.

The kafala system has been widely criticized. The flaws come from the minimal oversight of employers and their workers' lack of power and information. One example was the illegal practice, common among employers, of holding workers' passports while they were in Qatar. Some 90 percent of workers surveyed made this complaint. Employers saw this as a way of keeping their workers from fleeing the country and their jobs. Some migrants preferred that their employers keep their passports because they lacked a secure place to store them in the labor camps. Either way, the high number of migrants without passports testified to the poor enforcement of the law.

Other common complaints included not being paid on time, reported by one-fifth of migrants. Then there was "job switching," promising migrants one job when they signed a contract in their home country, only to put them to work in another when they arrived in Doha—at a lesser salary than the one promised. With no right to seek another job, without a passport and visa, and with the kafala system binding them to their sponsor, foreign workers had limited choices in seeking redress. The dramatically unequal power between workers and their sponsors underlay the inequities.

The poor treatment of foreign workers has not gone unnoticed. A number of Qatari government agencies oversaw the migrants' presence in the country. The Ministry of Labor had some three hundred inspectors investigating labor conditions. Within the Ministry, a national committee was dedicated to addressing workers' health, safety, and rights protection in collaboration with the International Labor Organization. The Qatar National Human Rights Committee aimed to demonstrate Qatar's commitment to rights for all its citizens by investigating complaints by foreign workers. Qatar Foundation launched a "Migrant Workers Welfare Charter" setting standards for the treatment of migrants and a benchmark of best practices.

The Qatar 2022 Supreme Committee, with oversight for Qatar's World Cup games, publicly committed itself to the safety, health, and dignity of all workers engaged in the $100 billion worth of construction projects. Winning the World Cup bidding process in December 2010 turned the international spotlight on Qatar and its treatment of the increasing numbers of workers recruited to prepare for the games. Despite the government's public deference to international standards and pressures, implementation remained in the hands of private businesses that had the usual economic incentives to maintain their substandard practices.

Migration of large numbers of workers was both necessary and potentially dangerous to Qatar's state and culture. The additional scrutiny from overseas had led to some publicized reforms and considerable expansion in available housing but no real change in the tight controls and impoverished conditions of the labor force. The power of employer-sponsors, the restrictions on migrants' mobility, and the potential for abuse in working conditions, stayed untouched.

On December 12, 2016, Law 21 of 2015 went into effect, declaring the end of the kafala system. The phrase "sponsorship" had been removed but as a number of human rights groups noted, the underlying system remained in place. Although the government could grant exit permits for migrants, foreign workers still needed to ask their employers for permission to leave the country. It was easier for some people to switch jobs but the need for a "no objection certificate" from an employer had not been abolished. There was a penalty for employers who held employees' passports but it was okay to hold them if the employee granted his written permission—an easily exploitable loophole. Amnesty International called on Qatar to abolish exit permits, free workers from requiring their employers' permission to change jobs, and completely ban passport confiscation. Late in 2016, a government minister urged the international community to withhold final conclusions until there had been time to see the new law in action.

Georgetown Involvement

An Egyptian graduate of GU-Q recalled her surprise at the treatment of migrant workers in Doha. Despite growing up with servants, she found the situation in the Gulf much different. "In Doha, the separation between people was something I never experienced in other cities like Istanbul and Cairo," she recounted several years after leaving the city. "People don't speak the same language with the workers who serve them or share a common background. You don't have the easy banter I had with my cook and gardener when I was growing up. And because the workers in Doha don't have their family network, they suffer a poverty that is much worse from poor people elsewhere in the Middle East. The city is profoundly fractured, much more than other places I've lived."

Georgetown actually employed only a few of the dozens of workers (called "blue boys" for their uniforms) seen in the halls of the university. Under their contract, Qatar Foundation was responsible for hiring one hundred-odd cleaners, security guards, and food service staff. Some twenty low-wage laborers were direct hires by the university, including drivers, travel staff, and mail room workers. These employees worked for contractors who were held to standards—such as offering a paid trip home every year—by either Qatar Foundation or Georgetown. These contractors, in the words of a Georgetown report, "demonstrate little commitment to implementing these standards."

"They don't care," was how one Georgetown administrator who worked with Qatar Foundation described the Foundation's attitude toward migrant laborers. Two years earlier, the Foundation had issued a migrant workers' charter with a host of protections and rights along with a hotline for workers to use to protest violations. In addition, Georgetown had signed a service level agreement covering workers at the university. The problem, according to a staffer who worked on the issue, was that the Foundation didn't live up to provisions including wages, paid sick leave, medical care, and improved treatment of workers. Efforts at third-party audits of workers' contracts went nowhere. As for the workers' general welfare, this staffer concluded: "They [the Foundation] pay lip service."

The university was not exactly an innocent bystander when it came to the working conditions of its workers. The truth was that these workers would be too expensive for Georgetown to hire directly with the same benefits as its own staff. Claire Wait, the Director of Facilities Management, pointed out that Georgetown's cheapest employee with benefits cost the university $70,000 a year. For that price, the university could use a local contractor to hire six employees. Outsourcing was not only cheaper; it was necessary for the university to operate in Qatar, as one top Georgetown administrator admitted. Cheap labor allowed Georgetown to deliver classes, pay the staff, pocket its management fee, and maintain the viability of its educational enterprise.

This didn't mean Georgetown administrators were comfortable with the labor system they inherited or that they didn't try to moderate its most appalling aspects. Efforts were made by various deans to adopt the migrant workers' charter throughout Education City and to improve workers' lives. Migrant labor also offered an important lesson for students trying to live up to the Jesuit value of "men and women for others."

A concern for migrant worker safety was most visible in the construction of the Georgetown building in Doha. Prior to the start of construction, both of the Education City buildings built by the same architect who built Georgetown's had fatal accidents onsite. Dean Reardon-Anderson took the lead in pushing for worker safety on the building site. According to the dean, he told Qatar Foundation, "If we're going to build a building with Georgetown's name on it, we're not going to have dangerous activities." A labor safety committee conducted regular onsite safety checks; educated construction workers on safety; and rewarded them for maintaining healthy work conditions. Ms. Wait reported that of the eight million man-hours involved in construction on the Georgetown building, there were no serious injuries—a record for safety unmatched in Education City.

Student Social Action

Visitors arriving at Georgetown's orientation at the beginning of any recent fall semesters might have witnessed a rather unusual event. Sitting on the floor in the central dining area were most of the freshman class. They were eating a meal with cleaners, guards, and dining workers. The students had prepared the food and served it to the workers. Student Affairs sponsored the event to remind students that their education depended on the work of people who were invisible to them.

Some surprising conversations were overheard at one recent orientation dinner. One student was taken aback to hear a cleaner, Anthony, speak to him in fluent English about the need to study hard and take advantage of the resources available to him—lessons that were much less effective when delivered, as expected, by their deans. Several Qatari students afterward volunteered to tutor workers in Arabic.

In 2007, a Student Affairs staffer, Molly Logue, working with women students from the class of 2009, began the Hoya English Language Program (HELP). Its aim was to enlist students to teach English to security guards, cleaners, and other workers. The student response was enthusiastic and a loosely structured program of classes began. Broken down according to the workers' levels of English, classes were held twice a week with certificates for achievement given at the semester's end.

At a special-awards dinner, the certificates were handed out to students and workers. The dinner in spring 2013 underlined the idealism and innocence of the effort. Part of the rationale for the classes was to encourage migrants to feel they were part of the community, as well as engaging students with these workers' lives. But the memory that lingers from the hour-long dinner and awards was the awkwardness of the evening. Georgetown students and staff sat at their own tables while workers sat at other tables. Besides the awards—which the workers came to the stage to accept, a few with tears—there was little interaction between the groups. All the assembled seemed pleased with their achievements but there was little sense that new relationships or understandings had been formed across steep class and cultural divisions.

There was a debate over how much these classes accomplished by teaching English for two hours a week, especially given that many of these workers were barely literate in their own language. In 2011, the program was revamped and tightened, with the name changed to Hoya Empowerment and Learning Program (still HELP). Teaching expanded to include financial literacy and computers. In response to Qatari students' interest, Arabic programs were added. Part of the effort aimed to build workers' self-esteem and pride. As they began to trust their teachers, migrants began to share their concerns. The hope, as one organizer put it, was "to set the stage for a concerted effort to advocate and fight for them and their rights."

And those teaching these workers were affected by their experience. Ann, who taught in the program, spoke to me later about it: "My class was cleaners, mostly Nepalese. We tried to teach them phrases they could use at work—like the words for cleaning materials such as 'mop' and 'bucket'—and, 'Where's the bathroom?'"

She also gained insights from the workers themselves: "They told me how they were taken advantage of by their contractors. They had to work weekends at places other than Georgetown and for no extra pay. They were afraid to complain and had no one to complain to. And they worried about losing their jobs, because they said people in their home countries were in line to take these jobs."

My wife also recalled the warmth and appreciation shown her. "At the end of each class, I stood at the door, thanked them, and shook their hands. I found them shy but grateful for what we were doing. The English classes gave many of them the confidence to speak up in class, to smile, to greet me in the halls, and to hug me at their award ceremony."

Going beyond HELP were a couple of innovative programs. One, called Labour Equations, aimed to confront students with the living conditions of Qatar's foreign laborers. Activities included photo expeditions to migrant camps, interviews of workers, film screenings, and discussions. These were later broadened to include student trips to the Philippines and the United States to study migration. The effort was led by Uday Rosario in the Office of Student Development. Pushing the edge of activism further, the Human Rights Club worked on repatriating Nepalese workers who had been stranded in Qatar after conflicts with their employers.

This student activism came in for criticism. Phone calls, thought to be from the security or interior agencies of government, asked the students to stop or face the consequences. Since most were on scholarships from that same government, many decided to limit their involvement. Some faculty members were upset with the efforts for migrants. One Arab teacher warned organizers "not to bite the hand that feeds you."

But it was just this hands-on education that Georgetown's administrators—including Dean Reardon-Anderson and Brendon Hill—were most enthusiastic about. It brought students to the migrant camps that some of them denied even existed in Doha. One student recalled going out to the camps over several weekends with Rosario to document workers' lives and understand their perspective on the challenges they faced. He praised Rosario, a tall, ponytailed Indian, for getting students to humanize and respect the people they were examining: "Uday constantly pushed me to excel and work hard at achieving my dream of improving conditions of migrant workers in the country, as ridiculous as the notion was to a freshman in college."

Professor Ganesh Seshan was encouraged by this attention to workers to undertake a study called the Qatar Migrant Family Survey. Ganesh, an Indian convert to Islam who had previously worked at the World Bank, sought ways to promote financial literacy among migrant workers. Using students, the professor set up a study that found that even a single workshop focused on budgeting and savings succeeded in motivating migrant workers to save more and involve their spouses back home in money decisions. Later videos and curricula were produced to educate workers on their finances. But when Seshan left the university in the summer of 2016—his unorthodox projects hadn't helped his quest for a long-term contract with the university—no one picked up the project of distributing these videos to workers.

A former Georgetown student, Ashok, who worked with Seshan, remembered a construction worker telling him that after attending a class on financial planning, he quit smoking because he realized its impact on his savings. Ashok went on to talk about how these experiences with workers had changed his career choices. Born in Doha to parents from Kerala, he had been hired for the survey because he knew Hindi. The project gave him a chance to earn a bit of income for college; his task was to learn about migrants' income, expenses, living conditions, and education. To do this, he interviewed workers, waiters, taxi drivers, and clerks at the malls and stores where they gathered. He listened and learned.

Ashok, a serious young man with an intense look that came through his rimless glasses, was now a graduate student studying public policy abroad. He had remained close to his family and worried about their future in Doha. He had also retained his interest in international migrant labor, perhaps because of his research with Professor Seshan: "It was a powerful experience for a young aspiring student at Georgetown, as I met people who were three times my age sharing with me how difficult life had been in Qatar." He smiled but not with a happy look, recalling one immigrant from nine years ago:

"I distinctly remember a clerk named Ahmed at a store who used to be a professor at a university in Egypt, who was swindled out of most of his life savings by a recruitment agent. He was promised a high-paying job in Doha but upon arrival here he learnt that he was duped.

"He had no option but to look for other work and was able to secure this job in a perfumery in a major mall in Doha, where he works long hours and waits to return back to Cairo. He was just biding his time in Doha before he makes enough money to return home. Unfortunately, instances such as this are not unique and many others had also reported such instances of exploitation."

I shifted the discussion slightly to the impact these research encounters had on him as an eighteen-year-old. He paused before answering. "When the surveys were completed, I was left with a need to learn more about why this was happening, and what could be done about it. . . . Georgetown certainly gave me the environment to thrive, and not just understand the causes of social issues but also the confidence in believing I could do something about it."

To the Future

My wife is crying. Who is responsible for this? Are the government? Or this company? . . . This money we want is not for our pleasure, it's to pay back debts. Why can they not understand this?—Worker with Krantz Engineering, *The Dark Side of Migration*

The siting of the 2022 World Cup in Qatar initiated a huge building program estimated at upwards of $100 billion. (In contrast, South Africa spent $2.7 billion for its 2010 World Cup and Brazil an estimated $14 billion in 2014.) The resulting influx of low-income workers pushed the government to improve their conditions of work and living. This was most apparent in the large construction projects undertaken to house workers. In new compounds, invariably shown to visiting foreign delegations interested in workers' welfare, laborers lived two or three to a room with shared kitchens, game rooms, and swimming pools, as well as entertainment and shops nearby. Large employers such as Qatar Rail and Maersk helped build these modern showcases. Not so visible were the smaller contractors and numerous laborers still living in drab dormitories in the Industrial Area.

The adoption of international standards for workers' living and working conditions also accelerated. Large companies have followed Qatar Foundation's lead in adopting the Worker's Charter, and put the best face on their treatment of workers. Workers' medical care stayed hit-or-miss. Many employees still didn't have the Hamad Medical Card that enabled residents to gain access to health-care services. This forced them to the emergency care departments of hospitals for any medical problems. Much as in America, actually.

Georgetown generally acted as an enlightened employer for its low-income migrant labor. It followed international standards for workers, insisted on safe conditions in the construction of its new building, and advocated Qatar-wide protections for them from abuse by contractors. In a recent survey of workers at Georgetown, the university came off as a good recruiter, informing migrants of their rights and intervening on their behalf with the companies that directly employed them. Professors researched the recruitment and treatment of these workers, set up financial workshops, and elevated the subject of international migration to a topic worthy of academic discussion. Student groups joined in by teaching laborers English and other subjects; a few of them went further by investigating and writing about the living conditions and exploitation of these workers.

So Georgetown is "off the hook," at least in a public relations sense, in its posture toward low-income workers. But whether its actions for impoverished people—individuals with whom it coexisted and on whom it depended—lived up to its liberal, religious, and educational principles, was another question. And whether its activities materially changed the depressing conditions of service that these workers faced in one of the world's wealthiest countries, raised another set of challenges.

A fair answer was that issues of migrant labor were not considered a priority in what the university was doing in Qatar. In administrators' eyes, they were making a strategic and worthwhile choice to preserve the institution's viability on these foreign shores. For academics, migrant issues brought up the issue of "value compatibility" between a liberal university and the often-medieval conditions that surrounded it—what one student bluntly called "living a lie." More realistically, Qatar's treatment of its migrant workers confronted Georgetown with a "reputational risk."

As an elite institution being amply compensated to deliver higher education in a region where it was needed while enhancing its global brand with scholarly research, Georgetown was probably living up to expectations. But the university had the intellectual resources that could make a difference in the lives of people who served it. These laborers—living at the margins, separated from their culture and families—didn't have the capacity, organization, or resources to change their life conditions. Georgetown could help. It could

211

encourage changes, not only as a privileged employer promoting standards for their treatment but also as a source of intellectual firepower, an academy of progress for the world around it.

The focus could be on the workers directly and on the groups trying to aid them. Instead of individual professors researching the laborers' challenges, the university could consider improving workers' lives a goal in itself. Georgetown could initiate a study to determine how workers could improve their lives. It could promote projects for faculty, staff, and students to formulate solutions to the grinding poverty, family separations, powerlessness, and exploitation these laborers faced. These intellectual resources could be centralized and mobilized for social concerns usually only raised in commencement speeches.

Given these workers' poverty and isolation, the university could offer forums to bring together individuals who were weak and divided but who collectively could have a powerful voice. If the goal were to empower workers and their families, then using information online could help.

Allowing workers or labor representatives in the Gulf to communicate with workers back home would give prospective migrants the tools they needed to understand the reality they were entering; it could elevate their ability to negotiate their contracts fairly. They needed help finding out what visas cost; what housing actually looked like; what savings programs were available; who the good employers were; which recruiting agencies could be trusted; and how to talk candidly with experienced workers from their own country. Using the university's communications facilities and resources, websites could be set up to post relevant information for reaching laborers before and after they arrived in Qatar. This could be labeled public education.

Social media could help workers act for themselves rather than waiting for institutions to establish standards that might or might not be honored in practice. Correcting the misinformation that confused many workers would help them make better decisions for themselves and their family. Georgetown would stand not only as an employer but also as an intellectual resource for people with difficulties participating in and benefiting from a global marketplace. It could offer its scholars' expertise via consultations with international companies that wanted to improve their workers' conditions. Georgetown had the capability and the standing to undertake these activities. Whether it was willing to take the initiative depended on the choices made within the academic community, by its leaders and members.

*

An example of such progressivism made headlines on September 1, 2016, when Georgetown's President DeGioia issued an apology to descendants of slaves who had labored constructing university buildings in Washington and were sold in 1838 to repay the school's debts. He also promised preferential status in admissions to their offspring. Georgetown was the first American university not only to recognize its ties to slavery but also offer compensation to descendants.

Hopefully, the migrant workers who benefit Georgetown in Qatar will not have to wait 180 years for the university to recognize the moral issues involved in the use of their labor.

CHAPTER 11

Does American Liberal Education
Have a Future Abroad?

In spring 2014, my contract was up and I was saying good-bye to Doha and to teaching at Georgetown. Prior to departing, I gave an informal talk in the faculty lounge and later presented an academic talk on the meaning and future of liberal education in Doha.

In the earlier talk, I looked around the crowded lounge and thanked the audience, noting I hadn't realized so many people would be so glad to see me leave. However, unlike at funerals, at retirement the body got to talk.

I acknowledged I had gone from being selected as Outstanding Faculty Member three years earlier to being voted Most Sarcastic Teacher at that year's Diplomatic Ball. The direction of my classroom performance was, alas, clear.

I apologized to my faculty neighbors who were subjected to the American country music sounds of Merle Haggard, Willie Nelson, Don Williams, and Allison Krauss that I insisted on listening to on Pandora with my door open.

I went on to recount, with similar sarcasm, how the last eight years in Doha had changed me.

Whereas once, as a sixties radical, I had dismissed limousine liberals, I recognized that I had become one. I now appreciated monarchs who were reasonable, stable, and paid on time. I now eagerly embraced conspicuous consumption. Although I never did much

214

around the house—you could ask my wife—now, thanks to the abundance of servants, I did nothing.

I no longer needed a free press. The local papers were fine with me. Why contaminate your mind with real news when you could read about cannibalism in Pakistan, witchcraft in Yemen, or crucifixions in the Philippines?

I liked the Qataris, so much in fact that I had begun to drive like them. I never stayed in lanes, accelerated into roundabouts, and viewed pedestrian sidewalks as just an unused lane for traffic. I accepted that bigger, more expensive vehicles *always* had the right of way. I mocked seat belts.

Wrapping up the talk, I took cheap shots at Arab colleagues' accents, the dean's tendencies to go on and on in his faculty talks, and a Lebanese colleague's eagerness to ascribe global warming to Israeli actions. I concluded by expressing my pride in the work we had done as well as respect for my coworkers and friends.

In my longer talk, I tried to determine what narrative best explained the motives, impact, and likely future of our academic transplant. How narrow or broad would be the consequences of this educational transfer from America to Qatar? What significance did this experiment hold for other universities? Would it last here? Could it be copied elsewhere?

Although the discussion came out of my experience at Georgetown's School of Foreign Service in this Gulf state emirate, the broader questions spoke to the role and future of American higher education abroad. Specifically, I wanted to address the issues behind this Arab outreach, how universities like Georgetown operated in foreign arenas, and what lay ahead for these overseas transplants.

To do so, I drew on my political science background to illustrate five models explaining the Georgetown experience, hinting at plausible future directions for Georgetown and other universities. With luck, they provided an impetus for further tinkering with this still-novel experiment.

215

1. *Extension of an American World Order:* The biggest of the Big Pictures involved geopolitical power. In this model, American universities were an extension of the world's sole superpower. Qatar had two American air bases and seven American universities. The bases supplied security via soldiers, weapons, and training. The schools provided education and skills via teachers and the infrastructure of a university. Arguably, in its role as the latter-day Rome of the civilized world, America was providing the world's best of both for its wealthy, strategically located ally.

The bases and the universities underlined American dominance and Qatari vulnerability. The bases, built and paid for by the Qataris, offered the hosts defensible borders that they couldn't secure themselves against larger, threatening neighbors: Saudi Arabia and Iran. Americans got forward positioning of troops and supplies as well as a communications command center for conducting military actions in the region. The bases allowed the Doha regime flexibility in its regional politics without endangering the physical security of this small state. The university educated its own youth—and the region's elite youth—at a level that allowed the students to earn international recognition and access to the globalized world of NGOs and corporations. It enhanced the Qatari brand and promised the country a step toward a "knowledge economy" not quite as dependent on expatriate professionals as it now was.

For America, the educational expansion was as much a sign of its preeminence as the spread of its military. American influence was enhanced by both. What international relations students called the "soft power" of ideas was encapsulated in these academic institutions, just as much as the "hard power" of economic ties and military weapons reflected America's pervasive global reach. Soft power shaped the preferences of others by introducing common values into the mix of relations between states. Soft power had the added benefit of shaping graduates with shared outlooks, similar approaches to organizing the world, and networks of personal relations enhancing future careers. Education provided an intellectual compatibility that in the long term could knit different cultures together. The product (education) and customers (students and host government) in this transaction underlined both sides' firm support for the liberal world order.

Although easy enough to denounce as imperialism, this was hardly an asymmetric, oppressive relationship. A degree of peace, prosperity, and stability accompanied the American presence in this part of the world, and the leaders of the Arab Gulf states publicly acknowledged the advantages that came with these ties. Post-9/11 America was acutely sensitive to the need to influence the political direction of the youth of this region. Indeed, the loudest complaints of late have come from leaders in the region alarmed at the Obama and Trump administrations' tendency to denounce past interventions and reduce present American involvement. The region still leaned toward acceptance of American weapons and education, at least until either were applied in practice.

One objection to this model was that universities were an inadequate instrument for achieving American foreign policy goals. The academics sent abroad to spread the Pax Americana gospel were most likely to be liberal scribblers busily dissenting from the past, current, or future spread of US influence. Many of the scholars who dominated the study of history, politics, media, regional studies, and literature had spent their careers critiquing if not denouncing the American imperium and its policies. As vehicles of American foreign policy, my colleagues—assuming they had any impact at all—were seldom helpful. Their progressive sympathies were usually such that they emphasized the shortcomings, hypocrisies, and victims of America's international outreach—of which there were plenty.

On the receiving side of the imperial venture, the Qatari hosts were something other than a passive, colonized group. The Qatari leadership initiated this educational relationship and paid considerable sums to maintain it. As was made clear whenever some clueless Georgetown staffer wanted to decorate the walls of the new Doha building, this expensive structure was owned by the locals and was only on loan to their American guests. They freely—and as we saw, shrewdly—negotiated a detailed contract setting forth the terms of the deal. They neither stumbled into this liaison nor were compelled to enter it. However deferential they might be in their overall relations with the American government, with Georgetown the Qataris were affluent clients, striving to satisfy their own goals and interests. And in the international marketplace in which this educational boutique filled a personalized niche, the wealthy customer was usually right and often had the last word.

2. *The Expatriate Hire*: A second framework for understanding Georgetown's involvement in Qatar was the "micro" opposite of the "macro" global extension of American power. In this perspective, the university was simply another expatriate organization practicing its craft for this resource-rich host. In this model, there was no need to inflate the goals of the parties. The foreign institution functioned as well-compensated, globally approved hired help. It subcontracted educational professionals who were brought in to do a job—to provide a service unavailable locally. Foreign faculty, administrators, and staff, and the institution they operated under, were at best prestige imports, a Western brand resembling Prada or BMW with benefits to Qatar similar to what these more easily consumed upscale goods promised.

Education City provided an imported learning experience, keeping the region's students and the money they would have spent abroad at home. Ironically, this infrastructure spending was designed to *avoid* university education overseas. Part of the reason Georgetown and the other schools were invited to Qatar was to keep young Qataris, especially the family-treasured females, from being devalued by American college life. Western education was fine and held in high esteem. Sex, drugs, and rock 'n' roll was out of bounds for those raised in Wahhabi traditions.

Home delivery of higher education offered the promise of separating the positives of American classrooms from the negatives of American culture.

More concretely, these educational professionals delivered a credential that raised the market value of Qatari sons and daughters for careers, marriage, or just family bragging rights. And like other expatriates, they offered the prospect, however distant, of transferring skills that increased the viability of the domestic economy. Qataris hoped to someday assume management of the new, improved, and expanded society largely created by the professionals who had trained them. Perhaps they dreamed of expropriating the universities themselves and establishing a world-class, Qatari-run university. This remained a distant prospect.

This model required allowing the imported intellectuals to practice their craft unhindered. Other global technicians were hired to discover natural gas wherever they thought best to look; these intellectuals were licensed to teach and practice their craft in an open, tolerant academic setting. Arguably, educating students was not as important as producing liquefied natural gas but then it was not compensated as well either.

While this "expats for hire" model played down the impact of foreign academics on distant lands, it might also be inadequate. Those individuals occupying positions at universities were aware that they had not been invited just to fix something. Expat academics were not extracting a natural resource, constructing office towers, or delivering imports to be left behind. Those committing higher education were not just practicing their skills; they were transferring them as well. The aim was to change behavior.

By some lights, universities might be just another prestige consumer product but that's not how faculty saw it nor what their customers thought they were getting. Parents didn't send their kids to college merely to hang a degree on their walls. They expected growth and transformation in their precious young legacies who took their families' hopes into the future. University

education represented, in some form, global modernization—
and a promise of fitting into that changing world.

3. *Contract for a Foreign Service School*: Juxtaposed between these
   two opposing poles was the "professional contract" paradigm
   that focused attention on the agreement Georgetown signed to
   deliver a school for training diplomats. The School of Foreign
   Service in Washington was obligated to transfer an identical curriculum to train future bureaucrats from Qatar and the
   region in language, culture, history, etc. Graduates, after gaining
   this needed expertise, were expected to fill positions mostly in
   government. Qatar's aim was to improve the quality of ministries widely considered somewhat ineffective and inconsistent
   in implementing public policies. Georgetown's goals included
   reaping financial benefits, universalizing its brand, and expanding public affairs education overseas.

   This model matched the type of skills that the other schools
   in Qatar's Education City—the largest enclave of American universities overseas—were contracted to deliver. It also illustrated
   the perceived professional gaps that Qatar's leaders were trying to
   fill in their economy. For engineers, there was Texas A&M; com-
   puter/business professionals were produced at Carnegie Mellon.
   Virginia Commonwealth University trained art and fashion
   designers; Cornell's medical school combined premed and professional training for doctors; and Northwestern supplied journalism and communications experts. There was an aspiration,
   so far unrealized, to combine these professional segments under
   an overall education infrastructure, called Hamad bin Khalifa
   University, with designs of becoming a well-regarded regional
   center for higher learning. But for now, these six American universities offered targeted, mainly undergraduate degrees to fulfill
   Qatar's specific needs in a globalizing world. Educational goals
   aimed at producing professionals.

   There was an objection to this model: out of a couple hundred graduates in Georgetown's dozen or so years on the ground,

only a handful had ended up as Qatari diplomats. If the benefits were limited to this particular result, the costs were clearly exorbitant. Offering limited courses of training to current employees of targeted ministries would be a lot more effective. The results would be more visible and easier to measure for their impact on actual careerists.

In addition, very few of the faculty or students saw what they were doing as professional training. Most of the faculty was generally neither experienced in international diplomacy nor very concerned with teaching it. Their goals in teaching were far more encompassing and far less professional. They were more likely to embrace a mission of shaping liberal-minded, worldly individuals or proselytizing for their own discipline rather than filling slots in the bureaucracy. Nor did most of the students aspire to a career in Qatar government service—most looked to international public agencies, multinational corporations, and nonprofit organizations in which to apply their skills.

The professional goals of these undergraduate students were not that different from those at any other small, liberal arts American college ("ah dunno" being the most common response when students were asked about their future career). The implication was that, whatever the terms of Georgetown's contract bringing the school to Qatar or the official justification, it was masquerading as a professional school; and the same could be said about the Washington campus. In fact, the School of Foreign Service was as close to a liberal arts college as Qatar's Education City allowed. The nearest it came to promoting career goals was through a vague aim to populate the globalized world with critical-thinking professionals.

4. *Expanding Liberalism*: This led into what really got scholars' juices flowing. Justifying the university's residence in Doha was the not-very-disguised secular humanism that academics were accused of spreading: free and open scholarship in an unhindered search for truth. Underlying this process was the tolerance for individuals'

freedom of thought and expression. American universities, Georgetown among them, embraced the wide diversity of a global marketplace of ideas: "freedom for the thoughts we hate."

Maximum personal freedom for academic intellectuals inevitably meant the same for those groups who faced oppression for their gender, nationality, race, religion, sexual choices, or political beliefs. This tolerance of diversity was part of the liberal commitment to an open pursuit of the truth. It was the universal humanitarian objective for a liberal education in a flattening twenty-first-century world. Scratch a liberal and you'll find a missionary.

My colleagues were not being hypocritical when they declared: "I want to teach my students to think for themselves." Most thought that is what they were doing and they hoped it would lead to agreeable social consequences. Their lessons encompassed Western civilization's "great ideas," from Plato to NATO. They embodied the values of the scholarly life: the joys of research, the discipline of analysis, the satisfaction of reaching evidence-based conclusions.

To some extent, this focus on process—on building intellectual muscle and the rigor of mastering a discipline—was fair and accurate. But only to a point. No one expected young minds under their care to come to illiberal conclusions about racism, sexism, tribalism, religious intolerance, etc. To be honest with ourselves, we had come abroad to eviscerate these biases, certainly not to reinforce them. Faculty expected humanitarian results from their teaching. These students were not just learning about research procedures and methods of analysis. Substantive attitudes, liberal values, and supportive social behavior were expected as well. And faculty arrived with the hope that this next generation would apply liberalism in a lifetime of benevolent relations with women, minorities, and dissenters—not to mention with each other.

Most of those teaching abroad hoped that is what would result from their endeavors. Although not completely wrong, it was also not the whole story.

222

"Toto, I've a feeling we're not in Kansas anymore." Dorothy's iconic remark in *The Wizard of Oz* summed up the limits to this model when applied in the Middle East. Higher education's American transplants were not taking root in nurturing, liberal soil. The Arab Gulf states were not places that elevated individuals and guarded their rights. Where there were formally declared freedoms of speech, press, or religion, they were only grudgingly and inconsistently tolerated, often in deference to the wishes of small, governing elites. Societies throughout Asia and Africa placed the importance of family, religion, tribe, and nation far above the individual. Dissent that questioned dominant values and behavior had to pass through high barriers in societies where traditional norms and social stability had far greater weight than individual freedom.

Nor was it accidental that many transplanted liberal universities emerged in states run by autocratic governing elites: Dubai, Abu Dhabi, Singapore, and China. The traditional societies surrounding these autocracies were neither very liberal nor very tolerant of foreign approaches to a host of social issues: gender roles, religious nonconformity, political dissent, artistic freedom, liberal expression. It was a curious dilemma: if progressive ideas (e.g., public participation, universal suffrage, and freedom of speech) were implemented in these societies, the foreign universities—which mainly served the privileged offspring of leadership groups—might find themselves unwelcome. Indeed, populist programs for the general welfare would be elevated in the budget. It might be just as well that importing American higher education had never been put to a vote in the Arab Gulf states. As a dean at our school said, "The first thing a democratic government in Qatar would do is get rid of Georgetown."

The dearth of social and political mixing between foreign universities and Qatari society reinforced the point. Many faculty and administrators spent years in Qatar without being invited into a Qatari home. One newly arrived British scholar marveled at the contrast with his last overseas post in Pakistan where a foreign professor "had to be a sociopath not to be invited out to dinner four times a week." A common practice among American and European professors of public policy—consulting their counterparts in government departments—was totally lacking in Qatar. Community involvement in night classes had only recently been given a tentative trial by Georgetown. Sponsoring speakers at broad public forums had fallen off in recent years. As with other outsiders in this conservative Arab society, faculty were kept separate and walled off.

This segregation didn't have much to do with local hospitality and warmth shown to strangers, which Qataris invariably exhibited in social encounters (except for those on the highway). More to the point was the primacy of the ties students and their parents had with their communities of origin and how education at a foreign university complemented and reinforced those ties. As one of my colleagues, Josh Mitchell, observed in his insightful *Tocqueville in Arabia*, students from this region possessed an intense loyalty and obligation to their families, far greater than that found on American campuses. Students from the region differed from the ambitious careerists populating America's top colleges, Josh thought. That elite's laser focus on the individual was alien to societies where family, community, and religion were more highly valued.

When students in Doha emerged from the university, many of them—likely most—would return to the enveloping ties of faith, family, and custom. Many adopted a pose of integrating into global outlooks and identities. But this would largely be through "talking the talk"—speaking the language of liberalism they learned regarding gender diversity, religious tolerance, and progressive politics. But the actual roles they filled and the identities they found comfort in, "walking the walk"—social, tribal, and familial—would be the inherited ones with which they had arrived on campus. Although liberalism had facilitated the individual's liberation from these traditional identities, the goal of higher education for the traditional society—the Qatari client's constituency—was to protect these collective roles, not supplant them.

This conflict remained unresolved. It surfaced most clearly in the dilemmas facing women graduates as they tried to reconcile family roles and career goals. This was illustrated by the young Qatari woman, a former student, who came to my office to request a recommendation for graduate school in London. She wanted it not for a particular course of study but as a way to resist her parents' pressure to get married.

These were very different expectations placed on the same course of education: individual advancement versus the fulfillment of traditional group roles. The liberal educational model did not offer a ready reconciliation between these diverging choices. Studying the great works of Western civilization did not provide much guidance for graduates faced with resolving the dilemmas of career, marriage, and lifestyle. Finding work and a mate in cities far outside the Gulf was one route toward reconciling the conflict. Ironically, the elevated trust in teachers rendered by traditional societies led to a somewhat schizophrenic experience at school, honoring the very sages who promoted critical thinking about the societies that hosted and esteemed them. Teachers inadvertently acted as travel agents promoting alternative lifestyles in urban centers abroad.

5. *A Muddled Bubble*: The final model transcends the previous four paradigms. I call it a "muddled bubble." Caught between changing worlds, the school was forced to carve out an uncomfortable, potentially innovative space for itself. This structure was still being built without clear precedents. Georgetown in Qatar was an ongoing experiment situated at an intersection among evolving cultures. Like a bubble, it had both boundaries and autonomy; it was muddled with regard to the clash of cultures and civilizations along with all the confusion this entailed.

"Bubble" also referred to the school's need to be separated and protected from its US host institution and the territory in which it sat. Although the school began by imitating the institution that birthed it, this was a tentative stage. The aim was to reproduce what had been accomplished in Washington, guided by familiar history, people, and interests. This was consistent with Georgetown's contractual agreement with Qatar and both sides' expectations. It was reinforced by the initial leadership, drawn from the main campus rather than hired from outside. The first dean in Doha, China scholar Jim Reardon-Anderson, had served as an administrator at the Washington school, while his two successors, Mehran Kamrava and Gerd Nonneman, were both newly hired in Doha. The latter two also had Middle East credentials and regional experience. When Reardon-Anderson returned as dean in 2016, this was a step back to the tried-and-true but seen as an interim appointment by all concerned. The School's ever-binding ties to the region were seen in the appointment of a new dean on September 1, 2017. Ahmad S. Dallal, who came from Georgetown's Department of Arabic and Islamic Studies, had served as the provost of American University of Beirut.

The problem was that too much dependence on the metropole didn't allow an evolution to occur on the ground. This transferred institution of higher learning needed space to adapt and learn. This was also reflected in a faculty that increasingly took on the characteristics of the host country: fewer old white guys from Washington (like me) and a greater number of younger (and less exclusively male) experts with foreign accents, darker skin, and grounding in the region.

Examples abounded of this confusion and adaptation. In the classroom, teaching students for whom English was a second or third language required adjustments. American politics could not be taught to a class of foreigners as it would be taught to students exposed to years of American schooling and TV news. Nor did these students need the same lessons and insights for their careers. Teachers and administrators were usually the last to grasp this fact. Embarrassingly, it took me several years to realize that the Introduction to American Government course should be classified under comparative international politics because it was indeed a course in foreign government for most of our students.

Transplanted American universities also needed autonomy from their hosts as well as from the surrounding environment. However progressive the local leadership, it rested in part on support from the complex traditional societies in which it dwelled. In the Gulf countries, liberal education was an alien irritant under the skin of religious orthodoxy. As we saw in chapter 9, critical books about religion or sex—or even the political history of the country—were stopped in customs and banned by the Ministry of Culture. Professors were under pressure, subtle or explicit, to moderate their commentary on local politics. Withdrawing the visa of a Turkish professor at the request of a regional ally had to have a chilling effect on his colleagues. Repeated expressions of general support for academic freedom from the country's leaders were easily forgotten in the face of actions contrary to these pledges.

Coeducation and the social mixing of the sexes occurred within the academic walls but was barely tolerated outside (sometimes not even inside). Women students were upbraided by local security guards for showing their arms in the gowns they wore to formal school dances. Raising the number of Qatari male students without lowering admission standards was difficult because of the small pool of qualified Qataris. Yet serving the needs of the host (and sole donor) population was a necessary strategy for survival even within the walls.

Evolving a valuable educational experience was not enhanced when books were censored, the student body restricted, faculty pressured, speech and lifestyles punished.

This novel educational experiment required watchtowers manned by local Arab guardians committed to the ideas and lifestyles within its walls. The university needed autonomy not because of the certainty of the path ahead but because these new trails needed to be cleared to see where the university was going. Risk taking had to be encouraged, including the risk of failing. Attempting to impose orthodoxy had the effect of undermining the university freedoms required if this experiment were to succeed.

This paradigm was also "muddled" in that the faculty brought their teaching experiences and subject knowledge to the classroom but it was the students who carried their education into the future—and whose continuing support as alumni the school required to endure. Faculty and students—given the gaps of age, knowledge, and culture separating them—needed to adapt to each other.

Many foreign faculty initially suspected, as I did, that they were confronting students arriving with settled traditional loyalties to religion, tribe, and family. Yet as shown in the preceding chapters, those students qualifying for and desiring admission to a Western university weren't usually a smooth fit in the worlds they had come from. These loyalties and their identities were often in flux. Their alienation might be an underlying reason for seeking a "foreign" education.

Increasingly, students had their identities shaped by myriad locales, families, religions, media, music, teachers, travel, languages, culture, and friends. And their world was in transition. If my Arab colleagues were right, theirs was a world where tribalism was not as cohesive as it once was, where faith itself was up for debate, and where radical Islam was no longer quite as acceptable as a rhetorical default in the Internet age.

Globalization—operating through migration, travel, and social media—moderated biases toward Europe and America. In their home countries, groups of women, religious minorities, and bloggers organized, spoke out, and won public support. If foreign universities were an invading force, students were willing collaborators; indeed, they were the vanguard with their fingers on the pulse of the future.

Those of us lacking the prescience to understand this muddle as a coherent whole were left teaching and learning within a confused and chaotic jumble of contrasting ideas and interests. Teachers were also left with the need to govern uncertainty with humility, not conformity or zealotry. It provided no justification in retreating to orthodoxy. The uncertainty of the situation encouraged the need to take risks; to push to the edges of comfort zones toward the experimental. Few of us knew what would work in the changing world these students will inherit.

*

Since I am not responsible for implementing the school's strategy, I am free to offer unsolicited guidance for others. Signs on the Education City campus—courtesy of Qatar Foundation—urge passersby to Innovate. Now what on Earth does this mean? Does anyone have any idea how universities can encourage nonconforming creativity?

It was no use looking to America for an answer. Take three leading, recognized American innovators: Steve Jobs, Bill Gates, and Mark Zuckerberg. They shared a common college experience: all dropped out. And all spoke about how college served as more of a hindrance than a support for them. Not exactly a ringing endorsement for academia.

Steve Jobs told how, after he stopped attending courses as a registered student at Reed College, he still hung out on campus. Serendipitously, he drifted into a calligraphy and typefaces class. It changed his life. Jobs came to appreciate the beauty of print and design. He described how it altered and elevated his concept for the look of his pioneering computer, the Macintosh. He attended the class that would most influence him because he had the freedom of *not* being a student. How to encourage this kind of freedom?

I don't know if any institution could. Faculty in Doha were heard to complain that many students lacked curiosity. At the least, a university could strive to foster this curiosity. Methods for doing so could include minimizing course requirements and hiring professors who actually enjoy teaching students, while evaluating and offering assistance to improve the classroom skills for those who don't.

The answers lie in talented faculty taking risks and trying new approaches to teaching. Unfortunately, establishing a permanent faculty, while it allowed greater security for existing teachers, also reduced the flexibility in the classes that could be offered. It meant fewer faculty brought in from "the real world" outside academia, less experimenting in new courses, and greater conformity among a small, careerist faculty. As the faculty became more risk averse in their own careers, they might find it more difficult to encourage students to take chances in their own lives.

Encouraging student creativity should mean offering them a creative curriculum. One way might be having more cross-disciplinary classes team-taught to gain a diversity of views in the same class. Or hiring "new blood" in the form of experts with less conventional backgrounds brought in through temporary contracts to teach unusual classes on an array of subjects that couldn't be offered by existing faculty. And finally, students needed to be encouraged to take classes from other schools in Education City in subjects outside the limited foreign service curriculum.

New electives could be designed by faculty and/or students on topics such as climate change and pandemic diseases, tribalism in world politics, or how a free press operates in unfree states. Push students to leave the narrow confines of their small city-state for junior years abroad, while encouraging those practicing underrepresented religions (Evangelicals, Buddhists, Mormons, Jews) and foreign students of less-common ethnicities to spend their junior years in Doha. Or how about a multidisciplinary, comprehensive, senior seminar on the Arab world and the wider world: the history, the economic ties, the shared literature, the religious overlaps, the military conflicts, the domestic and international politics—with rotating lectures by historians, economists, literature teachers, and anthropologists. And make it pass-fail to encourage participation.

University faculty and administrators could at least ask the right questions—how to encourage curiosity, innovation, risk taking, excitement for learning—aimed at preparing for a shared, unknown future.

Nor should the university's mission in Qatar be limited to the ivory tower. Succeeding with those now inside the walls while ignoring the society outside was not a long-term formula for success. A

Western university in the Middle East was not an art museum with its educational product displayed for those few with the talent, resources, and inclination to buy an entrance ticket. It was a living organism that survived by the relationships it formed and sustained in the community. The learning the university provided was not just to be consumed but also to be shared.

The "bubble" needed to be permeable. The intellectual resources brought to the region should be used to develop social capital that provided benefits beyond the immediate academic consumers. There needed to be webs of engagement reaching out from the university. It was embarrassing and dysfunctional for there to be virtually no Qatari professionals working at the school besides students. Why weren't there Qataris following university employees around, learning how to do their jobs?

Education City began as a gated community largely because of security concerns. Its model originated in oil companies that built such compounds for living and working beginning in the 1940s in Saudi Arabia and the Gulf. This very "gatedness" now needed to be moderated, and the recent dropping of required IDs to enter campus was a start. Opening up to the wider society meant expanding the number of stakeholders committed to the school becoming a "developmental" institution. Recently initiated community classes, a sports degree aimed at local staff for the 2022 games, and a master's degree in emergency preparedness were positive steps in this direction. These initiatives hinted at how foreign universities could be sustained in the Arab Gulf.

Classes in Arabic would cement this orientation toward the region. These should include not only subjects related to the Arabic language or literature; they should encompass substantive topics in the politics and economics of the region and world. Such offerings would open classes to Qatar University students and encourage more faculty sharing and joint student events. They would also preempt the observation by a member of the Qatari royal family that when her son graduated Georgetown, he could no longer speak or use his native Arabic very well.

Transactional relationships with the surrounding world could more fully utilize the school's resources. These would include training and exchanges of local teachers, counselors, administrators, and staff; consulting ties with government agencies, local businesses, and nonprofits; night classes and online courses for midcareer professionals; and workshops and social media sites for low-income labor. In this way, it would mirror American universities' integration into their society with evening lectures, research in the community, social action projects, media programs, publications, alumni activities, interfaith meetings, and teacher-parent dinners. These would not merely be spin-offs; they would serve as vital supports for generating the social capital to enhance the nation and region, making Georgetown valued by both.

American universities moved abroad in an imperfect world. They existed in a realpolitik mix of mercenary globalization, regional and international politics, religious ideologies, newly affluent middle-class consumers, traditional societies, and a modernizing elite that hosted them. These educators, Georgetown among them, were providing a world-class buffet of subjects in places where they were ambivalently welcomed but badly needed.

Standing back, pointing out the hypocrisies and inconsistencies of unprepared institutions adapting to uncomfortable dilemmas—from badly treated migrant labor to religious fundamentalism—was to miss a unique opportunity to shape a critical region of the world and its future leaders.

We could do worse than begin with Steve Jobs's advice, borrowed from the *Whole Earth Catalog*: Stay Hungry, Stay Foolish.

CHAPTER 12

Time to Go

Before I built a wall I'd ask to know
What I was walling in or walling out,
And to whom I was like to give offense.
—Robert Frost

Following the signing of the new ten-year contract in June 2015, a grayish gloom settled over Georgetown's Doha campus. Part of this attitude could be blamed on the (relative) hard times that Qatar was going through, with a decline in oil prices and the rise of a younger, austere, conservative leadership. Part of it might have been the natural ebbing of the early ebullience of a start-up with a shiny new building and the glow of unbridled expectations. And some of it might just have been a more down-to-earth assessment of the uncertainty of the prospects that lay ahead.

One consultant to the Qatar leadership referred to Georgetown and Texas A&M as the regime's "darling schools." He attributed this to a sense in Doha that the home campuses of both schools were invested in their overseas branches and that they had sent high-quality people to staff their satellite schools. In his opinion, other schools in Education City had sent out administrators and academics they didn't want to keep on their main campuses.

None of this provided a guarantee for the future. At some point, this expat concluded, Qatari citizens would object to spending what were in fact astronomical sums for each student's education. Supporting the point, Todd Kent, who served as a dean at Texas A&M, said it cost $3 million to graduate one Qatari engineer (although this figure didn't include the value of the university's research facilities now permanently located in Doha). Qatari public opinion—as reflected in the Majlis—would eventually be heard by the leaders. And there were voices opposing excessive spending by elites for an education out of reach of the children of most Qataris.

As one close observer of Georgetown's presence in Doha put it, the school's fate lay in a race between the growth of its alumni and the growth of the Qatari population. The school's political future rested with the loyalty of its local graduates. Either the graduates would become influential enough to preserve its presence in Doha or citizens in opposition would grow more vocal and their objections overwhelm its narrow support. One political scientist who followed Gulf politics remarked that a winning coalition in Doha consisted of the support of the thirty-five families that were needed to stay in power. Yet another reminder of what a small place Qatar was.

Kent, who left Doha in 2015, thought the Qatar regime had lost interest in Education City. Pointing to 10 percent financial cutbacks at Texas A&M, he noted that student aid had to be reduced by 35 percent. Because of the poor primary and secondary public education available in Doha, his school was having problems finding qualified Qataris willing to undertake the study of engineering. The international corporations in Qatar were, he said, "not good partners" because they didn't see much advantage in having American schools nearby. Given that a tuition-based model of higher education wouldn't work, Kent was pessimistic: he concluded the financial constraints meant that by 2022, none of the American universities would still be in Doha.

These dour thoughts were reinforced by a sense that the local political climate had turned more conservative. This impression went beyond Qataris approaching Western women in malls to say their short-sleeved blouses were offensive. More relevant was the new emir, who was seen as responsive to the populace's orthodox sentiments. His mother, Sheikha Mozah, remained as head of Qatar Foundation but did not enjoy the influence she once held. The government cut Qatar Foundation's budget by 35 percent, reflecting a decline in oil prices and a sense of changing priorities. For instance, national security was not cut by the new emir, a former soldier.

The concern for security was understandable. Since the Arab Spring, "Qatar" had become a toxic word in much of the region. It had sided with the Muslim Brotherhood in Egypt and stuck with that movement even after the overthrow of its elected president. Its support for them and for militant jihadists in Tunisia, Libya, and Syria put it at loggerheads with Saudi Arabia as well as the military government in Egypt. Al Jazeera reporters gained a reputation for supporting uprisings and demonstrations from Syria to Bahrain, which the neighboring regimes surmised reflected the views of Qatari leaders. With the withdrawal of the ambassadors of Saudi Arabia, Bahrain, and the UAE from Doha in March 2013, followed by the ascent of Sheik Tamim in June 2013, the impression spread that Qatar was "over its skis" in its foreign policies. The new emir pursued a quieter, more pragmatic approach—he endorsed the military government in Egypt, restored relations with Gulf neighbors, denounced terrorism, and accepted the regional consensus that the Arab Spring had not initiated a new liberalizing era. These changes were either not believed or not enough to stop Qatar's neighbors from imposing an economic and diplomatic siege in the summer of 2017 that deepened the country's sense of isolation.

Under the young emir, not all higher education spending was reduced. There was increased interest in improving Qatar University. By switching the language of instruction to Arabic in 2012, the school was seen as welcoming average Qatari families whose children now had a greater chance to go to college. As a result, enrollment went from eight thousand to fourteen thousand in three years. The government increased its funding while making clear this was the national university responsible for producing educated, mainstream Qataris for the private sector's labor market.

None of this was to say that Georgetown suffered from faint praise. At the tenth anniversary events, the emir told Georgetown president DeGioia, "I look forward to the next twenty years." The president of Qatar Foundation went further: "I see this as a Catholic marriage." In other words: no divorce. Mixing metaphors, Dean Gallucci said he was confident "the branch has taken root." There is no "us" or "them" at the Doha campus, he added; Georgetown had created a "we."

The ten-year contract renewal underlined the commitment to continue the school. The same agreement cut the school's operating budget by 20 percent. Chief Operating Officer Amol Dani described the Qatari negotiators' attitude as: "We love you, Georgetown; we just want you to do more with less."

As a result of these cuts, staff reductions were planned. (In the near term, the faculty actually increased by 25 percent due to prior planning commitments but teaching positions were expected to decline by attrition in the future.) Scholarships for foreign students were cut and the school lost some already-admitted members of the class of 2019 who were preparing for their freshman year. Because the number of admitted Qataris rose, there were complaints that the overall quality of the student body had decreased. A remedial writing program was initiated.

Expansion efforts were put on hold. The push to extend the school into graduate studies was curtailed. Online programs attracting working professionals from the business sector for part-time degrees were discussed and then shelved. A much-ballyhooed effort to shoehorn a sports program under the Georgetown brand continued, if only because it was kept outside the Qatar Foundation budget. It aimed to train skilled labor required for hosting the 2022 World Cup. These attempts to expand Georgetown's offerings reflected the need for a new educational model and yet what that might be remained cloudy. The annual tuition, at $48,000 in 2015, was too high to expect many qualified overseas students to pay on their own. If more revenues were needed, the Qatari government stood alone as the likely source. Yet that source seemed to have reached a limit in its commitment to its foreign guest.

Dean Reardon-Anderson saw Georgetown as a "one-off" that was "not likely to be copied." The coincidence of unlimited Qatari funds, limited popular input from a citizenry indifferent to the benefits of the school, and the security blanket of the American military bases, was a combination not found in many other places in the world. Repeating this experience would require a vast fund-raising effort combined with a tolerance for intellectual freedom among the local population that seemed increasingly rare in the world, not to mention the region.

Dean Gallucci noted that if Georgetown weren't already established in Doha, the project probably couldn't be started now. (This brought to mind one scholar's observation that if the Bill of Rights wasn't already in the US Constitution, it probably couldn't be adopted today.) The period 2003–2004 in Doha and Washington offered a combination of the right people in the right positions at the right time, most of whom were no longer in place. Certainly, the money, vision, and unity offered by the school's Qatari sponsors were no longer there, nor was the citizenry's acquiescence in a time of cutbacks to be taken for granted. One senior Arab scholar with close ties in Doha thought Georgetown's present contract would not be renewed. Its education was viewed as too elitist and too liberal to be tolerated by Qatari public opinion.

That the relationship was still working was a tribute to the mindfulness and restraint shown by both sides of the university-government divide. Georgetown recognized early on that it couldn't insist on practices that would outrage the local population. An early suggestion by someone on the Georgetown side—that crucifixes in the front of each classroom would be consistent with main campus practice—was quietly shelved. One unidentified priest, after looking at the plans for the new building, asked, "Where are the Jesuit grave sites?" The query, referring to the graveyard located behind the Healy Building on the Washington campus, never had to be answered by the hosts because it was never asked.

Qatar, for its part, had to be aware of the sensibilities of this American institution of higher learning. That didn't mean agreeing with all the values incorporated in a twenty-first-century curriculum, but it did mean respecting the autonomy necessary for the guests to fulfill their contract. This would entail halting attempts to censor books requested by faculty and students, refraining from punishing faculty for political expression (even when pressured to do so by regional allies), and allowing social action programs that could impinge on sensitive areas including migrant rights. Recognizing that Georgetown was answerable to a number of constituencies outside Qatar was also to accept it had an interest in how Qatar acted within its borders and on the broader world stage.

Students and Their Futures

My friend Robert Wirsing said, "Our teaching does not mean delivering a barrel of goodies from Washington, DC, that will be happily devoured by students." He and others saw liberal education uncomfortably undermining many of the traditional values and assumptions with which students from the region began college. Although they resembled Americans in many ways and were at least their equal in brain power and ambition, these students still exhibited dramatic differences due to their country of origin. As one professor put it, "they're living in a mess." Their life experiences amidst this social strife had left them, unsurprisingly, with a great appreciation for order. They did not arrive at college as blank slates; many started out alienated from yet tied to the societies that produced them, suspended between pressures from family, tribes, nations, religions, and fractured cultures.

Apart from the pull of tradition, students attempted to balance competing aspirations and identities from media, liberal values, global travel, mass consumption, and social networking in multiple languages. One hope for higher education was that it would bring some coherence to the streams of global culture they had absorbed. Yet what they incorporated from their experiences in college didn't always bring the orderly sanity they had hoped for.

BB was in one of the first classes I taught in Doha, Introduction to International Relations. The daughter of a prominent Qatari family, she was a shy, polite freshman who seldom spoke in class. When she came to my office, it was always with a girlfriend. Her well-designed, embroidered, black abaya emphasized her slenderness and her privileged background. By her senior year, when she took my Media and Foreign Policy class, she laughed more and asserted herself in class debates. BB had become a presence. Her essay for the class, on global networks' coverage of the Iraqi war, was outstanding. She had grown into a creative, insightful student, willing to entertain unconventional ideas, all without losing her ability—visible in a number of Gulf women students—to charm the listener.

By her senior year, when she stopped by my office, she came on her own. After discussing classroom topics, she would chat about her life and future. Her father wanted her to go into the family business but she wanted to stay in academia, hopefully to teach someday. Our discussions continued sporadically after she graduated. I would see her at school events and she would talk fondly of her time at Georgetown. She had married shortly after graduating and had a baby. Other students described her husband as traditional and not well educated. When I last saw her, she was pregnant again, accompanied by a servant who held her first child. She spoke of continuing her Georgetown education and said she missed the intellectual free-for-all of the classroom. She promised to come by the office to get a recommendation and talk about teaching. She never did. The last I heard, she had given birth to a third child.

The image we carry around of ourselves is not necessarily reflected by the life we live. As I described earlier, the education of women might accelerate their alienation from the life they knew before college. Returning to their family might mean resuming these lives as adults in a comfortable, privileged setting. It might also mean living what one student called "a double life": enjoying relationships with men and women conducted on the sly, expressing dissenting opinions during dinner conversations, living at a distance from the people around them while never quite acknowledging the separation. Or it could mean the dimming in time of one's university-acquired secular liberalism and embracing traditional views and lifestyles.

The remnants of the language of liberalism were all that remained of a liberal education.

In a conversation on the Washington campus, a Georgetown political scientist compared the education of women on the Doha campus to the training African Americans received at Howard University in the 1940s before they returned to the Jim Crow South. His point was that their professional training from this historically black university was virtually useless in the segregated work environment they encountered back in their home states in the South. Most ended up in the less-racist cities of the North and West, where they could fulfill their career ambitions. Of course, the privileges and high status that female graduates enjoyed in the Gulf and elsewhere made comparing them with African Americans a bit far-fetched.

Some students absorbed and identified with the liberal values found in their education. These were the grads who "walked the walk" of liberalism. Many came from professional families in places like Egypt and Pakistan, some occupying lower social standing than their classmates. They traveled a greater distance to get to the university; perhaps that's why they more fully embraced the values and views they found when they arrived. It might also have separated them from the traditional pull of their home countries. Their career path lay outside the traditional worlds they knew.

Realistically, their futures lay in New York and Washington, Paris and London—the large, metropolitan cities of the globalized world. Even if they settled outside these urban centers, they would likely be tied to them via the multinational communities they ended up living and working in. They would use their educational credentials, motivated by a progressive vision of the future, to get jobs in the nonprofits, universities, international organizations, and multinational corporations where they would join other transnational elites largely drawn from backgrounds similar to theirs. As they married within these peer groups, their ties with their homelands, families, and cultures would strain, loosen, and perhaps break. Their education became another step in the process of detaching from societies and people, beliefs and values, among whom they were no longer comfortable or even welcomed. They no longer followed the same faith, spoke the shared language, or felt comfortable in the same clothing they did before.

The contrast was most easily seen, once again, in the educated women of the Gulf. They faced stark choices after they graduated. Going back to their families meant resuming the gender-segregated lives they had partially suspended while at college. Now in their twenties, they were expected to marry—and their mate would need to be approved by their parents if not chosen by them. Many used graduate education abroad as a means of deferring the detachment from their families and culture they saw coming. Yet this delay in making their painful choice of separation was for many a continuation of it. Their terms for reengagement with the societies they had left—not getting married, continuing their careers, living apart from family—might still prove too costly for either party.

The path they were on—from higher education to Western living—could threaten to undermine the societies from which they came. When a society could not retain the loyalty of the best of the next generation, it was weakening its chance of thriving in the future. Alternatively, liberalizing these societies offered a survival strategy. It allowed them to embrace their most valued resource and product: their educated youth. Harnessing this youthful idealism and energy meant creating more attractive, more livable, freer societies. It was not just fanciful to imagine these were also places that would have better chances of growing and succeeding in the coming era of uncertainties.

Of course, in the era of Trump, whether anyone overseas thought that Americans and their universities still had anything to teach illiberal societies about liberal education was someone else's problem to worry about.

Parting

It was time to go.

I was coming to the end of my third contract after eight years of teaching. I could apply for senior core faculty status but I didn't think of myself as permanent, and approaching seventy, I was ready for something else. I also noticed the corners of my lecture notes were bending, a sign of their age and my resistance to revisions. My class evaluations were still positive but I usually found my students more generous in their assessment of faculty than faculty were of students.

Ann was ready to leave and had been for most of her years in Doha. Always more sensitive to her surroundings than her spouse, she saw the flat desert setting a huge step down from the green, wooded mountains of her native Washington State. Yet she had good friends among the women expats in the compound and found teaching English to the migrant workers a worthwhile use of her time. She did, however, have a visceral, negative reaction to parts of Arab culture, especially its treatment of women. Never worried about being politically correct, she viewed women who covered themselves as locked into medieval customs that forced them into marriages as teenagers and never gave them the chance to live out freely chosen, individual lives. The more she learned about the migrant laborers, their forced separation from their families, and their poverty in contrast to the wealth of the indifferent citizenry they served, the more she found the society harder to live in and accept.

Ann wasn't the only one with this response to what she saw in Doha. In many ways, I was shielded from this by my status as an older, male, Western professor and by students who frequently showed me their best sides: modesty, respect, hard work, intelligence, and moderation. My job was also a big plus; it paid me well, was not nearly as demanding as Washington consulting, and allowed me considerable free time to write about American politics. We were also relatively close to exotic destinations—from Burma and Nepal to Oman and Tanzania—which we could visit on semester breaks and did.

As for me, I had arrived in Qatar with apprehension and ideals. My anxiety had since dissipated; I felt comfortable among strangers in a strange land. I no longer expected the worst. Perhaps—like my countrymen—as memories of 9/11 faded, so did the fears. I could aspire to "tikkun olam," the Jewish concept calling on individuals to repair the world through social action. Yet more than ever, I understood the limits of what I could accomplish.

Looking back, perhaps I learned the limits all too well. The ideals I arrived with had been sanded down by experience. In my best moments, usually in class, I saw myself less as a carrier of imported liberal wisdom and more the lead questioner of unexamined values, critically exploring those who ruled and those who were ruled over. I was leading a conversation in explaining the politics students faced in the world: what elites did to acquire and keep power and what the rest of us could do to understand and influence their control. Media, political parties, theories, education—all could be channels through which the world might be changed, with luck by students if they retained their ideals and were smart about how they used these instruments.

I failed where the university failed. We both aspired to global teaching—yet this seldom included learning from the world. One goal of a multinational university ought to be to enrich our understanding of different societies. Yet we assumed we were bringing in our valuable cargo of knowledge and that it needed to be guarded from local contamination. And in some aspects—research standards, admissions, academic freedom—this had merit. We shared our parochial outlook with religious fundamentalists on the other side of the wall, though they viewed us as a foreign contaminant concealed in the attractive cloak of education. The result was a mutual endorsement of walls, physical and intellectual, shielding Education City from the societies it was there to nourish. These walls separated people, silenced ideas, muted contacts, and interrupted communications.

Teaching in a foreign land could broaden academics' views of the world and how we approach our fields of expertise. An ongoing conversation could be sparked by the books and ideas that we discussed. That discussion could enrich the subjects that I was teaching: international relations, media and public policy, and American politics. Arab and Islamic experiences, as well as their scholars' insights into international relations, would have enhanced my students' understanding of a discipline they saw was dominated by European men and Western history. I couldn't teach any other way because I didn't know anything else. And only now, on reflection, did I see this as an unacknowledged gap.

I never did have that type of exchange. I never fully engaged the community in which I lived. I believe this was a loss to both sides.

This might also prove to be the key to validating the experiment of Georgetown in Doha: widening our own horizons; opening ourselves to the wisdom of those we'd come to teach. In our recruitment, research, debates, and daily affairs at the school, we needed to reach over the walls.

That was a shame. It had taken me all this time to know how—and what—to teach. And it was time to go.

Notes

Introduction
Edward W. Said, *Covering Islam* (New York: Vintage Books, 1997).

Chapter 2
Author, personal interviews with Robert Gallucci, Jim Reardon-Anderson, Patrick Theros, various Qataris working with Qatar Foundation. Janet H. Moore, "Interview with Robert L. Gallucci, Dean of the Edmund A. Walsh School of Foreign Service of Georgetown University," January 31, 2007. Nick Anderson, "Sheikha Moza: The Woman Behind Doha's Education City," *The Washington Post*, December 6, 2015. Financial aspects of Georgetown in Doha obtained from several administrative staff. Waleed Al-Shobakky, "Petrodollar Science," *The New Atlantis*, Fall 2008. Junie Nathani, Interview of Reardon-Anderson, *The Hoya*, February 27, 2004. Geoff Kelly, interview in *The Hoya*, May 20, 2005. Nick Anderson, "In Qatar's Education City, U.S. Colleges Are Building an Academic Oasis," *The Washington Post*, December 6, 2015.

Chapter 3
Much of the historical background in this chapter comes from the fine accounts found in Mehran Kamrava, *Qatar: Small State, Big Politics* (Ithaca: Cornell University Press, 2015). Allen J. Fromherz, *Qatar: A Modern History* (Washington, DC: Georgetown University Press, 2012)

245

was used for nineteenth- and twentieth-century history. Mari Luomi's *The Gulf Monarchies and Climate Change* (Oxford: Oxford University Press, 2015) was helpful for current economic information and budget figures. Also helpful were Lina Khatib, "Qatar and the Recalibration of Power in the Gulf" (Carnegie Middle East Center, September 11, 2013) and Justin Gengler, "The Political Costs of Qatar's Western Orientation," *Middle East Policy*, Winter 2012. Articles in the *Washington Post* on December 17, 2013, and December 6, 2015, discuss other universities that were approached. Sheikha Mozah's 2004 speech in Los Angeles was quoted in *The Pearl: The Magazine of the Embassy of the State of Qatar*, December 2004. The background on Qatar's quest for American universities is from Catherine S. Mangan, "Qatar Courts American Colleges," *The Chronicle of Higher Education*, September 6, 2002, and John T. Crist, "Innovation in a Small State: Qatar and the IBC Cluster Model of Higher Education," *The Muslim World* (The Hartford Seminary, 2014). Branding discussions were taken from Kamrava, *Qatar: Small State, Big Politics* and Marc Fisher, *The Washington Post*, December 17, 2013. On the 2017 boycott of Qatar, I benefited from Joost Hiltermann, "Qatar Punched Above Its Weight. Now It's Paying the Price," The *New York Times*, June 18, 2017 and Simon Henderson, "The Palace Intrigue At The Heart of The Qatar Crisis," *Foreign Policy*, June 30, 2017.

Chapter 4

Author, personal interviews with Patricia O'Connor, Katrina Quirolgico, and Clyde Wilcox. Author, "Plenty in Common," *The Chronicle Review*, February 20, 2009. Author, "Who's a Middle Easterner?" *The Washington Post*, June 17, 2012.

Chapter 5

Author, personal interviews with Rogaia Abusharaf, Amira Sonbol, Dan Stoll, Robert Wirsing, Nancy Wirsing, Sue Page, Amina Husain, Dean Gerd Nonneman, and Melanne Verveer. Helpful background information came from Shabana Mir, *Muslim American Women on Campus* (Chapel Hill: The University of North Carolina Press, 2014); Amelie Le Renard, *A Society of Young Women: Opportunities of Place,*

Power, and Reform in Saudi Arabia (Stanford: Stanford University Press, 2014); *Best Writing* (Texas A&M University at Qatar, 2014); and Robin Wright, *Rock the Casbah* (New York: Simon & Schuster, 2011).

Chapter 6
Author, personal interviews with Joe Hernandez, Katrina Quirolgico, Brendan Hill, and Todd Kent. John Mearsheimer and Stephen Walt, *The Israel Lobby and U.S. Foreign Policy* (New York: Farrar, Straus and Giroux, 2007). How the *New York Times* played down coverage of the Holocaust is covered in Laurel Leff, *Buried by the Times* (New York: Cambridge University Press, 2005). Tamar Lewin, "In Oil-Rich Mideast, Shades of the Ivy League," *The New York Times*, February 11, 2008. I benefited from reading Marwan Bishara, *The Invisible Arab* (New York: Nation Books, 2012) and Andrew J. Bacevich, *America's War for the Greater Middle East* (New York: Random House, 2016). I paid Al Jazeera back for its invites by endorsing its short-lived venture in America in "Al Jazeera Expansion into US Could Be Win-Win," *The Washington Post*, January 5, 2013.

Chapter 7
Author, personal interviews with Roger Bensky, Josh Mitchell, Brendan Hill, Jim Reardon-Anderson, and Amy Nestor. Anti-Defamation League, "Report: Sheik Yusuf al-Qaradawi: Theologian of Hate," May 3, 2013. *The Protocols of the Learned Elders of Zion* and Henry Ford, *The International Jew* (Johannesburg: Global Books) are available in Doha, where books such as the one you're reading are censored. Walter Laqueur, *The Changing Face of Anti-Semitism* (New York: Oxford University Press, 2006). Additional discussion of Jews in Islamic history is in Bernard Lewis, *From Babel to Dragomans: Interpreting the Middle East* (New York: Oxford University Press, 2004). "SFS-Q Israel/Palestine Trip Summary Report," 2008.

Chapter 8
Author, personal interviews with Robert Wirsing, Maya Primorac, Jonathan Cartmell, Jon Crist, and Brendon Hill. Andrew Gardner

and Momina Zakzouk, "Car Culture in Contemporary Qatar," in Donna Lee Bowen, Evelyn A. Early, and Becky Schulthies (eds.), *Everyday Life in the Muslim Middle East, Third Edition* (Bloomington, IN: Indiana University Press, 2014). Dane A. Wisher, "How to Drink in Qatar," *The Morning News*, January 4, 2016. *Doha News* variously. Andrew Mills, "Academics in the Persian Gulf," *The Chronicle Review*, February 20, 2009.

Chapter 9

Author, personal interviews with Mehran Kamrava, Gerd Nonneman, Birol Baskan, Patrick Laude, Amy Nestor, Frieda Wiebe, and Robert Wirsing. Letter from Amy Nestor to author, October 21, 2016. Letter to author from Frieda Wiebe, July 27, 2015. Frieda Wiebe, letter to Sheikha Nagla Faisal Al Thani, May 13, 2012. Fromholz and Khatib were quoted in Lindsey Ursula, "Qatar Sets Its Own Terms for US Universities," *The Chronicle of Higher Education*, November 22, 2013. Nick Anderson, "Northwestern Professor Raises Questions About Its Branch in Qatar," *The Washington Post*, December 18, 2015. Ian Philbrick, "DC to Qatar: A Georgetown Presence in Doha," *The Georgetown Voice*, January 29, 2015. Nick Anderson, "In Qatar's Education City, US Colleges Are Building an Academic Oasis," *The Washington Post*, December 6, 2015. Birol Baskan, "Ankara Torn Apart," *The Turkish Yearbook of International Relations*, Volume 42 (2011), pp. 1–25.

Chapter 10

Author, personal interviews with Clair Wait, Uday Rosario, Ganesh Seshan, Zahra Babar, and Mehran Kamrava. Zahra Babar, "Labor Migration in the State of Qatar," *Note de l'Ifri*, Center for Migrations, December 2013. Ganesh Seshan, "Migrants in Qatar: A Socio-Economic Profile," *Journal of Arabian Studies*, December 2012. Andrew Gardner, et al., "A Portrait of Low-Income Migrants in Contemporary Qatar," *Journal of Arabian Studies*, June 2013. Ian Philbrick, *Georgetown Voice*, January 29, 2015. *Viewpoints*, The Middle East Institute, Washington, DC, February 2010. Amnesty

International, *The Dark Side of Migration: Spotlight on Qatar's Construction Sector Ahead of the World Cup*, 2013. "Georgetown University Plans Step to Atone for Slave Past," *The New York Times*, September 1, 2016. Various online groups monitor migrant affairs, including *Just Here* (www.justhere.qa). Email, January 10, 2015, in "Maids: Out of Sight, Out of Mind," *Just Here*, July 10, 2013. "Portrayal of the 'Other': Migrant Workers Are Patronized, Marginalized, Vilified," *Just Here*, September 19, 2013. "Rights Groups Skeptical as New Labor Reforms Take Effect in Qatar," *Doha News*, December 13, 2016. Ian Philbrick, "DC to Qatar: A Georgetown Presence in Doha," *The Georgetown Voice*, January 29, 2015.

Chapter 11
Author, personal interviews with Robert Wirsing, Josh Mitchell, Waleed Al-Shobakky, Abbas Al-Tonsi, and Jeremy Koons. Joshua Mitchell, *Tocqueville in Arabia: Dilemmas in a Democratic Age* (Chicago: The University of Chicago Press, 2013).

Chapter 12
Author, personal interviews with Amol Dani, Robert Gallucci, Patrick Theros, Todd Kent, and Amira Sonbol. Ross Douthat, "The Islamic Dilemma," *The New York Times*, December 13, 2015. Virginia H. Aksan, "How Do We 'Know' the Middle East?" 2009 Presidential Address, Middle East Studies Association, November 22, 2009. Shanta Devarajan, "The Paradox of Higher Education in MENA," Brookings Institution, June 27, 2016.

Acknowledgments

Many of the students and colleagues who I interviewed and were most generous in helping me write this book wished not to be identified. Their hesitation in publicly expressing their views ought to give people of the Gulf a moment of pause to think about the state of free speech in their region. I thank them all.

While I thought about writing my reflections while I was in Qatar, the book started breathing in Adam Hochschild's class on nonfiction writing at UC Berkeley's School of Journalism, spring 2015. Adam and his students ably steered a fine line between critiquing and encouraging my early efforts at putting thoughts to paper.

Robert Wirsing, Connie Hall, and Ed Wasserman read the entire draft and offered valuable edits and advice. Other friends were generous in their support during the months of writing: Joel Koblentz, John and Pat Rea, Simon Branfman and Paula Kasler, Noah Griffin, Al Platt, Jeff Lape, Parker Lape, and Jill Caporale. Family, as always, was a foundation: Ed and Eva, Daniel and Adrienne, Priyesh and Laura.

My agent, John Willig, took the book and ran with it, skillfully and patiently. Carole Sargent of Georgetown's Office of External Publications offered kind support in the very beginning. Editors Joe Craig and Sebastian Thaler at Skyhorse were unreasonably helpful to the author in fashioning a finished book. In the actual construction of the story, there were those who gave generously of their knowledge and time, including Bob Gallucci, Patrick Theros, Jim Reardon-Anderson, Gerd Nonneman, Patrick Laude, Josh Miller, Brendan Hill, Jonathan Cartmell and Sue Page, Waleed Al-Shobakky, Kai and Katrin Scholz-Barth.

And to my wife, Ann, companion and soul mate, thanks for overcoming what you wanted in order to reach what we wanted.

Index